The
Greatest
Submarine Stories
Ever Told

Books by Lamar Underwood

The Bobwhite Quail Book

Bowhunting Tactics of the Pros

Classic Hunting Stories

Classic Survival Stories

Classic War Stories

The Deer Hunter's Book

The Duck Hunter's Book

The Greatest Adventure Stories Ever Told

The Greatest Disaster Stories Ever Told

The Greatest Fishing Stories Ever Told

The Greatest Flying Stories Ever Told

The Greatest Hunting Stories Ever Told

The Greatest War Stories Ever Told

Into the Backing

Man Eaters

The Quotable Soldier

The Quotable Writer

Tales of the Mountain Men

Theodore Roosevelt on Hunting

Whitetail Hunting Tactics of the Pros

The Greatest Submarine Stories Ever Told

Dive! Dive! Fourteen Unforgettable Stories from the Deep

EDITED BY LAMAR UNDERWOOD

THE LYONS PRESS
Guilford, Connecticut
An imprint of The Globe Pequot Press

The Lyons Press is an imprint of The Globe Pequot Press.

10 9 8 7 6 5 4 3 2 1

Printed in The United States of America

ISBN 1-59228-733-6

Library of Congress Cataloging-in-Publication Data is available on file.

Contents

Introduction

The movies made me do it. I had absolutely no control over what happened. The movies pushed me into becoming a submarine literature (or "sub lit") junkie.

Like many people, I usually read the book first, then seek out the movie. But way back in 1958, the novel *Run Silent, Run Deep* had somehow missed my must-read list until the film version sent me scurrying forth to get my hands on it. By then, I knew *everything* about the movie (because I had seen it three times) and nothing about the book—except that it was written by an actual U.S. Navy submarine commander and was no doubt very auto-biographical, despite being a novel.

Looking back on those distant years, I feel a debt of gratitude to that film, now mellow with age. Seeing it today, some may understandably ask why I found that particular movie so captivating. "Run Silent, Run Deep" was filmed in black-and-white, and while having powerful performances by Clark Gable and Burt Lancaster, it had special effects that would probably be laughed at now. Still, I found the film gripping, and I appreciate the fact that it sent me on patrols through many volumes of great reading about submarines and their crews. And I have continued to plunk down my money at the box office whenever a new submarine movie comes along.

I am hardly alone with my submarine movie habit. Submarine movies have been box office gold since the first time an actor peered into a periscope on a Hollywood set. "Run Silent, Run Deep," "The Boat," "The Hunt for Red October," "Up Periscope," "U-571," "Gray Lady Down," "Destination Tokyo," "Crimson Tide," "K-19: The Widowmaker," "The Enemy Below," "Operation Pacific," "Action in the North Atlantic," "The Cruel Sea." That's a plethora of titles, taken straight from memory. No doubt the list could be much longer. You might think my interest in sub films would have dimmed a little by now. No way. Point me to a new submarine movie, and I'm on my way.

Submarine movies—and the best submarine books—have story-telling qualities I find irresistible. First they are "caper" stories, as the film genre is called. The sub and the crew are on some "impossible" mission to achieve a great goal, such as sinking enemy ships, or delivering weapons or special operations forces or spies. There is always great drama aboard submarines: the interaction of the members of the crew with each other and with the officers as they go about their duties; the weight of command on the officers as they try to follow their orders while dealing with the sea and the enemy. Submarine movies are replete with action, both above and below the surface, as the boats clash with destroyers and airplanes and even other submarines. And then there is the sea itself, always there, always interesting; now a violent, threatening enemy; now a benign setting of incredible beauty. Film or book, I feel I can always count on a submarine story to hold my interest.

I had barely cracked open *Run Silent, Run Deep* when I began to realize that what I was reading had scant resemblance to the film version I had seen and enjoyed. No problem. While different than the film, the novel had its own agenda of drama, action, and storytelling power. Written by a commander who had been on attack subs in the Pacific in World War II, *Run Silent, Run Deep* crackled with intense realism. So much so that sub lit went onto my A-list of personal reading favorites. I just couldn't get enough submarine stories.

There are today, of course, many novels with storylines about submarines that have never made it to the silver screen. Nevertheless, they are eminently readable. You can type in the word "submarine" on your favorite web search engine and find enjoyable submarine novels with their settings and action ranging from World War II to the coming of the nuclear age. The most recent feature some current international crises at the core of the plot: terrorists armed with super weapons on their way to use them; military SEAL and Special Forces Operations on covert missions; practice exercises at sea that turn into real confrontations with enemy vessels; the "rogue" or berserk commander story, his sub on some evil journey.

Submarine dramas are not confined to the fiction shelves. Nonfiction titles are out there which put the reader into real-life submarines in battles, exploration, and survival situations, like the nightmarish horror of being trapped in a steel cocoon on the ocean floor. There are numerous biographies, diary-inspired accounts of great voyages, and moment-by-moment reports of rescues beneath the waves while the clock of doom is ticking.

If my own interest in sub lit had ever lagged—which in fact it never did—it certainly would have been rejuvenated by the publication of *The Boat* in 1975. Translated from the German *Das Boot*, this book was a towering literary achievement which carried the submarine genre to new levels of realism and readability. German filmmakers led by director Wolfgang Peterson took up the challenge of bringing the story to the screen with great zeal and skill. "The Boat" was the first film to realistically capture the cramped conditions of submarine life, the technical challenges of keeping the systems operating, the suspense of the attacks, and the skull-hammering blows of being depth-charged.

Although I have never had a ride on a submarine (I guess not very many civilians ever have), I have several times as a tourist boarded a World War II sub tied to the pier outside the Baltimore Aquarium. The USS *Torsk* is a U.S. Navy attack submarine that patrolled on missions against the Japanese in the Pacific. If you're interested in sub lit—and evidently you are—you don't want to miss touring one whenever, wherever you can at historical sites or naval "open houses." For me, the experience of boarding the *Torsk* is riveting, from the surface battle stations atop the conning tower, down the main hatch into the main control room, through the narrow passageway past the radioman's desk and panel, the galley, the officer's mess and their quarters, the crew's mess and quarters, to the forward and aft torpedo rooms. Here is the battlefield, if you will, the places where the officers and men performed their individual roles in the boat's duels with the enemy and the sea.

Easing through the narrow compartments—metal structures, pipes, and controls pinching in on both sides and from the ceiling itself—one cannot help but reflect on the kind of men who choose to serve in such an environment, far beneath the waves in the crushing pressure of unfathomable depths. Clearly, they are a special breed, ready to go to sea and live and fight in conditions that seem almost prison-like. Knowing that submariners of all nations, officers and men both, have always been volunteers, I can only shake my head in wonder at their courage.

Reflecting on that courage and the technical challenges of submarine operations, it seems to me that the submarine "reads" I have enjoyed most have a similar feel to my favorite aviation stories: They are not simply *about* subs or planes. They give the reader the sense of actually being aboard, a participant in a continuous drama unfolding.

In selecting the fourteen stories presented here, one of my goals has been to bring you both fiction and nonfiction that I think best represent the essential areas of submarine literature. With each selection, I try to explain my reasons for choosing the piece. Hopefully, you will find great reading reward in every story, and experience that magical sense of "a felt life" that puts you in a submarine.

Welcome aboard! Let's put out to sea.

—Lamar Underwood

"Paukenschlag"

BY HOMER H. HICKAM, Jr.

(Excerpted from the book *Torpedo Junction*)

This stirring account of the U-boat war off America's east coast in 1942 creates the perfect atmosphere for beginning our journey through tales of submarine action. Here, in plain sight of the American coastline, already seasoned by years of warfare against Britain and Europe, German U-boats begin sinking lone ships and attacking convoys. This was the beginning of submarine warfare action that would be chronicled in volumes of books, magazines, and newspapers before World War II ended in 1945. No other era saw as much submarine attack-boat action as did World War II in the Atlantic and the Pacific. Here is how it all began, with one word: *Paukenschlag*!

If lines were to be drawn on a map from Cape Race, Newfoundland, down the east coast of the North American continent and into the Gulf of Mexico and the Caribbean, they would coincide with perhaps the most congested sea lanes in the world. When the United States entered World War II, the industrial cities of the eastern seaboard were particularly vulnerable to the disruption of these lanes. Fuel was required to keep those cities from freezing during the winter, and most of that fuel was provided by ships hauling it from Curaçao and Aruba in the Netherlands West Indies, from Venezuelan oil fields, and from the Gulf of Mexico ports of Corpus

Christi, Houston, and Port Arthur, Texas. The United States military was also vulnerable. The oil reserves of the United States were simply not large enough to meet the sustained, high demands of world conflict. To cut her supply lines along the Atlantic coast and to the south would be, in effect, to defeat the United States, to freeze much of her population, and force her out of the war. In January 1942, five German Type IX U-boats set forth to accomplish all that.

Although Admiral Karl Doenitz, commander of the German U-boat fleet, was surprised by Pearl Harbor and the entry of the United States into the war, he quickly improvised a plan for an attack across the Atlantic. Sensing a great opportunity, he proposed sending twelve U-boats to American waters, six of which were to be the new Type IXs, which had greater fuel and armaments than the standard Type VIIs. Doenitz called this operation *Paukenschlag*, the word meaning "drumroll." The admiral's bold plan, however, was turned down. The Mediterranean and Norwegian fronts, he was told, were of first priority for his U-boats, and not some risky adventure across the Atlantic. Doenitz was disappointed but not surprised by the denial. It was simply a continuation of the bureaucratic battle he had fought for what he considered to be the proper operation of his U-boats since the beginning of the war.

Admiral Doenitz was an intense, studious man who had spent much of the years after World War I planning a huge force of submarines that would lay waste to convoys in the Atlantic. But on the day Britain declared hostilities against Germany, the *Kriegsmarine* had in its inventory only twenty-two U-boats large enough to operate in the open ocean. Ordered to blockade the British Isles and pin down the Royal Navy, Doenitz knew that all he could actually do while waiting for a promised increase in the numbers of his U-boats was to inflict a few wounds here and there using "hit and run" tactics. Still, his fiercely loyal commanders were able to spring several surprises on the Royal Navy, the most spectacular being the sinking of the battleship *Royal Oak* inside the British fleet anchorage at Scapa Flow. This success, perhaps more than any other, was the one that established the U-boat myth of reckless daring and made a hero of the *U-47*'s commander, Günther Prien. Doenitz did not mind the adulation given to one of his commanders. If it helped in his struggle to wage U-boat warfare and get more U-boats built, he minded nothing.

The first of what U-boat sailors would come to refer to as their "Happy Time" would be in the summer of 1940. The British had gone to the convoy system to defend their merchant ships as they brought vital supplies from the United States and Canada. This system had worked well during

World War I and, it was assumed, would be just as effective in World War II, especially with the new ASDIC "pinging" equipment that would allow defending destroyers to locate intruding submarines. Doenitz, however, had studied the convoy system and thought that he had found a way to defeat it. His tactic was to send his U-boats out singly but with orders to immediately radio command headquarters the moment a convoy was sighted. When this was done, other U-boats would be routed into the area and ordered to wait until night, surface, and attack. Doenitz reasoned that ASDIC would not be able to locate the U-boats on the surface and that night would allow them to get in close without being spotted by lookouts. To the dismay of the Royal Navy, this simple tactic worked spectacularly. In June, 284,000 tons of shipping were sunk, followed by 196,000 in July, 268,000 in August, 295,000 in September, and a stunning 352,000 tons sent to the bottom of the ocean in October. This was the time of the U-boat aces, of Prien and Endrass and Kretschmer and Schepke. Still, despite all their swashbuckling successes, the U-boat commanders were never lone wolves. Doenitz had them all very much in control, requiring them to check in with him daily so that he could route them efficiently and effectively.

The "Happy Time" did not last long. For one thing, Doenitz still did not have very many U-boats available. For another, the British started to install radar on their ships and gradually learned to fight at night. Using carefully coordinated air and ship operations, the Royal Navy was soon able to reestablish control over the convoy routes and, by January 1941, had reduced U-boat sinkings to 127,000 tons for that month. Doenitz's response was to call for a fleet of bigger and faster submarines. He could knock the British out of the war, he was certain of it, if only his recommendations were followed. The German government considered his proposals but decided against them. More submarines, primarily the old Type VIIs, would be produced, but the focus of the war would remain on the ground and in the air.

Doenitz knew that tenacity counted as much in bureaucratic battles as anything. After the initial denial of his proposed American attack, he reviewed the ninety-one U-boats then operational. Thirty-three were in the dockyards for repairs and maintenance and twenty en route to or from operations. Thirty-three more were on battle station, twenty-three in the Mediterranean, six off Gibraltar, and four off Norway. He could not touch any of these. But there were five U-boats, fortunately the long-range Type IXs that had no assignment and were ready to sail. Could these be used? Doenitz badgered his superiors again for *Paukenschlag*. He was granted his request but only on the condition that the U-boats be immediately recalled if required for the Norwegian campaign. Doenitz eagerly agreed and called in the commanders of the five *Unterseeboote*, briefed them, and wished them luck. He had no idea of the reception they would receive in American waters, but the commanders—the veterans Hardegen (*U-123*), Kals (*U-130*), Zapp (*U-66*), Bleichrodt (*U-109*), and Folkers (*U-125*)—were supremely confident. Between December 16th and 25th, the five U-boats left their French ports to cross the Atlantic. To ensure surprise, Doenitz ordered them to keep out of sight between Newfoundland and the American east coast unless a worthwhile target—ships of over 10,000 tons—presented itself. The operational area was to be the coast between the St. Lawrence and Cape Hatteras.

Despite Doenitz's caution, the United States was aware that the U-boats were probably coming. The moment they left occupied France, British agents warned London, which, in turn, passed on the information to Washington. Since the coast guard had come under the Department of the Navy's command early in 1941, the responsibility for the defense of the Atlantic coast had been given to 62-year-old Rear Admiral Adolphus Andrews, known to his friends as "Dolly." When this huge undertaking was given him, Admiral Andrews had already been on the active list for forty-one years, with a varied career that had made him one of the best-known flag officers in the navy. An '01 graduate of the Naval Academy, Andrews had, among many other assignments, been the commander of the presidential yacht *Mayflower*, the naval aide to President Coolidge, and the American representative to the Geneva Conference of 1927. A Texan, he liked to do everything on a grand scale. His large staff reflected his enthusiasm. They included Captain Thomas R. Kurtz (chief of staff), Captain S. B. Bunting (assistant chief of staff), Captain John T. G. Stapler (operations), Captains Harry E. Shoemaker and Stephan B. Robinson (convoy and routing), Captain Ralph Hungerford (antisubmarine warfare), Captain Henry M. Mullinnix (air), and Lieutenant Commander Harry H. Hess (submarine tracking). Before the war began, Admiral Andrews set up his headquarters in New York City, in the old Federal Building on 90 Church Street, and packed it with a communications center and plotting room from which he planned to manage American coastal defense. All he had to manage, however, were twenty ships, some of them no more than barges and the largest a 165-foot coast guard cutter, plus 103 obsolete aircraft, most of them down for repairs. This pitiful force was supposed to guard the First, Third, Fourth, and Fifth Naval Districts—over 1,500 miles of rugged coastline from the Canadian border to South Carolina!

Admiral Andrews hoped that the commander in chief of the U. S. Fleet, Admiral Ernest J. King, would eventually agree to his request for assistance from the rest of the navy. An entire fleet of battleships, cruisers, destroyers, aircraft carriers, and submarines operated out of Hampton Roads and Norfolk, Virginia. Admiral Andrews believed that those forces should be used in coastal defense, but King and his fleet admirals wanted to ensure that their ships were ready to do battle with the German surface fleet (at that time completely bottled up by the British) or be available to steam to the Pacific to fight the Japanese. In a complaint to King, Admiral Andrews pointed out that of the ships he had available, " . . . there is not a vessel . . . that an enemy submarine could not outdistance when operating on the surface. In most cases, the guns of these vessels would be outranged by those of the submarines." King told him to do what he could with what he had, so Andrews assigned his tiny floating force to patrols around important harbors and convinced the army to send planes from Mitchell Field and Langley Field on two daily sweeps over the ocean. He was aware that the army pilots had virtually no chance of spotting anything and, even if they did, would probably not be able to distinguish a German U-boat from an American submarine, but it was a beginning in what he hoped would be a continuing close cooperation between his command and the army air forces. The one concession made by Admiral King was to order fleet minelayers to mine the approaches to New York, Boston, and Portland harbors as well as the approaches to the Chesapeake Bay. Otherwise, Admiral Andrews was on his own.

According to the *North Atlantic Naval Coastal Frontier War Diary*, the first indication of the coming disaster began on 31 December 1941 with a dispatch from the First Naval District that a periscope had been spotted by fishing boats between Cushing and Ram Islands in Portland Channel. A week later, an army plane spotted a fleet of unidentified "destroyers and cruisers" 50 miles east of Cape May headed for the coast. No further word was received, and the fleet was written off as "probably fishermen." The next day, however, a "large, black submarine with a long conning tower and gun forward" was seen on the surface moving slowly northeast. It submerged when it was spotted by the plane. Admiral Andrews took this report seriously and asked for stepped-up surveillance. On the same day, 7 January 1942, the admiral received an intelligence report that "there are strong indications that 16 German submarines are proceeding to the area off the southeast coast of Newfoundland. The object of this operation is not understood." On the night of 11 January, the *Cyclops*, a large freighter, was sunk, apparently by torpedoes or mines about 300 miles off Cape Cod. Admiral Andrews rushed off to meet with Admiral King to again request assistance. King flatly turned him down. The navy would keep up routine patrols as always, but the bulk of the fleet would be kept ready for surface action. Frustrated, Andrews sent the army's First Bomber Command a memorandum that stated, "Submarines may be expected off our coast at any time. At least four are known to be about 300 miles east of Nantucket Light on 12 January, and are probably proceeding westward." On 14 January, Andrews's worst fears were confirmed with the report of a torpedo attack on the freighter *Norness* just 60 miles southeast of Montauk Point.

The U-boats had arrived.

★ ★ ★

A huge winter storm swept the North Atlantic as the *Paukenschlag* U-boats battled their way toward America. Unable to spend much time submerged due to the limitations of their batteries, the U-boats were forced to stay on the surface, taking the blows of massive waves and hurricane-force winds. Only when the batteries were fully charged and the crew close to madness would a commander finally give the order to dive for a brief respite. But the U-boats were too slow underwater and soon they were back on the surface, fighting westward.

There were others also out on that frightening sea. Frantic distress signals were received from dozens of damaged or lost Allied ships torn from their convoys. Following the orders given them by BdU (*Befehlshaber der Unterseeboote*—Commander U-boats), the U-boats ignored the easy prey. This was a secret operation, not to commence until Admiral Doenitz determined the time to be right. In the *BdU War Diary*, Doenitz wrote his hopes for *Paukenschlag*. "The entrance of America into the war has provided the commanders with areas which are not hemmed in by defenses and which offer much better chances for success." He still harbored doubts, however. "In retrospect," he wrote, "the defenses of these areas are unknown." Doenitz knew he had gambled much of his prestige on the operation. It had to work. Finally, when the U-boats were near the mid-point in their crossing, Doenitz sent the signal: "*Paukenschlag* will take effect January 13."

Perhaps the most ambitious and aggressive of the five commanders was Kapitänleutnant Reinhard Hardegen of the *U-123*. Hardegen was considered something of a braggart by his fellow U-boat commanders, easy to get started talking but difficult to stop. He had also been thought a coward by some, but after a serious aircraft accident, it seemed he had been transformed into a courageous and determined leader. Whatever the merit of these opinions, Doenitz obviously had respect for him, having given him a lead position in *Paukenschlag*.

Hardegen managed to be the first across, arriving off Newfoundland on the night of 11 January. While traveling south on the surface, one of his lookouts spotted smoke. Kaleun (abbreviated, affectionate term for Kapitänleutnant) Hardegen moved his U-boat toward the sighting and then submerged when a big freighter appeared over the horizon. He decided to attack her even if Doenitz had said to wait until the 13th to begin the American operation. Perhaps, Hardegen reasoned, he was still out far enough to sink the ship without alerting coastal forces.

The freighter, the 9,076-ton British steamship *Cyclops*, was struck by two of Hardegen's torpedoes. The first one stopped her, the second broke her in two, and she sank quickly. The *U-123* submerged and kept heading west while most of the crewmen of the *Cyclops* drowned in the cold Atlantic. Only 82 of the 181-man crew would survive.

Coming in behind Hardegen the next day, Kapitänleutnant Ernst Kals of the *U-130* officially opened *Paukenschlag* by sinking two small freighters off Newfoundland. Kals had been ordered to that area to catch commercial traffic going in and coming out of the St. Lawrence and also to attack outbound American convoys. He would obey those orders and stay put. Hardegen, however, was heading south. On the night of the 14th, he took the *U-123* into Rhode Island Sound and was amazed at the sight that confronted him. The American shore seemed a fairyland of glowing lights and street signs compared with blacked-out Europe. Automobile headlights moved up and down the coast, a coast clearly marked by dozens of bobbing, well-lit marker buoys. "It's unbelievable," he breathed to the lookouts on the conning tower with him. "I have a feeling the Americans are going to be very surprised . . ."

One of the lookouts hissed a warning. He had seen the Panamanian tanker *Norness*. Hardegen maneuvered until he had the tanker between him and the lights on shore and then sent two torpedoes streaking into her side. The radioman sent up a report. The tanker had identified herself and believed she had struck a mine. Hardegen was surprised. "You're certain they're saying a mine?"

"Yes, sir. They're sending it in the clear."

Hardegen just couldn't believe it. "A mine!" he exploded. "Nobody seems to be expecting any German U-boats around here!" Unable to resist making a little speech, he turned to the voice tube. "Listen to me, everyone! We're here like a wolf in the middle of a flock of sheep. We've just sunk a tanker, and the Americans still haven't realized that there's a submarine in the area. So much the better for us. Let's take advantage of the situation."

Hardegen waited for the *Norness* to sink, but she stubbornly remained afloat. His radioman reported that she was also continuously signaling for help. Another torpedo was sent into the listing tanker, and this time she broke in two, her stern sinking and her bow settling. Satisfied, Hardegen took the *U-123* down and spent the rest of the night running south until he was opposite Long Island, almost at the mouth of New York harbor. "We could make out many lights," he would write in his log, "probably a suburb of New York . . . Distance to downtown approximately 30 miles. Depth approximately 33 feet. Cannot get any shallower or the topside bridge will not be submerged when diving." Early on the morning of 15 January, he caught the British tanker *Coimbra* all alone and sent two torpedoes into her side. The *Coimbra* buckled and then blew up. "The effect was amazing," Hardegen wrote, "strong detonation, fire column reaching 200 meters and the whole sky was illuminated . . . Quite a bonfire we leave behind for the Yankees as navigational help . . ." There were no other ships or airplanes visible, and the shore lights continued burning placidly as if nothing unusual were happening. Hardegen found himself no longer being very cautious. He stayed on the surface and kept moving south.

When word of Hardegen's successes reached New York, Admiral Andrews ordered everything under his command to sea, including some ships never designed for anything beyond harbor traffic. Typical of these was the *YP 49*, a small, wooden-hulled ship used for twenty-three years by the coast guard to patrol the Philadelphia Naval Shipyard. By adding two 300-pound depth charges, the navy had made her into an official subchaser. On 16 January 1942, navy Ensign Lee E. O'Neill was ordered to take charge of the *YP 49* and sail her to Barnegat Bay on an antisubmarine patrol. O'Neill did as he was told, and the next day found the "Yippy 49" pitching and wallowing on a gray sea passing dozens of small coastal ships hugging the coast. After turning north for the return leg, the *YP 49*'s engine, clogged by sludge in the fuel tanks, caught fire and one of the enlisted men was badly burned. O'Neill had no choice but to head sputteringly for the coast guard base in Atlantic City for assistance. Even though barely able to move, O'Neill conscientiously kept looking through his salt-smeared binoculars for U-boats. None was seen. One, however, saw him. Kaleun Hardegen watched with disinterest as the small patrol craft passed. It was the ship behind that he had his eye on.

O'Neill was standing on the dock watching the coast guard mechanics when he felt a shock. When he looked up, he saw a small freighter no more than 1,000 yards away shuddering from the impact of a torpedo. She quickly sank upright, her masts showing in the shallow water. The coast guard abandoned their service-station chores and launched a small unarmed boat to go out and rescue the crew of what proved to be the freighter *San José*. Hardegen came to the surface in clear view of the Americans on shore to observe the damage he had done and then moved slowly away, still on the surface. All Ensign O'Neill could do was watch helplessly. It was all Admiral Andrews back in his New York headquarters could do as well.

While Hardegen was battering the Americans, Fregattenkapitän Richard Zapp and his *U-66* had ignored all shipping and gone straight to Cape Hatteras. Admiral Doenitz had assigned Zapp to perhaps the best area to find freighters and tankers. Hundreds of ships used the wide, warm Gulf Stream that swerved near Cape Hatteras to sail north to the ports of North America and Europe. Southbound ships, not wanting to sail against the Gulf Stream or swing too far out into the open ocean, were forced near the jutting North Carolina coast. It was a natural choke point. On the morning of 18 January, the *U-66* was in position, waiting. A lookout called Zapp's attention to a light on the southwestern horizon. The light was rising, turning into two lights, then three and more, red and green and white lights all over the deck of an approaching ship. "Recognize tanker with 3 masts, narrow medium-high funnel," Zapp wrote in his log. "Tanker is heavily loaded . . . did not tack."

Zapp was careful with his torpedoes, stalking the tanker for four hours until he was in position. The tanker was the *Allan Jackson*, bound for New York with a cargo of 72,870 barrels of crude oil. Second Mate Melvin A. Rand was on the bridge when he happened to look to starboard and saw the wake of something coming toward the ship. Although he found it difficult to believe, he thought it looked like a torpedo. "Hard to port!" he yelled at Seaman Randy Larson at the wheel, but it was too late. The torpedo struck the tanker in the nearly empty forward tank on the starboard side. A second torpedo was close behind, this one exploding between two full oil tanks. The *Allan Jackson*, engulfed in flames, began to break apart. Rand and Larson leaped from the bridge into the sea.

The *Allan Jackson*'s master, Captain Felix W. Kretchmer, was thrown out of his bunk and all the way across his cabin by the second torpedo. Trapped by fire, he was only able to get out of his cabin by squeezing through a tiny porthole. He headed toward the bridge but the tanker suddenly tore in two, the sea rushing up and sweeping him away. Boatswain Rolf Clausen had been playing cards in the messroom on the port side aft when the torpedoes struck. He and his companions rushed out on deck, lowered a lifeboat, and pushed it toward the stern where it seemed to be clear of flames. It was only at the last that they realized the reason for the clearing was because the tanker's huge propeller was still turning, creating a backwash. The propeller struck the boat and would have torn it to bits, but the *Allan Jackson* settled a little and the propeller dropped farther down into the water. In doing so, it also flushed out a clear lane through the burning oil. Someone prayed aloud as the lifeboat entered the fiery corridor. Heat blistered their faces and singed their hair but they kept going until, finally, the flames were behind. Almost instantly, the burning oil closed in, sealing the narrow escape route. Looking back, Clausen saw a man on fire leap from the ship.

The *U-66* eased to a stop while Zapp assessed the damage he had caused. He tried to identify the tanker with his searchlight but could not. It was too badly torn up to make an identification by silhouette, and burning oil had spread for almost a half a mile around the ship. No matter. Undoubtedly, the Americans would announce on the radio the next day what tanker it was. He took the *U-66* down.

Clausen and his fellow survivors kept rowing away. A shout led them to the radio operator, Stephen Verbonich, just before he went under. Three hours later, one of the men aboard the lifeboat spotted a bluish light to the east. Hoping it wasn't the U-boat, Clausen used a flashlight and turned it against the sail and blinked an SOS signal. Shortly before daylight, Clausen saw with relief that it was an American destroyer. He sent up two distress flares and the ship turned in their direction. It was the American destroyer *Roe* on normal patrol. The *Roe*, which had already picked up three *Allan Jackson* survivors, including Larson and Rand, took Clausen and his mates aboard, and then moved forward carefully. There were bodies floating in the water. A *Roe* lookout yelled that he thought he had seen one of them move. He had. Drenched in oil, Captain Felix W. Kretchmer climbed aboard the destroyer and stood straight on the polished deck. He had been in the water for over seven hours. He wasn't certain what had happened, he reported, but he thought his ship had perhaps hit a mine. Twenty-two men had lost their lives.

While the *Roe* returned to Norfolk with the *Allan Jackson*'s survivors, Zapp continued his hunt, moving the *U-66* out to sea a little, dropping down to the bottom for a day of rest, and then surfacing just as the Canadian passenger liner *Lady Hawkins* hove into view. The big ship was blacked out and tacking but made a perfect silhouette against the lit-up American shore. After six hours of stalking, Zapp sent two torpedoes after the fast liner. On the *Lady Hawkins*, the terrified passengers rushed for the lifeboats, but only three of the boats would get away before their ship sank. Three hundred passengers and crew would go into the water that night. Only ninety-six would survive after a torturous five days with little food or water.

Although Zapp and the *U-66* were enjoying being first off the North Carolina capes, Hardegen and the *U-123* had sunk four ships while moving south. Four ships! Hardegen pondered that fact. Where were the defenses? Where was the American navy? Except for O'Neill's tiny "Yippy," he had not encountered a single warship or airplane. The opportunities for success gave Hardegen no time to puzzle for long. On 19 January, he was at a position off Cape Hatteras despite the fact that BdU had assigned him only the New York and New Jersey coasts. Hardegen had no intention of allowing Zapp to have the exclusive rights to such an obvious killing zone as Hatteras. Besides, he believed that once a U-boat was at sea, a commander should always use his initiative and find the best spot for killing ships no matter what the orders. In this, he had the blessings of Admiral Doenitz. At 0207 (unless otherwise specified, all times given are Eastern War Time (EWT)), a big freighter was spotted. Hardegen backed off to get her between him and the bright lights of shore and then loosed two torpedoes.

It was the American *City of Atlanta*. After the torpedoes struck, the crew panicked. Men milled and yelled and frantically clawed at the lifeboats, trying to push them overboard. One, with eighteen men, was finally dropped but it immediately capsized, spilling the men into the sea. Hardegen was on the bridge and ordered a searchlight turned on. He had been surprised that the freighter had sunk so fast and had not seen anyone get off. He ordered one of his men to call out to see if there were any survivors. Again and again, the man called "*Kamerade! Kamerade!*," but there was no reply and Hardegen soon gave up, taking the *U-123* down. The next morning, the freighter *Seatrain Texas* would find only three survivors of the *City of Atlanta*. Forty-three men had been lost.

But Hardegen and the *U-123* were not finished for the night. At 0430, one of the lookouts whispered he could see another light, this one a white mast light coming up over the horizon to the north. Hardegen alerted the bow torpedo room to prepare for a salvo. More reports came from the lookouts. Three more ships could be seen coming up over the horizon. Hardegen decided, however, to concentrate on his original target. At 0500, the ship, moving very slowly and festooned with lights, sailed into Hardegen's cross-hairs.

The *Ciltvaira*, a Latvian ship, was the small freighter moving slowly in front of Hardegen. She was on her way to Savannah from Norfolk with a mixed crew of thirty-two Finns, Danes, Estonians, Dutch, Swedes, Romanians, and even a few Latvians aboard. There was also a ship's cat named Briskis and a puppy, Pluskis. Captain Karl Skerbergs had heard about German U-boats operating off the Atlantic coast but had dismissed it as fantastic. In any case, he believed the *Ciltvaira* was much too unimportant a target for a U-boat. They would be after bigger game, that much Skerbergs knew.

It was still dark outside when Captain Skerbergs was awakened by a loud "thump." He leaped out of bed. He thought his ship had hit a shoal, but the shouts of his crewmen outside his cabin quickly dispelled this theory. An explosion! Skerbergs guessed that the *Ciltvaira* had struck a mine. He grabbed his clothes and made for the bridge. The ship had stopped and was drifting. He looked out to port, thought he saw a light, but what light could it be? To starboard, he could see the light of a buoy. Which one? He found the bridge deserted except for the mess boy who was standing in a corner, looking very frightened. He calmed the boy and asked where the mates were. Just then, the first mate appeared and together, he and Captain Skerbergs tried to determine where they were. For some reason, none of the charts made any sense. Skerbergs suddenly felt his ship lurch. Was she sinking? He heard the sound of a lifeboat being released. He made his way out on deck with the first mate and saw that almost all of his crew had left the ship in the large standard lifeboat. They yelled at the captain to get off, that the ship was sinking. Skerbergs yelled back at them to return, but when he saw that they had taken Briskis and Pluskis with them, he knew they would not come back. Reluctantly, he gathered the remaining crewmen and told them to get the wounded and follow him into the other, smaller lifeboat. He was told then that two of the firemen had been killed by the explosion, whatever it was, but that no one else had been seriously injured. Captain Skerbergs ordered the two bodies wrapped in blankets and brought with them. Soon, the captain and the others found themselves adrift while the sun rose placidly and brilliantly over a flat, calm sea.

Hardegen, through with the *Ciltvaira*, turned after the other ships his lookouts had spotted. The three that had been there had disappeared, running in to shore, but five more had appeared, apparently unaware of the killing ahead of them. Believing that the closest tanker was too small to waste a torpedo on, Hardegen decided to use his deck gun. His second-in-command, Von Schroeter, was skeptical of the idea. "Attack while running up astern of them?" he questioned. "Can't be done, sir. For one thing they'd be bound to see us before we had fired the first shot and then we'd get it in the neck."

Hardegen reddened. "I don't give a shit!" he snapped. "Guns are not in my line but I have a hunch it will work . . . The bolder you are, the more likely your bluff will be successful."

Hardegen demanded full speed and, with a puff of black diesel smoke, the *U-123* pushed ahead, closing on the tanker. The deck gun fired once, then again. There was a spout of flame on the tanker's deck and then a huge boil of fire and smoke. The lookouts reported that the other ships had turned off their lights and were running away, so Hardegen decided to stay with the burning tanker. He ordered his *Obermaschinistmaat* to maintain maximum speed, but just as he did, the port diesel clanked to a stop with a broken cooling-water pump. A cursing Hardegen was forced to suspend the chase.

While the *U-123*'s machinists worked on the engine, the radioman brought Hardegen a message sent by the tanker. "Tanker *Malay* on fire after being shelled by U-boat," it read. "Please inform nearest naval command. Fire under control. Am making for Norfolk." The radioman added, "The *Malay* is 8,206 tons, herr Kaleun."

"Good God, I had no idea she was so big!" Hardegen exclaimed. He decided to catch her no matter what it took.

The *U-123* strained ahead, her one good engine giving her barely 15 knots. The smoke from the *Malay* was still visible and gave Hardegen something to chase. An hour later, the *Malay* could be seen. The fires were out. "It aggravated me that the tanker was OK again," Hardegen wrote, "and I intended to spoil their success." The *U-123*'s last torpedo hit the *Malay* in an empty compartment, flooding it. Three panicky crew members of the tanker attempted to launch a lifeboat while the ship was still steaming full ahead, but the instant the boat hit the water, it overturned and the men in it were lost. After the *Malay* came to a stop, another lifeboat, this one with fourteen men in it, was successfully dropped to the sea. An hour later, however, the *Malay*'s master, John Dodge, ordered the lifeboat back. The *Malay* could still make way. Hardegen, thinking that he had sunk the tanker, had already left to chase another ship. Amazingly, the *Malay* would yet manage to limp into Norfolk the next day.

The *Ciltvaira* was also still afloat. After her crew had abandoned her, a tanker, the *Socony-Vacuum*, happened upon the scene and took aboard the crew. Captain Skerbergs had barely gotten on the tanker when he looked back and saw the *Ciltvaira* about a mile away. He could see no discernible damage besides a slight tilt. Perhaps he could yet save his ship. He called for volunteers, got eight, and climbed back into the small lifeboat. Soon, he and the men were scrambling back aboard their freighter while the *Socony-Vacuum* motored on toward Charleston, South Carolina, with the rest of the crew, including Briskis and Pluskis. Carefully, Skerbergs climbed down toward the fireroom. He heard much gurgling even before he got there but he still had hope. Once there, however, he was disappointed. The *Ciltvaira* was broken open in the middle and was filling fast. Skerbergs scrambled back to the deck and ordered the lifeboat launched again. Another ship appeared, this one the Brazilian freighter *Bury*. Soon, Skerbergs was on his way to New York while behind him, his little ship kept filling with water. She was still afloat when Skerbergs, from the stern of the *Bury*, sadly watched her disappear below the horizon.

There was no sadness aboard the *U-123*. Quite the opposite. A general celebration was going on. The cook was called to fix the best meal he could. It was apparent to the crew of the U-boat that they and their commander had become something special. They were all aces. They had sunk six ships, believed it to be eight, without so much as an answering firecracker from the hapless Americans. "The night of the long knives is over," Hardegen wrote. "A drum roll for 8 ships, among them 3 tankers, with a total of 53,860 GRT. What a pity that when I was positioned off New York we didn't have two additional mine-laying U-boats closing everything down and 10–20 boats tonight in addition to ours. I believe each one of them would have been able to get her limit." More than ships had been sunk, too. He noted in his log that, as a result of his activities ". . . the entire telegram communications of Jews across the sea has stopped completely." He made a report to BdU announcing his success and Doenitz promptly replied: "To 'Drummer' Hardegen. Bravo! You drummed very well." Shortly afterwards, Doenitz also awarded Hardegen the Knight's Cross. A ceremony was held in the control room of the *U-123*, the crew presenting their commander with a homemade version of the decoration. Even though the *U-123* was out of torpedoes, Hardegen's glorious patrol wasn't over. On the way back to France, he would use his deck gun to sink two more ships.

After the initial losses in January, a worried Admiral Andrews ordered a review by his staff to see if any pattern to the U-boat attacks could be dis-
cerned. Cape Hatteras seemed to be the U-boat's favorite hunting grounds,
that was clear. Also, the U-boats were working primarily alone. This surprised
Andrews. Why were they not using the famous "wolfpack" tactics he had
heard so much about? His staff had no answer for that, but it was clear that
the U-boats were being given easy shots because the merchant ships were
keeping their running lights on at night. It was also believed that city lights
were being used by the U-boat commanders to silhouette their targets.

Admiral Andrews's task was to convince Admiral King of his needs.
He began to make a series of trips back and forth to Washington to argue his
case. First, Andrews told King, he wanted more ships and airplanes for patrol
duty. Next, he wanted the president to order a complete blackout along the
eastern shore. He had sent a member of his staff, a Captain McFall, down the
coast to observe the light intensity. McFall had come back and reported, "It is
possible for a submarine to select either the bow or stern of a ship as his target by the glare of lights." The people would understand, Andrews earnestly
explained, if they knew their lights were causing the deaths of men at sea.
Finally, Andrews wanted to move the commercial sea lanes 60 miles out to sea
around Cape Hatteras. This would spread the traffic out and make it harder
for the U-boats to find targets.

King and Andrews could speak plainly to each other. Both were from
the same Naval Academy class and had climbed up through the rungs of
command of a small navy. The officers of such a force invariably form a soci-
ety of their own, and the peacetime United States Navy had been no different. King and Andrews had crossed paths often. Both men were ambitious but
had different styles. Where Andrews recognized his own limitations and that
of other men, King was completely unsparing of himself and all others. King
had finally climbed to the position of Commander in Chief, U. S. Fleet on
20 December 1941. Three months later, he would also take on the additional
duties of the chief of naval operations.

King turned down the first two requests Andrews made with the
explanation that he still intended to keep his fleet intact and there were scientific instruments being designed that would take care of he U-boat problem. He did, however, allow a temporary movement of the shipping lanes, at
least through the month. Recognizing King's intransigence on the subject,
Andrews accepted the decision but then made an attempt to educate King a
bit on the mathematics of submarine warfare. From his studies of the British

battle against the U-boats, Andrews said, he had determined that nothing mattered so much as having as many ships and planes arranged against the submarines as possible. The British had succeeded only because they had put everything they had to sea, including converted trawlers. They had, Admiral Andrews told his dubious commander, actually defeated the U-boats in the North Atlantic, although it had hardly been recognized. The United States could do the same by following their example. What Andrews really needed, he said, were destroyers. Admiral King replied that this was not possible. He would have no destroyers to spare for the east coast, not now, probably not ever. He reminded Admiral Andrews that he had a war to fight in the Pacific as well. As far as King was concerned, the subject was closed.

Although Hardegen was heading back to France, Zapp and his *U-66* were still off Hatteras, determined to use the last of their torpedoes. Since sinking the *Lady Hawkins*, the *U-66* had sunk the American freighter *Norvana* and its cargo of sugar on the morning of January 22. Nothing was ever heard of the ship or its crew of twenty-nine again. Zapp had used two stern torpedoes on the diminutive freighter, ensuring its doom. "Steamer breaks apart midships and sinks within one minute," Zapp logged. He estimated it at 7,500 tons and 400 feet in length. The *Norvana* was, in fact, only 2,677 tons and 253 feet long.

The *Venore*, loaded with 22,700 tons of iron ore from Chile, was to be the *U-66*'s last victim of *Paukenschlag*. The *Venore*'s captain, Fritz Dourloo, had heard rumors of German U-boat activity all the way back at the Panama Canal. In fact, his second cook had been told by soldiers at the canal that four ships had been sunk right off Cape Hatteras. But the *Venore* was bound for Baltimore, so Dourloo had no choice but to sail up the east coast of the United States. The night of 23 January 1942, found her 80 miles off Hatteras, heading almost due north. Dourloo had decided to stay out that far, reasoning that if there were any U-boats, they would probably be working in closer. Lookouts had spotted another ship behind them earlier in the day and as the day wore on, the ship, the British tanker *Empire Gem*, began to catch up. At twilight, the tanker was only a mile off the starboard quarter. Ahead lay Diamond Shoals. Dourloo ordered only the dimmed sidelights turned on and proceeded through the darkness at 10 knots. The *Empire Gem* was still a little behind, her running lights fully on. Peter Karlson, the quartermaster, was at the wheel of the *Venore* with the captain beside him. Ahead of them, they saw a light blinking. Dourloo read the code. It was the Diamond Shoals Lightship and it was messaging for them to come nearer. Perhaps they were going to be ordered into a safe harbor for the night. After several minutes of running toward the light, it suddenly went out. Dourloo ordered Karlson back on his original course. Neither man said anything but both thought it. *Trap.*

If Zapp had, in fact, lured the *Venore* in closer, he made no mention of it in his log. He had, however, been wrestling with the problem of which ship to attack first. He had decided to go after the *Venore* because she appeared to be bigger, but just as he lined up, the *Empire Gem* suddenly changed course, running right in front of the *U-66*'s tubes.

The *Venore* was just beginning a turn when a terrific shock wave knocked everyone on the bridge to their knees. A column of fire climbed 500 feet into the night sky where the *Empire Gem* had been. Dourloo turned the *Venore* away from the burning tanker and pointed her bow directly toward shore. It was their only chance. Better to hit the shoals than take a torpedo. Dourloo looked back. The U-boat was following. He ordered his radioman to call the coast guard station at Ocracoke and alert them to the *Venore*'s situation. The radioman, Vernon Minzey, did so, adding the plaintive comment, *Think Swimming Soon.*

While the *Venore* raced for shore, many of her confused crew prepared to lower the lifeboats. No orders had come to them, but after seeing the *Empire Gem* explode, they were all certain the *Venore* was next. Before a boat could be swung out, however, there was a slight concussion aft. Just then, a man erupted from somewhere below and ran screaming all the way to the stern and jumped off. Two lifeboats were swung out, dozens of panicky men climbing aboard. The *Venore* was still grinding on at full speed. As soon as the boats hit the sea, they were torn apart, planks and bodies smashing against the side of the ship. It happened so quickly not a single whimper was heard from the crewmen. A third boat was dropped, this one with only two men aboard. Somehow, it avoided hitting the *Venore* and was seen swirling away into the darkness.

Since the *U-66* had torpedoed the *Empire Gem*, Zapp had busily tried to cut off the speeding *Venore*. From 1,000 meters, he had sent two bow torpedoes after her with one hit. Disappointingly, however, the "iron ore freighter," as Zapp referred to the *Venore* in his log, had kept going. Although the *U-66* was in hot pursuit, Zapp saw that he was going to lose the race and decided to fire another torpedo even though he was more than a mile behind. To hit the fleeing freighter would take an extraordinary shot.

Third Mate Andy Jackson was on the bridge when the torpedo plunged into the Number 9 ballast tank of the *Venore*. Zapp had made his shot. The ship listed sharply to port, the deck going completely under. When she righted, a huge torrent of water, thrown high into the air by the torpedo, cascaded down to wash across the decks. Captain Dourloo went outside and unleashed a liferaft and threw it overboard for any men who might be in the water. He told Jackson to go to the remaining lifeboat. Jackson complied, finding Minzey, the radio operator, along the way. Together, they made their way to the lifeboat station only to find that the boat had already been lowered under the direction of Chief Mate Mulligan. Mulligan yelled up at them to come down the falls. Jackson got tangled in the ropes and fell headlong into the boat. Minzey, who only had one arm, also lost his grip but missed the boat and fell into the sea. He did not come up. Three days later, the twenty-one survivors in the lifeboat were found by the tanker *Tennessee*. The remaining twenty-two crewmen, including Captain Dourloo, remained missing forever.

As for Fregattenkapitän Zapp and the crew of the *U-66*, they had at last used all their torpedoes. They were triumphantly sailing for France, while Kals in the *U-130* and Folkers in the *U-125*, unsuccessful in finding targets farther north, moved into the Hatteras killing grounds. In quick succession, the *U-130* sank the *Veranger*, the *Francis E. Powell*, and severely damaged the tanker *Halo*. The *U-125* found Hatteras to be profitable as well, running the tanker *Olney* aground and sinking the freighter *West Ivis*. Cape Hatteras, the Graveyard of the Atlantic, was starting to be called a new name by the freighter and tanker crews: Torpedo Junction.

On 25 January 1942, Admiral Andrews was given a message from Admiral King. It read "Atlantic Fleet aircraft within limits your respective coastal frontiers hereby made available to you to assist actively in combatting enemy sub actions."

Admiral Andrews reacted with satisfaction. His battle was finally being recognized! He immediately relayed the message to his staff and commanders at sea. On the same day, three utility planes from the Atlantic fleet pool were assigned to the airfield at Elizabeth City, North Carolina, the first addition to the small force of unarmed coast guard airplanes stationed there. Cape Hatteras would be their patrol area. On 27 January, Andrews assigned twelve more planes there for patrolling. The next day, he attempted to provide for Elizabeth City in a different way. In a letter to Admiral King, he wrote, "It is understood that there are approximately twenty PBY-5s belonging to the Royal Air Force now at Elizabeth City, N.C., and that due to lack of crews these aircraft are not all in transit. In view of the immediate demand for long-range patrol planes, it is suggested that arrangements might be made for temporary assignment for six of the PBY's . . . until such time as suitable replacements can be furnished." Admiral King's reply was negative but not abruptly so. "Shortage of patrol type aircraft for specific duty under Naval Coastal Frontier Commanders is recognized," his letter to Andrews said, ". . . provision is made in the current aircraft program for patrol squadrons which will be allocated to the Naval Coastal Frontier Commands." Admiral Andrews now felt he had the attention of his commander. But he would keep asking and pushing even if it made him the most unpopular officer in the navy. He only had to check his teletype machines each morning to see the obvious. There was a battle being fought for which he was responsible, and it was a battle that was being lost. He was going to fight back with whatever he could.

While Admiral Andrews wrestled with the problems of his command, Admiral Doenitz was beginning to realize the success of his. In his private office, Doenitz nervously ruffled through the papers on his desk as Kapitänleutnant Hardegen concluded his report. Nodding approval, the admiral waved Hardegen to a chair and then slowly made his own assessment. It was obvious, he said, that the combat conditions off the American coast should be exploited. But there was a problem. The High Command. Always the High Command. Doenitz was as angry as Hardegen had ever seen him. "Can anyone tell me," he said in his high-pitched voice, "what good tanks and trucks and airplanes are if the enemy doesn't have fuel for them? Once again, I've tried to explain this simple fact to them . . . our sole mission should be to sink as much tonnage as possible, as quickly as possible, and in the place where we can do it most efficiently." Doenitz clasped his hands so tightly his knuckles whitened. His lips were tightly pursed. "Well, gentlemen, I've received an answer . . . 'You are oversimplifying,' they say. It seems to me that these fine gentlemen have forgotten what Napoleon said: 'War is a simple art and consists entirely in performance.' "

Paukenschlag, then, would continue, but at nothing like the level Doenitz wished. In fact, just as six more U-boats were gathered to cross the Atlantic, Hitler himself diverted them to the Norwegian fjords to stop a British invasion he intuitively believed was coming. Doenitz protested, but the Fuhrer's order was law. Admiral Andrews had no way of knowing it, but Adolf Hitler had given him at least a little more time to gather what resources he could to stop the U-boats.

"Second Attack"

BY LOTHAR-GUNTHER BUCHHEIM

Translated from the German by Denver and Helen Lindley
(Excerpted from the novel *The Boat*)

Film audiences all over the world have been captivated by the film version of *The Boat*—*Das Boot* in German—but no doubt many have overlooked and missed the reading rewards that await them in this stunning book. An international best-seller when it was published in 1975, *The Boat* was heralded as the best-ever vivid and realistic portrait of a U-boat submarine crew in action. The author served on a U-boat as an official naval correspondent after earlier navy service as a lieutenant on mine sweepers and destroyers. His recollections of every detail of submarine life are shared in engaging prose, crackling with drama and suspense.

The time is the late fall and early winter of 1941, when German U-boats were stalking British convoys on the Atlantic. The early successes of the U-boat wolf packs have now been tempered by more skilled British destroyer operations and their sonar, Asdic. In the sequence presented here, The Boat has been on the surface through the evening dusk, waiting for darkness, carefully stalking a convoy of ships and tankers, guarded by fast, prowling corvettes. The crew is at battle stations. The time for attack is near.

It should be noted that, as in most U-boats, the crew here is made up of 18- and 19-year-olds, with the officers not much older. The captain is the "Old Man" at 30. The casualty rate for these young men was very high: of the 40,000 German sailors who served on U-boats in World War II, 30,000 never returned.

The moon has turned even whiter, icier. All around its sharply defined halo the sky is clear. But one of the clouds on the horizon is advancing on it, looking like the vanguard of a whole horde.

I only have eyes for this particular one. It's moving in the right direction, but after a while it slows down until it's hardly rising at all; then it turns threadbare and starts to unravel. As we watch, it dissolves. All that's left is a veil of vapor.

"For chrissake!" hisses the navigator.

But then another cloud prepares to free itself from the horizon, even heavier and fuller than the first.

The wind pushes it a little sideways, exactly the way we want it to go. No one is cursing any longer, as if cursing might upset it.

I abandon the cloud to concentrate on the horizon. In my glasses I can make out the bow, stern, and midship superstructures of the freighters.

The Commander tells the First Watch Officer his plan. "Charge them and fire. After firing, turn instantly to port. If that cloud keeps rising, I'll go in for the main attack!"

The First Watch Officer gives the instructions for the calculator, which is operated by one man in the tower and a second in the control room.

"Tubes one to four stand by for surface firing!"

All four torpedo tubes are flooded.

The bow compartment reports over the speaking tube: "Tubes one to four clear for surface firing!"

"Connect TBT and target position calculator. Firing will take place from bridge!" orders the First Watch Officer.

The words come smoothly. So he can do it. He's got that much by heart.

The mate at the calculator in the tower acknowledges the orders.

The Old Man behaves as though all this liturgical antiphony has nothing to do with him. Only the tension in his stance betrays his acute awareness of everything that's going on.

The First Watch Officer now reports to the mate in the tower: "Enemy position bow right—angle fifty—enemy speed ten knots—range ten thousand feet—torpedo speed thirty—depth ten—position changing."

The First Watch Officer doesn't need to worry about the proper lead angle for the torpedoes. The position calculator computes that. The calculator is connected directly with the gyrocompass and the TBT column, along with the torpedoes, whose steering mechanism is thus continuously adjusted. Every change in the boat's course is automatically translated for the torpedoes. All the First Watch Officer has to do is keep the target in the crosshairs of the glasses on the TBT column.

He bends over the eyepiece. "Ready for comparison reading! . . . Variation . . . Zero!"

"*Must* work," the Commander murmurs. Once more he glances up at the moon. The second cloud has stopped, like a captive balloon that has reached its predetermined height. Three handbreadths below the moon: There it hangs, and doesn't budge.

"One good push!" The navigator shakes his clenched fist; an outburst of feeling from so quiet a man as Kriechbaum amazes me. But there's no time to muse over the navigator; the Commander jerks his face sharply around and orders: "Full speed ahead! Hard a-port! Commence attack! Open torpedo doors!"

From below come the shouted repetitions of the commands. The bow is already beginning to swing along the horizon—seeking the shadows.

"Midships!—Steady as she goes! Hold ninety degrees!" The boat is racing straight at the dark shapes, which are growing larger by the second.

The plowshare of the bow cuts into the shining sea, hurling aside great masses of sparkling water. The wave surges, glints with a thousand facets. The foreship rises. Immediately spray sweeps over us. The diesels are running at full speed. The bulwark quivers.

"Find your target!" the Commander orders.

The First Watch Officer remains bent over the sight.

"There, those two overlapping ones, we'll take them. Have you got them? To the left, beside the single freighter! The big one will need a double shot, the others singles. Fire a double, one at the forward edge of the bridge and one just ahead of the aftermast!"

I'm standing close behind the Commander.

"Tubes one to four clear!"

My heart is hammering in my throat, and I can't think straight. The roaring engines, the shadows, the silver sea, the moon, the final charge! We're meant to be a U-boat—let's pray everything goes right.

The First Watch Officer keeps the target in his sights. His mouth is downturned, his voice matter of fact and dry. He's constantly revising his figures. He already has his right hand on the firing lever.

"Connect tubes one and two—angle sixty-five—follow changing angle!"

"Request angle!"

"Angle seventy . . . angle eighty!"

Close beside me I hear the Commander say, "Tubes one and two, permission to fire!"

Seconds later the First Watch Officer orders, "Tubes one and two fire!"

I strain all my senses: no report—no jolt—nothing! The boat races on, even closer to the freighters.

They've noticed nothing!—nothing!

"Connect tube three!"

"Tube three—fire!"

"Port ten!" orders the Commander.

Once more the bow moves, searching, along the chain of ships.

"Connect tube four!" from the First Watch Officer. He waits until the new target is in position and orders, "Tube four—fire!"

It's at this moment, close beside the target steamer, that I discover a long, low ship—a shadow that's not as dark as the others—probably painted gray.

"Hard a-port! Connect stern tube!" That was the Commander. The boat heels heavily as she turns. The shadows move to starboard.

The navigator calls, "Vessel veering this way!"

I see that our stern is now aimed at the shadows. But I also see that the light-colored shape is narrowing. I can even see the thread of her bow wave.

"Tube five—fire! Hard a-starboard!" shouts the Commander. The boat has barely swung toward the other side when orange-red lightning blazes up, followed in a fraction of a second by another flash. A mighty fist strikes me in the knees, and a sharp whistling goes through me like cold steel.

"They're firing, the bastards! ALARM!" roars the Old Man.

With one jump I'm in the hatch and let myself fall through. Seaboots land on my shoulders. I leap away, jammed up against the chart table, doubled over with pain. Someone goes rolling across the floor in front of me.

"Flood!" shouts the Commander, and immediately afterward, "Hard a-port!" There's a dash of water from above. Our high speed is forcing the boat down at a steeper angle than usual, but the Commander still orders, "All hands forward!"

"That was damned good!" he exclaims as he catches up with us.

I have some difficulty realizing that this is praise for the enemy artillery. The cavalcade of men goes stumbling through the compartment. I catch terrified looks. Everything begins to slide. The leather jackets and the binoculars on their hooks to right and left of the hatch are standing out from the walls.

The needle of the depth manometer sweeps over the scale, till the Chief finally orders the hydroplanes reversed. The jackets and binoculars sink slowly—very gradually—back toward the walls. The boat returns to an even keel.

I can't catch the Commander's eye. "That was damned good"—anything better and we'd have been done for. I can think of only one thing: the torpedoes—what about the torpedoes?

"Just as I thought—it was a destroyer," says the Commander. He sounds short of breath. I can see his chest heaving. He looks us over as if to assure himself that everyone's present, then mutters, "The return engagement is about to begin."

The destroyer! At such close range! The Old Man must have known for some time that the pale shadow was no freighter. The Tommies' destroyers are light gray, just like ours.

There's a destroyer coming hell for leather straight at our diving point! "The return engagement!" It's going to be a pretty explosive one.

"Take her down to three hundred feet—slowly," orders the Old Man.

The Chief repeats the order in a low voice. He's crouching behind the hydroplane operators, his eyes fixed on the manometer.

A whisper: "Now we're in for it!"

Make yourself heavy, make yourself small, shrink!

Our torpedoes! Did they all miss? Can that happen? Five of them? A double and two singles and the stern tube as well while we were turning. Admittedly the shot from tube five was hastily aimed, but the others! Why no explosion?

The Chief brings his head even closer to the round eye of the manometer. On his forehead, sweat sparkles like pearls of dew. I see the single drops link up, making trails down his face like snail tracks. He wipes his forehead impatiently with the back of his hand.

We've barely moved an inch.

They'll be above us any moment now.

What went wrong? Why no explosions?

Everyone stands silent, brooding. The needle of the depth manometer moves another ten divisions.

I try to think clearly. How long since we dived?—How fast was that destroyer moving?—Misses!—All misses!—These shitty torpedoes!—The familiar suspicions—Sabotage! What else could it be? Faulty steering mechanisms, the bastards! And any minute now the Tommies will be ripping our asses up! The Old Man must have been out of his mind. What he did was a torpedo boat attack! On the surface! Straight up and at 'em. They can't have believed their eyes! How many yards' range was it, anyway? How many seconds for a destroyer to reach us at top speed? Those garbled steering orders! The turn!—Crazy: The Old Man had ordered hard a-port just as we were diving. That's something you never do. What can he have been up to? Then I get it: The Tommies saw us diving away to starboard. The Old Man was trying to fool them—let's hope they're not as crafty as we are!

The Old Man rests one thigh on the chart chest. All I see of him is his bent back and the dim white of his cap over the upturned collar of his fur-lined vest.

The navigator's eyes are almost completely closed: slits carved in wood with a sharp chisel. He's sucking his lips between his teeth. His right hand holding fast to the housing of the sky periscope. Six feet away, the control-room mate's face is no more than a pale blob.

A dull, smothered sound breaks the silence—like a stick hitting a slack drumhead.

"That one got it!" whispers the Commander. He raises his head abruptly, and I can see his face. His eyes are squinting, his mouth stretched wide.

Another dull concussion.

"And that one too! Damned slow running time," he adds dryly.

What is he talking about? Torpedoes? Have two of them hit?

The Second Watch Officer has straightened up. His fists are knotted and he's baring his clenched teeth like an ape. It's obvious he wants desperately to shout. But he only swallows and chokes. The grimace stays frozen on his face.

The needle of the depth manometer keeps moving slowly over the dial.

Another drumbeat.

"Number three!" says someone.

These dull detonations—is that all there is to it? I squeeze my eyes shut. All my nerves seem to be concentrated in my ear canals. Is that all there's going to be?

Then there's a sound like a sheet being slowly torn in two, followed by a second sheet being rapidly ripped to shreds. After that, a violent rasping of metal, and now all around us nothing but tearing, grating, knocking, cracking.

I've been holding my breath so long that I have to fight for air. Dammit. What's happening now?

The Old Man raises his head.

"Two of them going down, navigator—there *are* two, wouldn't you say?"

The noise—is that the bulkheads bursting?

"They've—had—it!" The Old Man drags the words out in long breaths.

No one moves. No one gives a victory yell. The control-room mate is standing beside me, motionless, in his usual position, one hand on the ladder, head turned to face the depth manometer. The two hydroplane operators: stiff folds in rubber suits, sou'westers gleaming with moisture. The pale eye of the manometer: the pointer steady now. Then I register: the hydroplane operators are actually still wearing their sou'westers!

"Damned slow running time. I'd already given up." The Commander's voice is back to its usual dark growl. The breaking and cracking, roaring and tearing show no sign of coming to an end.

"Now *there's* a couple of boats you can write off for good."

Then a shattering blow knocks me off my feet. In the nick of time I catch hold of a pipe to break my fall. There's a crash of breaking glass.

I pull myself upright, automatically stagger forward a couple of steps, jostle against someone, collide with a hard corner, and collapse into the hatch frame.

This is it. The reckoning! Mustn't let yourself go! I press my left shoulder hard against the metal frame of the hatch and make myself as heavy as I can. I use both hands to seize the pipe that runs under my thighs. My own special space. My hands touch the smooth enamel paint and feel the rust on the underside of the pipe. An iron grip. Like a vise. I stare intently at the back of my left hand, then my right, as though staring could make them grip all the harder.

Where's the next?

I raise my hunched head very slowly, like a turtle, ready to retract it instantly when the expected blow comes. All I hear is someone sniffing violently.

My eyes seem to be drawn magnetically to the Commander's cap. He takes a step—and his cap and the red and white scales on either side of the water gauge become part of a single image: clowns' striped whips. Or the oversized lollipops that stand like flowers in jars in the windows of Parisian confectioners. All-day suckers. Or the beacon lighthouse that we saw on the port bow as we left the harbor. That was painted red and white too.

The hatch frame almost bucks me out. An enormous detonation tries to shatter my eardrums. Then blow after blow, as if the sea were a mass of huge powder kegs being set off in quick succession.

A multiple drop.

Christ, that was accurate! That was their second charge. They're no fools, and they didn't fall for our bluff.

My guts contract.

Outside, nothing but rearing, gurgling, rumbling! Undersea whirlpools seize the boat, tossing it violently this way and that. Luckily, I'm so firmly wedged I might as well be in a gyrowheel.

Suddenly the gurgling of the water, pouring back on itself to fill the vacuum left by the explosions, ebbs away, but we can still hear the dull roaring, knocking, and breaking up of the other boats.

The Commander laughs like a madman. "They're certainly going down—well, that saves us a parting shot. Too bad we can't watch the tubs go under, though."

I blink in exasperation. But already the Old Man's voice is matter of fact again. "That was the second strike!"

I become aware of the voice of the hydrophone operator. My powers of perception must have been partially suspended. The operator must have been giving continuous reports, but I haven't heard a word.

"Destroyer bearing thirty degrees to port. Getting louder fast!"

The Commander's eyes are fixed on the operator's lips. "Any change?"

The operator hesitates. Finally he reports, "Sound receding astern!"

The Commander immediately orders an increase in speed. Now I can finally clear the fog from my brain, follow what is going on, and think with the others. The hope is that the destroyer will cross our course a good way astern, which is obviously what the Old Man's after.

We still don't know which way the destroyer will turn in its renewed attempt to pass overhead—the Old Man must be guessing that it'll be to port, for he has the helm put hard to starboard.

The chief mechanic Franz comes into the room. His face is chalk-white. Beads of sweat gleam like glycerin on his forehead. Although there are no waves to worry about, he hangs on first with his left hand, then with his right. "They've got us!" he blurts out. Then he shouts for safety cassettes for the gyrocompass.

"Stop that racket!" the Commander rounds on him angrily.

Four detonations in quick succession, almost a single blow. But the deep whirlpools don't reach us.

"Astern—way astern!" the Old Man jeers. "Not as easy as all that."

He props his left leg against the chart table, then undoes the buttons of his collar. He's making himself comfortable. He pushes his hands into the pockets of his leather trousers and turns to the navigator.

Another single detonation—not close, but the echo is remarkably long. The bubbling and roaring seem never-ending.

Through the dull hubbub comes the Old Man's voice. "They're spitting in the wrong corner."

The destroyer certainly seems to have faulty bearings—another couple of distant detonations. But we're still tormented by the acoustical aftermath of every bomb—even those that explode several thousand yards away. The enemy knows how demoralizing this can be, even if the bombs fall wide of the mark.

"Take this down, navigator."

"*Jawohl*, Herr Kaleun."

" '22.40 hours proceed to attack'—22.40 hours is right, isn't it, navigator?—'proceed to attack. Columns running in close formation'—yes, close formation. How many columns we don't need to say. 'Destroyers clearly visible up ahead and on the moonlit side ...' "

How's that? Clearly visible? Destroyers clearly visible up ahead ... So there's more than one? My mouth goes dry. The Old Man didn't say a word about it. On the contrary, he was acting the whole time as if there were no escort on the side we were attacking.

" '... clearly visible.' Have you got that? 'Attack on starboard side of second column'—got that too?"

"*Jawohl*, Herr Kaleun."

" 'Moon very bright ...' "

"You can say that again," murmurs the Second Watch Officer, but so softly the Commander can't hear him.

" '... very bright—but not bright enough to necessitate underwater attack ...' "

I have to get up to make way for the men who ended up in the bow compartment when "All hands forward!" was ordered, and who now want to get back through the hatch. They tiptoe past like tightrope walkers to avoid making any noise.

The Old Man orders the boat down farther and to hold depth and course for about five minutes. And when the hydrophone operator announces a new attack he takes us deeper still. He's betting that the people in the destroyer won't have caught this second maneuver and therefore that they'll be setting their canisters to go off at the previous depth . . . the one we were holding just long enough to make sure their sound men got a good reading.

New reports from the operator. No doubt about it: the destroyer is on our heels.

Despite the urgency in the operator's voice the Old Man gives no new orders to the helmsman. I know: he's postponing any change in course until the last moment, so the destroyer that's speeding after us won't have time to copy our maneuver. Hare and hound! Only when the dog is about to snap—when he's sure the hare is already in his jaws—does the hare swerve, but the dog can't make the turn: His own momentum is too great.

The analogy doesn't totally fit our case, I admit—we're not as fast as the hare, and our turning circle is too big. Indeed, it doesn't fit at all: The destroyer can always turn faster than we can. But if it's running full speed and wants to change course, it too is thrown off. A tin can like that simply has too little draft.

"Not bad shooting. Azimuth damned good. They just aimed a little too high . . ." Then the Old Man orders, "Hard a-starboard. Port motor full speed ahead!"

All the auxiliary machines have long since been turned off: the radio transformer, the ventilators, even the gyrocompass. I hardly dare breathe. Quiet as a mouse. What does that mean, "Quiet as a mouse?" The cat up there—we mice down here? Anyway, don't move!

They really should have got us on the first attack—they were so close to our diving point. But the Old Man was too clever for them. First he turned our narrow silhouette toward theirs. And then the turn to starboard—and the dive, but with the rudder hard a-port. Like a player taking a goal kick who looks at one corner of the net and kicks at the other.

The Old Man favors me with a nod. "We're not through with them yet. Tough lot. They're no beginners."

"Really," is all I manage.

"Though they must be getting a trifle annoyed by now," he adds.

He orders us down farther; five hundred feet. Going by the operator's reports, the destroyer must be following us around on a leash. At any moment they can signal their engines full speed ahead and start attacking. What we need is a faster boat.

The Old Man orders higher speed. This involves all sorts of risks, because the faster the motors run the more racket they make. The Tommies must be able to hear our E-motors just by using their ears. But the Commander's prime concern is probably to get out of range of the enemy's direction finder.

"Destroyer getting louder!" the operator announces in a low voice.

The Commander whispers an order for us to reduce speed again. So it didn't work. We didn't manage to break away. They're still after us. They're not going to let themselves be shaken off; they'd rather let their scows wallow along without protection. After all, positive location of a U-boat is no everyday occurrence.

A gigantic sledgehammer hits the boat. At almost the same instant, the Old Man orders the bilge pumps turned on and the speed increased. As soon as the tumult outside ebbs away he has the pumps stopped and the motors reduced to slow. "Thirteen—fourteen," the navigator counts, and makes two new marks on his slate. So that was two bombs. I count: first we had four. Then the second drop, the multiple ejection, was counted as six. Does that check? I recalculate.

Another three, four blows—so violent that the floor plates clatter. I feel the detonations right down to my stomach. Cautiously I turn my head. The navigator's chalking up four.

The Old Man hasn't budged an inch. He holds his head so that he has one eye on the depth manometer and his left ear turned toward the sound room.

"They really don't seem to like us." That from the ensign. Unbelievable: He actually said something. Now he's staring at the floor plates: The sentence must have escaped him involuntarily. Everyone heard. The navigator is grinning, and the Old Man turns his head. For an instant there's a trace of amusement on his face.

The pebbles. At first it sounds like no more than a handful of coarse sand thrown against our port side. But now it's garden gravel, three, four scoops, one after the other. Their Asdic. It feels like being suddenly lit up from all sides, as if we were lying exposed on a huge stage in full view of the audience.

"Swine!" mutters the control-room mate half to himself. For a moment I hate them too, but after all, who or what are "they": the hard singing of the screws, the hornet buzz, the rattle of gravel against the boat's side? That shadow, the narrow silhouette that was only a shade brighter than the freighters—that's all I've been able to see of the enemy . . .

The whites of their eyes! For us, that's pure rubbish! We've lost our sight. No more seeing—only listening. Ear against the wall! So why no new report from our eavesdropper-in-chief? The Commander is blinking impatiently. Nothing?

All ears harken unto Thee, O Lord, for Thou wilt bring great joy to those who trust in Thy word—or something like that. The Bible Scholar would have the exact quote; he's hardly recognizable in the dusky light. The hydrophone operator raises his eyebrows. That's another sign: won't be long before everyone's ears are busy again.

They have ears, and hear not. One of the Psalms of David. I'm all ears. I am one gigantic ear, all my nerves a single listening knot; they've twined themselves like fine elfin hair around hammer, anvil, and stirrup.

A box on the ears—we've had plenty of those—lend a willing ear— walls have ears—pull the wool over someone's ears . . . Of course, *that's* it: they want to skin us, pull our hide over our ears.

How do things look on the surface now?

There's sure to be a murderous amount of illumination. All searchlights on, and the sky studded with parachute flares so that the archenemy can't escape. All cannon barrels lowered and ready to be fired at once if they succeed in forcing us to the surface.

The operator reports, "Destroyer bearing twenty degrees. Getting louder fast!" And after a short hesitation, "Commencing attack!"

Two ax blows hit the boat broadside. More wild roaring and gurgling. Then two more blows in the midst of the raging tumult.

I've opened my mouth the way artillery men do so that my eardrums won't burst. After all, I was trained as a naval gunner. But now I'm not next to a cannon; I'm on the other end, in the midst of the bursting shells.

There's no getting away from here. No use throwing yourself flat. Digging in—that's a laugh: what we have under our feet are iron floor plates covered with cunt patterns, as Zeitler calls the thousand little shapes. I exert all my self-control to suppress claustrophobia, the damnable urge to flee in any direction. Keep your feet nailed to the floor! I pray for lead in the soles of my shoes, like those bright, barrel-shaped toy figures that always bob up again however you knock them down. Thank god, I can remember what they're called. Standup men . . . standup men, incense men, humming tops, fancy nutcrackers. Bright pretty toys.

When you think about it, I'm well off. I can't be knocked over either. The frame of the hatch in which I'm crouching is the best place to be at a time like this.

I loosen my grip on the pipe. Apparently it's safe to relax. Ease the muscle cramp, move the jawbone, rest the skeleton, relax the belly muscles, let the blood circulate. For the first time I realize how painful my contortions have been.

Our every move is defined by our opponents. The Tommies can even decide what positions we must assume. We draw our heads in, huddle waiting for the impact of the detonation, and stretch and loosen up once the roaring begins outside. Even the Old Man is careful not to unleash his derisive laughter except during the gurgling that follows the explosions.

The operator half opens his mouth. Immediately I catch my breath again. What now? If only I knew where the last series fell, just how far from the boat the bombs exploded or how far we are from our diving point! After our first unsuccessful attempt to break away, it seems as though the pursuit has gone around and around in circles—first to the right, then to the left, up and down, like a rollercoaster ride. We haven't made any ground at all. Every attempt so far to break out sideways and find cover has been spotted by the enemy.

The operator closes his mouth and opens it again. He looks like a carp in a tank at the fish store. Open, shut, and then open again. He announces a new attack.

And then immediately calls "Asdic!" hoarsely from the sound room. He could have saved himself the trouble. Everyone in the control room has heard the *ping-ping*. As have the men in the bow compartment on top of the torpedoes, and aft in the motor room and diesel room.

The enemy has got us trapped in the tentacles of the direction finder. Right now they're turning steel hand wheels and searching through three dimensions with pulsing beams—*zirp—zirp—ping—ping* . . .

The Asdic, I remind myself, is only effective up to a speed of about thirteen knots. During a fast attack the destroyer no longer has directional contact. At higher speeds the Asdic suffers major interference from the destroyer's own noises and the commotion of its screws, which is an advantage for us, since it gives us a last-minute opportunity to make minor changes in our position. But the Commander up there is also capable of figuring out that we won't stand still and wait for the attack. Only: which way we move is the one thing his directional boys can't tell him. There he has to use his intuition.

One break for us is that our enemy and his clever machines can't tell exactly how deep we are. In this, nature is on our side: water is not simply water; right down through our present depth it forms layers like sedimentary rock. The salt content and the physical characteristics of the individual layers are never the same. And they scatter the Asdic. All we have to do is move suddenly from a layer of warm water into a cold one and the Asdic becomes inaccurate. A layer of dense plankton will influence it too. And the people up there with their apparatus can't correct their plotting of our position with any confidence because they don't know where these damn layers are.

Herrmann is working away at his wheel.

"Report!" says the Old Man in the direction of the sound room.

"Sounds bearing three hundred fifty degrees."

In less than five minutes the screws are audible to the naked ear.

Ritschipitschipitschipitschi—that's no full-speed attack. The destroyer is moving just fast enough to be able to go on tracking us, and the Asdic echoes loud and clear.

A fresh attack. Four, five detonations. Close. Against closed eyelids I project jets of flame, towering St. Elmo's fire, the flickering gleam of chrysoprase, cascading sparks around dark-red central cores, dazzling white naptha flames, whirling Chinese pinwheels, blinding surges, amethyst beams piercing the darkness, an enormous fiery holocaust loosed from rainbow-haloed fountains of bronze.

"Exercise maneuvers," whispers the Old Man.

I wouldn't call them that.

A gigantic fist comes down and shakes the boat. I feel the thrust in my knees as we're jolted upward. The needle of the depth indicator jerks back. The light goes out, and there's the sound of breaking glass. My heart is pounding—finally the emergency light goes on.

I see the Old Man biting his lower lip. It's the moment of decision. Does he take the boat down to the depth where the last bombs exploded or up a few hundred feet?

He orders a turn and a simultaneous dive. Back down the rollercoaster again. One—two—three—but where? Up? Down? Left? The last surge made it sound as if the bombs had been forward and to port of us. But were they above or below the boat? Here we go again. The operator resumes his reports.

The blow hits me right on the third dorsal vertebra. Followed by another—and another: two straight punches to the back of the head and the neck.

Smoke is beginning to swirl out from the helmsman's station. To crown everything else, are we going to have a fire? Are those cables beginning to smolder? And won't that cause short circuits?

Calm down! Nothing can happen to this scow: *I* am on board. *I* am immortal. With me on board the boat is immune.

No doubt about it—the instrument panel is on fire! The sign on the Minimax: *Keep calm! Fight fire from below.* My brain keeps repeating: immune—immune—immune.

The control-room mate springs into action and almost disappears in the flames and smoke. Two or three men go to his assistance. I notice that the boat is bow heavy—more and more so. I hear, "Valve—bilge duct broken." But that can't be all there is to it! Why doesn't the Chief trim toward the stern? What else are our trim tanks for, if not to act as a balancing rod?

Although the destroyer must be quite close, the Old Man orders full speed ahead. Of course! We already have too much water in the boat; we can no longer manage to keep her buoyant. We need the power of the screws and their pressure on the hydroplanes to make the boat stern heavy fast. Otherwise the Old Man would never create such a racket: at this speed it's like having a cowbell around our neck. Dilemma: to sink or speed up. The Tommies up there must be able to hear us—motors, screws, and bilge pump—with their own ears. They might just as well turn off their Asdic and save the current.

In addition to his complicated course calculations, the Old Man now has to worry constantly about the boat's depth. We're in a tricky situation. If it were only a question of surfacing, that wouldn't take much: "Don rescue gear," and blow the tanks with everything we've got. Don't even think about it!

Everything's wet, covered in condensation.

"Driving-shaft gaskets making water!" someone shouts from the stern. Immediately followed, from forward, by ". . . valve leaking!" I'm no longer paying much attention. Why bother worrying about which valve it might be.

Four detonations in quick succession, then the mad gurgle and roar of the black flood rushing into the huge hollows torn out by the bombs.

"Thirty-three—four—five—thirty-six," the navigator counts in a loud voice. That time it was close!

We're now at four hundred feet.

The Old Man takes us deeper and turns the boat to port.

The next detonation slams my teeth together. I can hear sobbing. The new control-room assistant? Surely he's not going to have a fit of hysterics?

"Nice shooting!" the Old Man jeers loudly as the next detonations surge over us.

I tense my stomach muscles as if to protect my organs against a ton of pressure. It's some minutes before I dare release my left hand from its grip on the pipe. It rises of its own volition and brushes across my forehead: cold sweat. My whole back feels equally clammy. Fear?

I seem to be seeing the Commander's face through a fog.

It's the smoke from the helmsman's station still hanging in the room, although the smoldering has stopped. There's a sour taste in my mouth and a dull pressure somewhere in my head. I hold my breath; it only makes the pressure worse.

Any moment and it'll be time again—the destroyer will have completed its circle. The pack of hounds has to grant us this brief respite whether they want to or not.

There's the Asdic again. Two or three sharp rattles of pebbles. A cold hand creeps under my collar and runs down my back. I shudder.

The pressure in my head becomes unbearable. What now? Why is nothing happening? Every whisper has died away. The condensation pitter-patters at steady one-second intervals. Silently I count them. At twenty-two the blow lands, doubling me over with my head crumpled against my chest.

Am I deaf? I see the floor plates dancing, but it's seconds before I hear their metallic clatter, mixed with a yowling, groaning sound and a high-pitched screech. The pressure hull! It can't be anything else. The boat heaves and pitches in the rearing eddies. Men stagger against one another.

Another double blast. The boat groans. Clattering scraping sounds.

The Tommies are being economical. No more carpeting—instead, always two bombs at a time, probably set for different depths. I dare not relax my muscles—the hammer lands again with enormous force.

A gurgling, coughing gasp quite close to me turns into a moan. Sounds as if someone has been hit. It confuses me momentarily, but then reality asserts itself: don't be crazy, no one gets shot down here.

The Old Man has got to think up something new. No chance of sneaking away. The Asdic won't let us go. They've got first-class men sitting up there at the controls, and they're not easily bluffed. How much time do we have left? How much do the Tommies need to circle?

Lucky for us that they can't drop their bombs overboard whenever they want. They have to be running at full speed before they fire. If those bastards could use their Asdic to sneak up right over the boat before dropping their cans, this cat and mouse game would have been over long ago. As it is, they have to attack at high speed so as not to blow themselves out of the water when their bombs go off.

What's the Old Man up to now? It's making him frown. I can tell from the way his brows are twitching that he's deep in concentration. How long will he go on waiting? Can he pull off another last-minute swerve to escape the advancing destroyer?—and in the right direction?—at the right speed?—and the right depth?

It's high time he opened his mouth and gave an order. Or has he given up? Thrown in the sponge?

Suddenly a sound like canvas being ripped. The Commander's voice crackles out at the same moment: "Bail!—Hard a-port! And gun those goddam motors!"

The boat leaps forward. The noise of the bilge pump is drowned in the roar that fills the sea around us. Men stagger and clutch the pipes. The Old Man doesn't budge. The navigator clings to his table.

The Old Man's gamble suddenly dawns on me. He's ordered us to hold a straight course, even though we've been spotted. A new wrinkle. A variation he hasn't tried on the Tommies before. Obvious: The Commander of the destroyer wasn't born yesterday. He doesn't come rushing blindly to the spot where they've located us. They know our tricks. They know that we know they're attacking; they know that we know they can't use their Asdic at high speed, that we'll try to escape their line of attack and also change depth. Whether we feint to port or to starboard, whether we head up or down is something they can only guess at. They have to rely on luck.

And so the Old Man stops playing tricks for once and simply holds his course and depth until the next drop. Bluff and double bluff. And just when you think you're lucky—bang! You get it up the ass!

"Time?" asks the Commander.

"01.30 hours," the navigators replies.

"Really?" There's astonishment in his voice. Even he seems to be finding the dance a trifle drawn out.

"Most unusual," he murmurs. "But they probably want to be absolutely sure."

For a while nothing stirs. The Old Man orders us deeper. Then deeper still.

"Time."

"01.45 hours!"

Unless my ears are really playing tricks on me, even the compass motor has been shut off. Not a sound in the boat. Only the pitter-patter of condensation ticking off the seconds.

Have we made it? How far have we gone in a quarter of an hour's silent running? Then the stillness is broken again by the hideous noises that the Old Man calls "creaking in the beams": Our steel cylinder is being brutally tested for resistance by the pressure at these depths. The steel skin is bulging inward between the ribs. The interior woodwork groans.

We're down at 650 feet again, more than twice the shipyard guaranty, creeping along through the blackness at a speed of four knots with this vast column of water sitting on top of us.

Operating the hydroplanes becomes a balancing trick. If the boat sinks any lower, its tortured fabric may no longer be able to withstand the external pressure. A matter of inches could be crucial. Is the Old Man counting on the Tommies not knowing our maximum diving depth? We ourselves never mention this magic number in feet but say, "Three times r plus sixty." An incantation. Could the Tommies really not know how much r is? Every stoker knows; probably fifty thousand Germans do, all told.

No reports from the operator. I can't believe we've escaped. The bastards are probably lying in wait, engines stopped. They know that they were almost directly above us. The only thing they couldn't calculate was our depth, and the Old Man has taken extreme measures about that. The Chief moves his head back and forth uneasily. Nothing seems to rasp on his nerves so much as the creaking in the woodwork.

Two detonations. Bearable. The gurgling is cut short at a stroke. But our bilge pump keeps going for several seconds more! They must have heard the damn thing. You'd think someone could build quieter ones.

The longer we remain at these depths, the more tormenting the thought of how thin our steel hull is. We aren't armor-plated. All we have to withstand the pressure of the water and the shock waves of the explosions is a mere inch of steel. The circular ribs—two every three feet—are all that give our thin-walled tube the meager powers of resistance that enables us to stay alive down here.

"They're taking one helluva time to get ready," whispers the Old Man. We must be dealing with some really clever bastards if even he admits it.

I try to picture what's going on up there. I have my own memories to help me, for after all it's not so long since I was one of the hunters, on a destroyer myself. It's the same game on both sides except that the Tommies have their highly perfected Asdic and we have nothing but our sound gear. It's the difference between electronics and acoustics.

Listen—make a run—drop the bombs—circle—listen—make a run—drop more bombs—try setting them for shallow depths—then for deeper ones—then the star act: the spread—launch at least a dozen canisters simultaneously—like drumfire. The same thing the Tommies do.

Just endure, last out each round. How long has it been so far? I still don't dare move. This time I'm one of the hunted. Trapped in the deep. On a boat with no more torpedoes in its tubes. Defenseless, even if we manage to surface.

★ ★ ★

It hasn't gotten to the point yet where we have to surface. The Old Man, sitting there so relaxed, doesn't look at all as though he were at the end of his tether. But the grin has gone from his face.

The operator whispers, "More propeller sounds at one hundred twenty degrees,"

"Now we're in for it!" the Old Man mutters. There's no doubt about it.

"What's its present bearing—the second sound?"

His voice has become urgent. Yet more computations to be made in his head.

A report from astern: "Diesel air valves making water badly!" The Old Man exchanges a glance with the Chief, who disappears aft. The Old Man takes over the hydroplanes.

"Forward up ten," I hear him order in a murmur.

I become aware of a strong pressure in my bladder. The sight of the stream of water must have prompted it. But I don't know where I can relieve myself.

The Chief reappears in the control room. Aft, there have been two or three breaks around the flanges. His head seems to have developed a nervous tic. A leak—and he can't pump: the enemy up there have seen to that. The auxiliary pump must be kaput anyway. "Glass case of the auxiliary bilge pump cracked," I hear amid the roaring chaos. The glass in the water gauge has broken, too. It's madness.

The Old Man orders both motors full ahead again. All our high-speed evasive maneuvers are doing is reducing the capacity of our batteries. The Old Man's gambling with our supplies. If we have no more battery juice, if we run out of compressed air or oxygen, the boat *has* to surface. The game will be up—nothing more we can do . . . The Chief has blown compressed air into the diving cells again and again in order to give us the buoyancy he could no longer achieve with the bilge pump alone.

Compressed air has an extremely high market value: Given our present circumstances, we're in no position to start manufacturing more. Using the compressor is out of the question.

And how about the oxygen? How long can we go on breathing the stench that permeates the boat?

The sound man gives one report after another. I too can hear the Asdic rattle again.

But it's still not really clear whether we have two pursuers now in place of one.

The Old Man pushes a hand under his cap. He probably doesn't have much grasp of the situation either. Hydrophone reports give practically no information about the enemy's intentions.

Or could they in turn be fooling us with their own noises? Technically it would be possible. Our having to rely completely on the operator's perceptions is preposterous.

The destroyer seems to be making a wide circle. No further word about the second series of noises, but this could mean that a second ship has just been lying there silent for some time.

The pause continues. The First Watch Officer glances round uncertainly. Crumpled face. Sharp nose, white about the nostrils.

The control-room mate is trying to pee into a big can. He fumbles about laboriously trying to get his cock out through his leather trousers.

Then—without warning—a crash. The half-filled can drops from Tin-ear Willie Isenberg's hand and spills onto the floor plates. The place instantly stinks of urine. I'm surprised the Old Man doesn't start cursing.

I breathe very shallowly so as not to encounter the steel band around my chest, not to inhale too much of the stench. The air is terrible: the hot

smell of diesels running at full speed . . the stink of fifty men . . . our sweat—
the sweat of fear. God knows what else has gone into this miasma of odors.
Now the air smells of shit too. Someone must have lost control. Sweat and
piss and shit and bilge—unendurable.

I can't help thinking of the poor bastards in the stern. They can't see
the Commander, draw comfort from his presence. They are really caged in.
No one to signal when the infernal din is going to break out again. I'd rather
die than be stuck back there between the reeking, hot engine blocks.

So it does matter, after all, where one's battle station is. Even here
there are the privileged and the underprivileged.

Hacker and his crew working in the bow compartment at the
tubes—no one tells them our course either. They hear neither the orders to
the helmsman nor the signals to the engine room. They don't know what the
sound man reports. They have no notion which way we're moving—or
whether we're moving at all. It's only when an explosion suddenly hurls the
boat upward or slams it deeper down that they feel it in their stomachs; and if
we go very deep indeed they can hear the telltale "creaking of the beams."

Three detonations. This time the gigantic sledgehammer came from
below. I catch a glimpse of the depth manometer in the beam of a flashlight.
It jumps backward. I can feel it in the pit of my stomach. We are being hurled
upward in a high-speed elevator.

If the boat is five hundred feet or so down, the pressure waves from
depth charges are supposed to be at their worst if they go off another hundred feet below that. How deep are we now? Six hundred feet.

There is no flexible steel underneath us. Nothing really to protect
the engines! They are the most vulnerable to explosions from below.

Six more bombs. Again so close under our keel that I can feel the
twisting force in my knee joints. I'm standing on one end of a seesaw while
someone drops blocks of stone on the other end. The needle jerks backward
again. Up and down—just what the Tommies want.

This attack has cost them at least a dozen bombs. There must be a
mass of fish up there, floating on their sides, their air bladders torn apart. The
Tommies could collect them by the netful. Something fresh for the galley.

I try to take long, regular breaths. For a good five minutes I breathe
deeply, then four bombs explode. All astern. The sound man reports a decrease in strength.

I concentrate on imagining how one could reproduce all of this, this
entire scene, in papier mâché for the stage. Everything very exact. Scale one

to one. It would be easy: just remove the port wall—that's where the audience would sit. No elevated stage. Everything face to face. Direct view of the hydroplane station. Shift the sky periscope up front to give the whole thing perspective. I fix in my mind the positions and attitudes of the actors: the Old Man leaning against the periscope shaft—solid, heavy-set, in his ragged sweater, his furlined vest, his salt-flecked boots with their thick cork soles, the stubborn tangle of hair escaping from under his old battered cap with its tarnished trim. Color of his beard: sauerkraut, slightly rotten sauerkraut.

The hydroplane operators in their rubber jackets—in the heavy unyielding folds of their foul-weather gear—are two stone blocks that might have been hewn out of dark basalt and polished.

The Chief in half profile: olive-green shirt with rolled-up sleeves, crumpled dark olive-green linen trousers. Sneakers. Valentino hair slicked back. Thin as a whippet. Expressionless as a wax doll. Only his jaw muscles constantly working. Not a syllable, only the play of the jaw.

The First Watch Officer has turned his back to the audience. One senses he doesn't want to be observed because he isn't in complete control of himself.

Not much of the Second Watch Officer's face to be seen. He's too heavily muffled up, standing motionless, his eyes darting everywhere, as if searching for an escape hatch—as if they're trying to get away, to be free of him, to abandon him, leave him eyeless, while standing rigid by the periscope.

The navigator keeps his head down and pretends to be checking his stopwatch.

Only some minor sound effects: a low humming and the occasional drip of water on the metal plates.

All easy to reproduce. Minutes of silence, complete immobility. Only the constant hum and the dripping. Just keep everyone standing there frozen—until the audience becomes uneasy . . .

Three detonations, no doubt astern.

The navigator apparently has a new method of keeping score. Now he draws the fifth mark diagonally through the first four. That saves space and makes it easier to follow. He's already on his sixth row. I can't remember just how our conscientious scorekeeper tallied the last salvos.

The Old Man goes on calculating uninterruptedly: our course, the enemy's course, an escape course. With every report from the sound room, the basic factors in his calculations change.

What's he doing now? Will he have us steer straight ahead? No, this time he's trying another turn: hard a-port.

Let's hope he's made the right choice, that the Commander of the destroyer hasn't decided on port too—or on starboard, should he be steering toward us. That's the way it is: I don't even know whether the destroyer is attacking from forward or astern.

The figures that the operator is calling out are becoming jumbled in my head.

"Dropping cans!" The operator has heard the splash of more bombs hitting the surface of the water.

I hold tight.

"Man the bilge pump," the Old Man orders, enunciating with great care although the explosion hasn't yet come.

The noise! But it doesn't seem to bother the Old Man.

A whirlpool of detonations.

"Saturation pattern!" he says.

If it doesn't work with single charges or with series of them, they simply lay down a carpet.

Unshrinkable!

With half my mind I ask myself where I dug up the English word "unshrinkable." Finally I see it machine-stitched, in gold thread, on the label of my swimming trunks, under the words "pure wool."

A carpet! A spool begins unwinding in my head: hand-knotted, exquisite Afghan design—flying carpet—Harun al Rashid—Oriental bullshit!

"Much too good for us!" sneers the Old Man. In the worst of the noise he orders the speed increased. "Now they're reloading!" Contemptuously, he explains the absence of new detonations. "The more you use, the more you lose."

A golden maxim, like something straight out of the messroom calendar. The quintessential lesson of a dozen depth-charge attacks: "The more you use, the more you lose."

The Commander orders us up. What does that mean? Are we going to surface? Is the next order to be: "Prepare escape gear!"?

Atlantic Killer—a title for a film. Show a hairline crack in an egg. That's all it would take on our eggshell—just one crack. The enemy can leave the sea to do the rest.

The efforts we used to make to get rid of garden snails. The black shiny giants, the night snails, we would collect in buckets to be emptied into toilets and flushed away. Drowned in the cesspool—that did the job. Stepping on them is as disgusting as chopping them up. An explosion of green slime.

As children we played the cremation game. Away with the hearth fender, little pails of rainworms dumped onto the red coals—and in a second the worms were transformed with a loud hiss into twists of black ash.

Rabbits. You hold them firmly with your left hand and give them a blow on the back of the neck. Neat and clean: only a little twitching—as though electrocuted. Carp you hold with your left hand sideways on a board and give them a heavy blow on the snout with a stick. It makes a crunching sound. Quickly slit open their stomachs. Careful with the gall bladder, the gall mustn't spill out. The swollen air bladders gleam like Christmas tree ornaments. Funny thing about carp: even when they're cut in two there's still life in them. It used to frighten us as children when the halves when on jerking for hours on end.

I could never bring myself to kill doves, even though it's easy to do. You simply tear their heads off. Clamp them between index and middle fingers—a small twisting motion and crack and away! Roosters and hens you hold high on the wings with your left hand, directly under the shoulder blades, as it were. And then quickly press them sideways on the block and guillotine them with the ax. Let them bleed, but be sure to keep a firm hold, or they'll fly away without their heads. A bloody mess.

New sounds: propeller noises—a high whistling, audible throughout the boat. I see the new control-room assistant trembling all over. He's slumped down over the water distributor. Someone else—who is it?—sits down on the floor plates. Doubled up, a dark lump of flesh and fear. The others are huddled in a variety of postures, making themselves as small as possible. As though hiding would do any good now.

Only the Old Man sits in his usual way, casual and relaxed.

A new detonation! My left shoulder hits something so hard that I nearly cry out.

Two more.

"Start pumping!" the Old Man orders above the roar. We can't lose the destroyer. Damnation, we can't shake her off!

The Chief stares glassily out of the corners of his eyes. He looks as if he can hardly wait for the next series of bombs. Perverse: he *wants* to bail, and to do that he *needs* the bombs.

The boat can no longer be held without continuous bailing. Bilge pump on when there's roaring outside, bulge pump off when it stops. Again and again—on and off—on and off.

Waiting—waiting—waiting.

Still nothing? Nothing at all? I open my eyes but keep them firmly fixed on the floor plates.

A double blow. Pain in the back of my neck. What was that? Cries—the floor shudders—the floor plates jump—the whole boat vibrates—the steel howls like a dog. The lights have gone again. Who cried out?

"Permission to blow tanks?" I hear the Chief's voice as though through wool.

"No!"

The beam of the Chief's pocket flashlight wavers over the Commander's face. No mouth. No eyes.

Tearing, shrieking, shrill screaming—then more shattering blows. The orgy of noise has hardly ebbed when the chirp of the Asdic is back again. In our deep-sea aviary, the chirp that rings of betrayal. Rasps the nerves more than anything else. They couldn't have come up with a worse sound to torment us. Like our own Stuka's siren scream. I hold my breath.

Three o'clock plus how many minutes? I can't quite make out the big hand.

Reports. Fragments of words both from forward and aft. *What* is leaking badly? A drive-shaft gasket? Of course, I understand, both shafts go through the pressure hull.

The emergency lights go on. In the half-darkness I see that the control room is full of men. What now? What is happening? Which men are these? They must have come in through the after hatch. I've been sitting in the forward one. They couldn't have got through *here*. Damn this dim light. I can't recognize any of them. Two men—the control-room mate and one of the assistants—half block my view. They're standing as stiff as ever, but everything behind them is in motion. I hear the scuffling of boots, panting breath, sharp snorts, a few mumbles curses.

The Old Man hasn't noticed yet. He keeps his eyes on the depth manometer. Only the navigator turns his head.

"Breach in the diesel room," someone shouts from the stern.

"Propaganda!" says the Old Man without even turning around, and then once more with deliberate clarity, "Prop-a-gan-da!"

The Chief starts in the direction of the diesel room but stops short and looks at the manometer.

"I demand a report!" snaps the Commander, turning away from the manometers and seeing the crowd in the semi-darkness around the after hatch.

As though by reflex he draws his head in and bends forward slightly. "Chief, just give me your light," he orders in a whisper.

There's a stir among the men who have come into the control room from astern. They shrink back like tigers in front of their trainer. One of them even succeeds in raising his leg behind him and groping his way back through the hatch. It looks like a circus act. The flashlight in the Commander's hand catches only the receding back of a man hastening through the hatch toward the stern, rescue kit under his arm.

The face of the control-room mate is close to mine. His mouth a dark hole. His eyes wide—I can see the full circle of his pupils. He seems to be screaming but there is no sound.

Have my powers of perception gone mad? I don't see the control-room mate as frightened, but as an actor imitating the fear of a control-room mate.

The Commander orders both motors half speed ahead.

"Half speed ahead both!" comes the voice of the helmsman from the tower.

The control-room mate seems to be coming out of his coma. He begins to glance around furtively but won't look anyone straight in the face. His right foot feels its way cautiously over the floor plates. His tongue moistens his gray lower lip.

In a soft voice the Old Man sneers, "Wasting their tin cans . . ."

The navigator has come to a dead stop, his hand holding its piece of chalk. He looks frozen in mid-movement, but it's only hesitation. He doesn't know how many marks to jot down for the last attack. His bookkeeping could get scrambled. One error—and the whole thing would be down the drain.

He blinks as if to shrug off a dream, then makes five bold strokes. Four straight up and down, and one through the middle.

The next explosions come singly—sharp, ripping bursts but with little after-roar. The Chief has to shut down the pumps quickly. The navigator starts on the next group of chalk marks. As he is drawing the last one, the chalk falls from his hand.

Another great blast. Once more, a rattling over badly laid rails. Rumbling across switches, then bumping through broken stone. Metal screams and shrills.

If a rivet should give way now, it could—as I well know—plow straight through my skull like a bullet. The pressure! A stream of water breaking into the boat could saw a man in half.

The sour smell of fear! Now they've got us in the wringer, by the short hairs. We've had it. *It's our turn now.*

"Sixty degrees—getting stronger—more sounds at two hundred degrees!" Two, then four explosions in my head. They're going to rip open our hatches, the filthy swine!

Groans and hysterical sobbing.

The boat is jouncing like an airplane in a pocket of turbulence.

They're carpeting us.

The impact has knocked two men down. I see a mouth shrieking, flailing feet, two faces masked in terror.

Two more explosions. The sea is a single raging mass.

Subsiding roar and then suddenly silence. Only essential sounds: the sonorous insect hum of the motors, men breathing, the steady drip of water.

"Forward up ten," whispers the Chief.

The whine of the hydroplane motors pierces me to the bone. Must *everything* make so much noise?

Isn't the Old Man going to change course? Aren't we going to turn again? Or will he try to break out of the circling pattern by steering straight ahead?

Why doesn't the sound man say something?

If he has nothing to report, it can only mean that there are no engines running on the surface. But the bastards can't have gone so quickly that he didn't catch them at it. So they're lying there doggo. We've seen that happen a couple of times before. Still, the noise of the destroyer's engines has never been absent this long . . .

The Old Man maintains depth and course.

Five minutes pass, then the operator's eyes suddenly open wide, and he turns his hand wheel furiously. His forehead is deeply furrowed. They're about to attack again. I no longer listen to his reports but try to concentrate on nothing but keeping my seat. A sharp double crack.

"Boat making water!" A cry comes from astern in the roar following the explosion.

"Express yourself properly," the Commander orders the invisible man in a hiss.

Making water! This miserable naval jargon! Sounds like manufacturing something: "creating" it, and yet making water is about the worst thing that can happen in our situation.

The next one seems to hit me below the belt. Don't scream! I clench my teeth until my jaws ache. Someone else cries out for me, in a falsetto that goes right through me. The beam of a flashlight sweeps around in search of the man who screamed. I hear a new noise; the chattering of teeth like the quick rattle of castanets, then sniffling, snorting. There are men sobbing too.

A body lands against my knee and almost knocks me over. I feel someone hauling himself up, seizing me by the leg. But the first man, the one who fell against my knee, seems to be staying flat on the floor plates.

The emergency light over the navigator's table has not gone on again. The darkness provides a cover under which panic can secretly spread.

More racking sobs. They come from someone crouching on the water distributor. I can't see who he is. The control-room mate is suddenly there, giving him such a blow on the back that he cries out.

The Old Man swings around as though bitten by a tarantula and snaps in the direction of the water distributor, "Report to me when this is over!"

Who? The control-room mate? The man he hit?

When the light improves I see the new control-room assistant is silently weeping.

The Old Man orders half speed.

"Half speed ahead both!" the helmsman acknowledges.

This means that the boat's buoyancy can no longer be maintained at slow speed. Too much water has seeped in astern.

The propeller noises can be heard more clearly than ever. A roaring rhythmic beat. As counterpoint, the sound of a milk cooler, and over that a whirring egg beater and the buzz of a drill. Full speed!

The needle of the depth manometer moves a few marks further. The boat is slowly sinking. The Chief can no longer stop it—blowing the tanks would make far too much noise and pumping is out of the question.

"One hundred ninety degrees!" the operator reports. "One hundred seventy degrees!"

"Steer sixty degrees!" orders the Commander and pushes home the tight-drawn steel cable of the sky periscope. "Let's hope we're not leaving an oil slick," he remarks as if by accident. Oil slick! The words flash through the room, echo in my mind, and at once leave iridescent streaks on my closed eyelids. If oil is rising from the boat, the enemy has as good a target as he could possibly wish for.

The Commander bites his lower lip.

It's dark up there, but oil smells even in the dark—for miles.

There's a whisper from the sound room. "Destroyer sounds very close!"

The Commander whispers back, "Slow ahead both—minimum hydroplanes!"

He takes off his cap and lays it beside him on the chart chest. A sign of resignation? Have we reached the end?

The operator leans way out of his compartment as though about to make a report. But his mouth remains shut. His face is rigid with tension. Suddenly he takes his earphones off. I know what that means: noises everywhere, so there's no longer any point in trying to determine where they're coming from.

Now I can hear them myself.

A crashing, exploding roar, as though the sea itself were collapsing. Finished! Darkness!

"Are there ever to be any proper reports?" I hear an unrecognizable voice say before I open my eyes again.

The boat is becoming perceptibly stern heavy. In the beam of a flashlight the telephone cable and some oilskins swing out from the wall.

A few more heartbeats, then a voice penetrates the stillness. "Motor room—shipping water!" Immediately followed by more reports: "Bow compartment flanges holding—diesel room flanges holding fast." Finally the emergency light. The needle of the depth manometer moves with terrifying speed over the dial.

"Full ahead both!" the Old Man orders. Despite the desperation implicit in this command, his voice is matter of fact and calm.

The boat lungs forward: the batteries have connected up, one after the other.

"Forward hydroplane full up! Aft full down!" the Chief orders the operators. But the indicator doesn't move. It's frozen.

"Aft hydroplane out of action," reports the control-room mate. Ashen-faced he turns toward the Commander with a look of complete trust.

"Recouple for manual," the Chief orders, so calmly that we might as well be on maneuvers. The hydroplane operators rise and throw their entire weight against the hand wheels. The white needle of the indicator suddenly trembles—thank god, it's moving! The mechanism isn't damaged and the hydroplane isn't jammed; only the electrical control has failed.

The loud humming of the motors. Full speed—that's insanity! But what else is left for us to try? Running silently, we can no longer hold our present level. The motor room is making water—an inrush of water at our most vulnerable point.

"Both E-motors falling below full power!"

The Old Man reflects no more than a second, then commands, "Examine both batteries! Test the accumulator bilges for acid!" No doubt about it: some of the battery cells must have cracked and run dry. What next? What more can happen?

My heart almost stops as the First Watch Officer moves to one side, revealing the depth manometer. The needle is still moving slowly forward. The boat is sinking, even though the motors are running on all the power still available.

It's only seconds before there is a sharp hissing sound. The control-room mate has released the compressed air. Our buoyancy tanks are filling.

"Blow them full!"

The Chief has sprung to his feet. He's breathing in short gasps. His voice vibrates. "Trim forward! Move, move!"

I don't dare stand up for fear my legs will fail me. My muscles are like jelly, my nerves are quivering. Let the final blow ball! Give up! Call it a day! This is unendurable!

I realize that I'm slipping into dazed indifference. Nothing matters. Just get it over with—one way or another. I summon up all my strength to pull myself together.

Damn it all, don't let go.

We have risen 175 feet. The indicator comes to a halt. The Commander orders, "Open exhaust three!"

Terror wells up me. I know what this order means. A surge of air is now rising toward the surface and forming a bubble that will betray our position. A torrent of fear. To ward it off, I murmur, "Immune! Immune!"

My heart keeps pounding! My breath comes in gasps. I hear a muffled command: "Shut off the exhaust!"

The navigator turns his head to the Old Man. I can see his full face: a wood carving. Pale, polished linden wood. He sees me and thrusts out his lower lip.

"Hysterical women," growls the Old Man.

If the E-motors aft are swamped, if there should be a short circuit . . . how could the screws turn? Without propellers and hydroplanes both working, we're done for.

The Commander impatiently demands reports from the motor room.

I catch only fragments: ". . . made watertight with wooden wedges—sole-plate broken—lots of water, cause unknown."

I hear a high whimpering sound. Seconds pass before I realize that it's not coming from the enemy. It's coming from somewhere forward. A high undulating wail.

The Old Man turns a disgusted face in that direction. He looks as if he might explode with rage at any moment.

"One hundred fifty degrees—getting louder!"

"And the other—the first one?"

"Ninety degrees; sixty degrees; holding steady!"

Christ, now the fuckers have got together. They're tossing the ball back and forth, and the ball is the Asdic bearing. Our original pursuer is no longer acting under any handicap. While he's attacking at top speed—which puts his own Asdic out of action—his colleague can idle along, taking bearings for him. And then radio the figures to him.

The Old Man's face is contorted, as though he had taken too long to swallow an especially bitter pill. "This is a crime!"

For the first time, the sound man shows signs of nervousness. Or does he *have* to turn his wheel so violently to find out which of the two sounds is getting louder?

If the second Commander up there is an old hand, if the two of them have worked together before, they'll exchange roles as often as possible in order to outfox us.

Unless I'm completely mistaken, the Old Man is steering toward the enemy in a tight curve.

★ ★ ★

04.00. Our attempts to break away have lasted—how many hours? I've lost count. Most of the men in the control room are sitting down: elbows on knees, heads in their hands. No one even looks up any longer. The Second Watch Officer is staring at the floor as if he could see mushrooms growing out of the floor plates. The graduated circle of the sky periscope has been torn loose and dangles on a wire. There is the tinkle of falling glass.

But wonders never cease!—The boat remains watertight. We're still moving, still buoyant. The motors are running, our screws turning. We're making headway, and we still have power for the rudder. The Chief can hold the boat: it's actually on an even keel again.

The navigator is bent over the chart table as though he is fascinated by it; his head is close to it, and the points of the dividers—which are clasped in his right hand—have bored into the linoleum.

The control-room mate has stuck two fingers into his mouth, apparently about to whistle on them.

The Second Watch Officer is trying to imitate the Commander's equanimity. But his fists betray him: they're firmly clenched around his binoculars—he still has the glasses hanging around his neck—and he's flexing them very slowly at the wrists, first one way, then the other. His knuckles are white with strain.

The Commander turns to the operator, who has his eyes closed and is twisting the wheel of his apparatus from side to side. Having apparently singled out the sound he was looking for, his maneuverings taper off almost to nothing.

In a subdued voice he announces, "Destroyer noises receding at one hundred twenty degrees!"

"They think they've finished us off!" says the Commander. That's the last one of them—but what about the other?

The Chief is in the stern, so the Commander himself is still in charge of the hydroplanes.

The whining has ceased. All that comes from the bow compartment is an occasional spasmodic sobbing.

The Chief reappears, his hands and forearms black with oil. Snatches of his half-whispered report reach me. "Flange of outer gas vent . . . condenser . . . two foundation bolts broken . . . already replaced . . . firmly wedged with wooden pegs . . . flange still leaking—but it's minor."

Beside the Commander's desk lies a carton of syrup, mashed and trodden all over the floor. The accordion is spread open in this disgusting mess. All the pictures have fallen off the walls. I take a cautious step over the face of the C-in-C.

In the Officers' Mess, books lie strewn among towels and spilled bottles of apple juice. The silly straw dog with glass eyes that's supposed to be our mascot has landed on the floor too. This is where I probably ought to start cleaning up—do something to occupy my hands. I bend over; stiff joints; I go down on my knees. Christ! I can actually move my hands. I'm making myself useful! Quietly, quietly, be careful. Don't hit anything. It must be way past four o'clock.

I've been cleaning up for a good ten minutes when the Chief comes through: greenish rings under his eyes. Pupils dark as lumps of coal, cheeks sunken. He's at the end of his tether.

I hand him a bottle of fruit juice. It's not just his hand; his whole body is trembling. He perches on a ledge while he's drinking. But as he puts the bottle down he's already on his feet, staggering slightly like a boxer, badly shaken and completely exhausted, but pulling himself up out of his corner one more time. ". . . It won't work," he mutters as he disappears.

Suddenly there are three more explosions, but this time they sound like beats on a slack drumskin. "Miles away," I hear the navigator say.

"Two hundred seventy degrees—moving away slowly!" the operator reports.

To think that somewhere there is dry land, hills and valleys . . . people are still asleep in their houses. In Europe, that is. In America they're still sitting up with the lights burning, and we're probably closer to America than we are to France. We've come too far west.

Absolute silence in the boat. After a while the operator whispers, "Destroyer bearing two hundred sixty degrees. Very faint. Slow revs—seems to be moving away."

"They're running silent," says the Commander. "Dawdling as slow as they can. And listening! Where in hell's the second one? Watch it!"

This is addressed to the hydrophone operator. So the Old Man no longer knows precisely where the enemy is.

I can hear the chronometer ticking and the condensation dripping into the bilge. The operator does a full sweep—and another, and another—but gets no bearing in his instrument.

"I don't like it," the Commander mutters to himself. "Don't like it at all."

A trick! It has to be. Something's wrong: it sticks out a mile.

The Old Man stares straight ahead, expressionless, then blinks quickly once or twice and swallows hard. Apparently he can't decide on a course of action.

If I only knew what the game was. No more explosions—no more Asdic—the Commander's continued play-acting—what to make of it?

If only I could ask the Old Man straight out, in four plain words, "How do things stand?"

But my mouth seems to be riveted shut. I'm incapable of thought. Head's a volcanic crater, bubbling evilly.

I feel thirsty. There must still be some apple juice left in the locker. I open it carefully, but shards of china fall out. All that damn banging around. Most of the cups and saucers are broken. A coffee pot has lost its spout. Looks idiotic without it. Fortunately the bottle of apple juice is intact. Apparently it was what smashed everything else. Quite right too: Smash everything around you so as to stay whole yourself.

The framed photograph of our launching is still lying under the table, broken. Sharp slivers of glass still sticking in the frame. I must have missed it while I was cleaning up. I manage to get hold of it but can't be bothered to loosen the glass daggers, so it goes back on its hook just as it is.

"No more noises?" asks the Commander.

"No, Herr Kaleun!"

Slowly it gets to be 05.00.

No noise. Hard to understand. Have they really given up the chase? Or are they considering us as sunk already?

I feel my way back into the control room. The Commander is consulting in whispers with the navigator. I hear, "In twenty minutes we surface!"

I hear it, but I can't believe my ears. Do we *have* to surface? Or are we really safely out of the shit?

The operators starts to say something; he's about to make a report—but he stops in mid-syllable and keeps turning his wheel. He must have caught a faint sound, which he's now trying to track by fine-tuning his apparatus.

The Old Man stares into the operator's face. The operator moistens his lower lip with his tongue. In a very low voice he reports, "Noise bearing sixty degrees—very faint."

Abruptly the Old Man climbs through the hatch and crouches down beside him in the gangway. The operator passes him the headset. The Old Man listens and the operator turns his wheel very gently back and forth along the scale, and gradually the Old Man's face grows stern.

Minutes pass. The Old Man remains tied to the hydrophone by the cord of the headset. He looks like a fish on a line. His orders to the helmsman are to bring the bow around so that he can hear better.

"Stand by to surface!"

His voice, grating and determined, has startled others than myself. The Chief's eyelids twitch.

Stand by to surface! He must know what is and isn't possible! Noises still audible in the hydrophone and he's getting ready to go up?

The hydrophone operators sit hunched over their tables. The navigator has finally taken off his sou'wester. His mask-like face looks years older, the lines in it carved even deeper.

The Chief stands behind him, his left thigh resting on the chart chest, his right hand on the pillar of the sky periscope, his torso bent forward as though to bring him as close as possible to the needle of the depth manometer that is slowly moving backward over the scale. With every mark it passes we are three feet closer to the surface. It moves very slowly, as if to give us time to experience these minutes at leisure.

"Radio clear by now?" asks the Commander.

"*Jawohl*, Herr Kaleun!"

The watch is already assembled in oilskins and sou'westers under the tower hatch. Binoculars are being polished—much too vigorously, or so it seems. No one says a word.

My breathing has steadied. I've regained the use of my muscles. I can stand without being afraid of staggering, but at the same time I can single out every muscle, every bone in my body. The flesh on my face feels frozen.

The Old Man intends to surface. We're going to breathe sea air again. We are alive. The bastards didn't kill us.

"The Last Cruise"

BY NORMAN POLMAR

(Excerpted from the book *The Death of the USS* Thresher)

The time is 1963. The age of the nuclear submarine has arrived. The great submarine battles of the Atlantic and the Pacific have been in the history books for twenty-some years. Now military operations are aimed at deterring possible Russian aggression. The most advanced submarine in the American fleet is armed to fire missiles and is nuclear powered to patrol the farthest reaches of the oceans. This submarine is named the *Thresher* and is called the "ultimate hunter-killer" submarine. On April 9, the *Thresher* puts out to sea for a routine test dive.

A t 3:45 on the morning of April 9, 1963 the piers of the Portsmouth Naval Shipyard were cold and damp. The darkness was broken here and there by the glare of streetlights and floodlights. Resting quietly in the waters of the Piscataqua River, the nuclear submarine *Thresher* was securely moored to Pier 11 at the shipyard. Inside most of the submarine's compartments it was bright as day. Power lines connected with the shipyard provided electricity for lights, radios, cooking, and a dozen other household duties. The submarine's nuclear power plant was still.

Fifteen minutes before the hour of four, Lieutenant Commander John S. Lyman, the *Thresher*'s engineer officer, began the four-hour countdown required for starting up the submarine's atomic power plant. Two hours later he requested permission to pull the first control rods which would start the reactor "cooking." These rods were made of special metals that absorb neutrons from the uranium 235 "fuel" in the reactor. As the rods were removed, fewer neutrons are absorbed until there are enough "free" neutrons to split other atoms. The atom-splitting produces still more neutrons that make possible a sustained nuclear reaction.

Lieutenant Commander Harvey, the *Thresher*'s commanding officer, gave permission to pull the rods.

A nuclear "fire" was silently lit.

At 6:15 the engineer officer reported to Harvey that the reactor had gone "critical," meaning it had reached the point of self-sustained nuclear fission. An hour later, the submarine's turbo-electric generator was producing electricity to feed the innumerable pieces of equipment that did everything from cook eggs to compute torpedo firing angles. At 7:30, the engine room notified Harvey that the full power of the submarine's remarkable propulsion system was ready to respond to orders.

One by one the lines holding the *Thresher* to Pier 11 were cast off. Soon there was nothing connecting the 129 men aboard the submarine with the shore. Normally only a 104-man crew plus perhaps a few men for training would be aboard. But, because the *Thresher* was going out on post-overhaul trials, there were also shipyard personnel and representatives of the Atlantic Fleet Submarine Force, the Naval Ordnance Laboratory, and civilian firms with special equipment in the submarine. In all, there were 12 officers and 96 men assigned to the submarine; a Submarine Force staff officer; three officers and 13 civilian employees from the Portsmouth yard; a specialist from the Naval Ordnance Laboratory in White Oak, Maryland; and three civilian factory representatives.

Four men who would normally have gone out in the *Thresher* that morning stayed ashore: Lieutenant Raymond J. McCoole, 33, was not aboard the *Thresher* on her final voyage because his wife had suffered a minor accident at home. The morning before—20 hours before the *Thresher* was to go to sea—McCoole's wife Barbara called him at the shipyard and said: "I feel terrible about calling you, but something dreadful has happened." She explained that while opening a bottle of rubbing alcohol some had spurted into her eyes.

McCoole quickly found Lieutenant Commander Pat Garner, exec of the *Thresher*, and explained what had happened. Then McCoole rushed back to his home, eight miles from the shipyard. His wife had flushed her eyes with water, but they still burned and she could not see clearly. He took her to a nearby hospital where she was given emergency treatment, and her eyes were bandaged.

The McCooles had five children, their ages then ranging from six months to nine years. With Barbara having to keep her eyes bandaged for several days, McCoole could not leave her alone. He phoned the yard and explained what had happened. Garner told him to stay put. McCoole said he wanted to make the cruise and would try to find a nurse to stay with the family. Reportedly Garner replied: "I'm ordering you to stay with Barbara. . . . Besides, we can use the room for one of the civilian technicians. Don't worry, Ray, there'll be plenty more trips for you."

Three enlisted men assigned to the *Thresher* were also ashore when she sailed. Garron S. Weitzel, 27, an interior communications electrician second class, had been attending navigation school at Dam Neck, Virginia, since January. He was scheduled to return to the *Thresher* in June. Frank DeStefano, a 29-year-old chief machinist's mate, had been sent to Washington for an interview with Vice Admiral Rickover in preparation for further assignment in the Navy's nuclear power program. He was also in line for a commission. Raymond Mattson, 34, a torpedoman's mate first class, had been ordered ashore for treatment of a nervous condition.

The large black submarine that was the *Thresher* eased away from the pier slowly. She steamed south, around New Castle Island, out of sight of the sprawling shipyard, and into the open sea off Odiorenes Point. As she met the running sea, she wallowed. The *Thresher*—shaped somewhat like a giant fish—was designed for high submerged speeds. On the surface her hull design made her cantankerous and unsteady.

As the *Thresher* pulled away from the New England coast, she began a series of surface trials that included tests of her communication and navigation equipment. East of Boston, at 9:49 A.M. the *Thresher* rendezvoused with the submarine rescue ship *Skylark*. The *Skylark* would escort the *Thresher* on her diving tests as was the custom in the Navy. The *Skylark* would provide a communications link to shore and, if the *Thresher* ran into trouble, try to assist her.

Skippered by Lieutenant Commander Stanley W. Hecker, the 205-foot *Skylark* was designed to help men escape from sunken submarines. Rescue ships have six anchors and several buoys so they can moor directly over a sunken submarine. On board are divers and elaborate equipment to bring them down to investigate a stricken submarine and, if possible, to attach hoses to pump in air for breathing or to expel water from the submarine's main ballast tanks to "blow" the submarine to the surface. On the deck of every rescue ship is a submarine rescue chamber. This device, developed in the late 1920s, is a two-chamber diving bell that can be sent down to a stricken submarine, attached to a hatch, take on survivors, and carry them to the surface. In the first—and so far only—use of the chamber, 33 men were brought up from the sunken U.S. submarine *Squalus* in 1939. (Another 26 men lost their lives when flooding compartments in the submarine were closed off to save the rest of the crew.)

The *Squalus* sank in 240 feet of water. The rescue chamber can theoretically help submarines in water as deep as 850 feet. Thus, if anything was to happen to the *Thresher* while over the continental shelf—the submerged coastal area where the water is less than 600 feet deep—the *Skylark* might be able to save anyone trapped in the stricken submarine. But if the submarine went down in deeper waters, and crewmen were alive, there was no means of rescuing them.

The *Skylark* had orders to meet the *Thresher* and escort the submarine on her diving tests. No agenda of the *Thresher*'s tests had been given to the *Skylark*. Later the rescue ship's commanding officer related, "I had no information as to the capabilities of the *Thresher* such as her depth, speed, and range. In fact, the UQC [Navy jargon for underwater telephone] was the only equipment on the *Skylark* of known capability with submarines."

With the *Skylark* standing nearby, the *Thresher* made a shallow dive, checking for leaks and testing various equipment. After this initial shallow test dive, the *Thresher* came to the surface. Throughout this shallow test dive conversations were carried on between the *Thresher* and *Skylark* with the UQC, which is actually like an underwater "acoustic" radio. The quality of communication between a surface ship and a submarine varies as sea conditions and distance between the ships change. As water temperature and density change between the two ships, the sound waves are often deflected and distorted, and what is received by the surface ship is sometimes garbled.

As the *Thresher* again wallowed on the surface, Harvey released the *Skylark* and directed the rescue ship to rendezvous again with the submarine the next morning for deep-dive tests some 200 nautical miles east of Cape Cod. The deep-dive tests were to be conducted beyond the continental shelf where the water drops off rapidly to more than 8,000 feet. While the *Thresher*'s diving capability did not approach that depth, she did need more than the 600 feet of depth available over the continental shelf.

About 3 P.M. on the afternoon of April 9 the *Thresher* again slipped beneath the waves and headed for the rendezvous point. En route various tests were conducted, including a full-power run with the submarine making about 30 knots. That night, as the *Thresher* sped toward deeper water, she transmitted a routine radio check to Atlantic Fleet Submarine Force Headquarters at Norfolk, Virginia.

At 6:35 on the fateful morning of April 10, the *Thresher* came up to periscope depth some ten nautical miles from the *Skylark*. It was the last time Wes Harvey saw the light of day. At 7:47 A.M. the *Thresher* notified the *Skylark* by underwater telephone that she was preparing to dive to her test depth. Here the term "test" is somewhat misleading. The test depth of a nuclear submarine is the maximum depth at which she is designed to operate and fight. Before the *Thresher* entered the yard for her nine-month overhaul she had been to her test depth some 40 times. That depth—long considered highly classified—was 1,300 feet. (At the time the Navy would officially say that U.S. nuclear submarines could dive "deeper than 400 feet.")

Submarine skippers have strict orders not to go below the craft's test depth except in the most dire emergency. Below test depth the fittings and pipes on the submarine begin to give way. Deeper, the tremendous pressure would begin to "pull" the submarine's hardened steel like taffy. Through the ruptured pipes, fittings, and hull, tons of water would shoot in, flooding the submarine in seconds or driving her to depths where the intense pressure would smash her in.

But Lieutenant Commander Harvey had no intention of taking his submarine below her test depth. During her test-depth dive the *Thresher* would level off at certain depths to check for leaks and to test equipment. She was to notify the *Skylark* of changes of course, depth, speed, and, in any event, make a UQC check every 15 minutes. The telephone messages would be recorded in the written logs aboard both ships.

Thirteen minutes before the hour of 8 o'clock the *Thresher* reported to the *Skylark* by underwater telephone that she was beginning her test-depth dive. Five minutes later, the *Thresher* reported being at 400 feet and checking for leaks.

Two minutes later—at 7:54—the *Thresher* told the *Skylark* that future references to depth would be made in terms of test depth to prevent discussions from being intercepted by any craft that might be in the area, especially the numerous Soviet trawlers that cruise off the American coast. Thus, references to test depth were given without using actual figures.

At 8:09 A.M. the *Thresher* reported she was at one-half her test depth; at 8:35, "minus 300 feet." Eighteen minutes later, a message said the submarine was proceeding to test depth.

At 9:02, the *Thresher* asked for a repetition of a course reading, according to Lieutenant (junior grade) James D. Watson, the *Skylark*'s navigator, who was talking with the submarine. He later said the *Skylark* had good communication with the *Thresher* at the time. Ten minutes later the two vessels made a routine check.

Then, "about a minute later," according to Lieutenant Watson, the *Thresher* reported: "Have positive up angle. . . . Attempting to blow up." Others aboard the *Skylark* who heard the message remembered it differently. Lieutenant Commander Hecker recalled the voice over the underwater telephone as having said: "Experiencing minor problem. . . . Have positive angle. . . . Attempting to blow." Roy S. Mowen Jr., a boatswain's mate third class, recalled the *Thresher*'s last message as: "Experiencing minor difficulty. . . . Have positive up angle. . . . Attempting to blow. . . . Will keep you informed."

The *Skylark*'s written log—the official record—recorded that at 9:12 a "satisfactory" underwater telephone check was made. Subsequently, it showed the submarine reported: "Have position up angle. . . . Attempting to blow up." Contrary to Navy procedure, the exact time of this message was not recorded.

Thus, it is known only that just after 9:12 the *Thresher* indicated she was having some kind of difficulty. Then the men aboard the *Skylark* listening to the UQC heard the sounds of air under high pressure.

At 9:14 the *Skylark* told the *Thresher* she had no contact. The submarine was asked to give her course and bearing to the *Skylark*. There was no reply. Hecker, skipper of the *Skylark*, told the man at the microphone to ask: "Are you in control?" When there was no reply, Hecker took the microphone himself and repeated the question three times.

But nothing was heard from the submarine until 9:17 when a garbled message was heard. To Hecker the message was unintelligible. But Watson believed that last garbled message from the *Thresher* ended with the distinct words "test depth." Seconds later, Watson heard a sound he remembered from his World War II days—"the sound of a ship breaking up . . . like a compartment collapsing."

Taking careful check of his position at the time of the last communication with the *Thresher*, Hecker patrolled the area, listening attentively for some reply to his continued calls to the submarine. At 10:58, the *Skylark* began dropping small signal grenades into the water. This is a pre-arranged signal with submarines to surface in case communications are lost. At almost the same time, Hecker ordered a radio message sent to New London, where the *Thresher* was assigned to Submarine Development Group 2 which in turn was part of Submarine Flotilla 2.

Far from being an alarm, the message tended merely to indicate a communications failure: UNABLE TO COMMUNICATE WITH *THRESHER* SINCE 0917. HAVE BEEN CALLING BY UQC VOICE AND CW QRB CW [dot-dash code] EVERY MINUTE EXPLOSIVE SIGNALS EVERY 10 MINS WITH NO SUCCESS. LAST TRANSMISSION RECD [received] WAS GARBLED. INDICATED *THRESHER* WAS APPROACHING TEST DEPTH. MY PRESENT POSITION 41–43N 64–57W CONDUCTING EXPANDING SEARCH.

The message was sent with an "operational immediate" priority. This meant it was to be sent and delivered as fast as possible. The two higher priorities in naval communications are reserved for vital emergencies, such as contact with enemy forces. The *Thresher* was not in emergency, not yet at least. The wording of the *Skylark*'s message would put the Navy's search procedure in action.

But sending the "operational immediate" signal took time. The *Skylark* is an auxiliary ship, not a warship with elaborate radio equipment that can flash a message around the world in seconds. Her communications link to the shore was a transmitter broadcasting dot-dash signals. As Robert L. Cartwright, radioman first class, tapped out the fateful message, atmospheric conditions made transmission difficult. Several times the radio operator at New London had to interrupt the *Skylark*'s transmission with requests to repeat portions of the message.

It took one hour and 58 minutes to send the brief message from the *Skylark* to New London. Captain J. Sneed Schmidt, commander of Submarine Flotilla 2, received the *Skylark*'s message at 1:02 P.M. as he returned from lunch. "I had two officers from Norfolk as my guests," he recalled later. "The chief handed me the paper and said, 'Here's a message you've got to see right away.' I looked at it, read it aloud, and said, 'Now gentlemen, you can see the importance of this. You'll excuse me while I get going.' "

Captain Schmidt later recalled that he had no feeling of disaster as he read the radio message. "It's happened many times before where ships have lost communication. I get messages like this every week on the average."

But there was no question that action must be taken "just in case." The direct "hot line" from New London to Atlantic Fleet Headquarters at Norfolk quickly carried the text of the *Skylark*'s message to the top operating commanders on the East Coast. Within the hour, Vice Admiral Elton W. Grenfell, commander of all submarines in the Atlantic, and Captain Schmidt were discussing the *Skylark* message by phone. "We agreed that this doesn't look good," Schmidt later said.

Another Norfolk-based flag officer, Vice Admiral Wallace Beakley, was told of the *Skylark* message at 1:32 P.M. Five minutes later, in his capacity as Deputy Commander-in-Chief of the Atlantic Fleet, he ordered the nuclear submarine *Seawolf*, the diesel-electric submarine *Sea Owl*, the rescue ship *Sunbird*, and an aircraft to the scene of the *Thresher's* last reported position. Shortly afterwards the salvage ship *Recovery* and additional aircraft were ordered into the search.

Back at New London, Captain Frank A. Andrews, the commander of Submarine Development Group 2, climbed into a helicopter and was flown out to the large destroyer *Norfolk* that was cruising off Cape Cod. After taking him aboard, the sleek *Norfolk* picked up speed and headed to the search area while Captain Andrews made preparations for taking charge of the various ships, submarines, and aircraft racing eastward to join the hunt for the *Thresher*.

The Navy's No. 1 officer, Chief of Naval Operations George W. Anderson, was told of the *Thresher* situation about 3:40 P.M. Admiral Anderson had been attending a meeting of the Joint Chiefs of Staff in the Pentagon, which concluded at 3:35. While he was walking back to his office from the meeting, Atlantic Fleet Headquarters phoned his office on a "hot line" circuit. Admiral Claude V. Ricketts, the Vice Chief of Naval Operations, took the call and was told that communications between the *Skylark* and *Thresher* had been lost and that the submarine might be in trouble. Ricketts immediately sent his senior aide to find Admiral Anderson and inform him of the message.

The aide, Captain H. B. Sweitzer, encountered Admiral Anderson in the corridor outside of the E-ring office of Secretary of the Navy Fred Korth. Admiral Anderson stepped into Korth's office and repeated the message he had just received. After a brief conversation, Korth called the White House to speak to Captain Tazewell T. Shepard, the President's naval aide. Fifteen minutes later Captain Shepard was in Mr. Kennedy's office.

John F. Kennedy—the first American president to have worn the uniform of a naval officer—asked first how many men were involved. Shepard did not have the exact number involved, but told the Commander-in-Chief that the normal complement of such a submarine was about 90 men. "The President asked me to keep him informed of the search efforts," Captain

Shepard was to recall later. "He was very distressed at the possibility that the submarine may have been lost."

Far to the north, the Canadian Navy was asked to stand by to assist in whatever operations might be necessary. The *Thresher's* last reported position was only about 100 nautical miles off the tip of Nova Scotia. Canadian Navy Headquarters at Halifax on the Nova Scotia peninsula quickly alerted one of the submarines based there to stand by to get under way. As the submarine's skipper ordered his crew rounded up, a rumor began to spread that a U.S. submarine was in trouble.

A newsman at television station CJCH heard the rumor and the station interrupted its program with the bulletin: "U.S. submarine reported in danger of sinking or in trouble on the high seas."

The secret was out.

★ ★ ★

There were those who knew what happened to the *Thresher*. Five, perhaps ten, maybe a score of men, and just possibly as many as 129. All were dead. Thus the theories of what killed the *Thresher* initially ran the gauntlet of possibility from enemy action to human error to the failure of a piping system.

It is known that at 7:47 A.M. on April 10 the *Thresher* was operating close to the surface when she rendezvoused with the rescue ship *Skylark* some 220 nautical miles east of Cape Cod. The day before the *Thresher* had conducted her shallow dives. At first she had gone down to about 60 feet (depth of keel), close enough to the surface to allow her to keep her extended radar mast exposed for contact with the *Skylark*. That first dive was made in about 185 feet of water. As the *Thresher* continued her shallow diving trials, she headed east and into deeper waters. It is believed she went down to about 400 feet in the course of the dives on April 9. The *Thresher* also made a full-power run at that time. The tests were acceptable to Lieutenant Commander Harvey, and he advised the *Skylark* that he was going ahead with the planned dive to the *Thresher's* maximum operating or "test" depth on the morning of the 10th. About 12 hours were to be devoted to the deep dives. If all went well the *Thresher* would be tied up safe and sound at Portsmouth about 4 P.M. on April 11.

The transit from the shallow dive area to the meeting with the *Skylark* on the morning of the 10th was probably made at about 200 feet. According to the Navy, "she was probably at such depth as to avoid shipping, with occasional periscope depth. There was no set depth [for such a transit by nuclear submarines]." Since Commander Harvey had already made a careful shallow test dive on April 9, he had no hesitation about diving the *Thresher* rapidly to 400 feet on the morning of April 10. The remainder of the deep dive would be cautious, and all instruments would be scrutinized as the submarine slowly went deeper and deeper.

At 7:54 A.M. on the 10th the *Thresher* reached 400 feet and advised the *Skylark* that future references to depth would be made in terms of test depth—1,300 feet. There was always the possibility that a Soviet surface ship or even submarine could be in the area and able to intercept the relatively primitive UQC underwater telephone. Outside of a small circle of Navy officials and civilian engineers, and a large, but closed-mouth, group of submariners, the *Thresher's* test depth was classified at that time.

The *Thresher* slowly went deeper. Beyond the 400-foot mark the *Thresher* descended by small increments, probably 100 feet at a time. She reported being at one-half test depth at 8:09 A.M. Thus it can be assumed that at 8:09 the *Thresher* was at about 650 feet.

At 8:35, the *Thresher* reported her depth at "minus 300 feet" or roughly 1,000 feet. Carefully the *Thresher's* crew checked the submarine's watertight integrity and conducted various tests, in part similar to those of the shallow dive the day before.

At 8:53, the *Thresher* reported she was proceeding to test depth. The *Thresher* had probably remained at "minus 300 feet" for 18 minutes, checking equipment and conducting tests, or perhaps she had gone slightly deeper during that time without actually reporting the change of depth to the *Skylark*. Possibly the *Thresher* went down another 100 feet in this period.

At 9:02 and again at 9:12, routine communications took place between the *Thresher* and the *Skylark*. Reviewing the previous estimates of depth, it appears that the *Thresher* would have descended another 100 feet by the time of the 9:02 or 9:12 message if she were going down 100 feet at a time:

Estimated Time	Time Interval	Depth
7:54		400 feet
8:09	15 minutes	650 feet
8:35	24 minutes	1,000 feet
8:53	18 minutes	1,000–1,100 feet
9:12	19 minutes	1,100–1,200 feet

These estimates must be assumed to be the maximum depths reached by the *Thresher* during the time periods indicated, for it is entirely possible that she remained at the same depth during a time interval to conduct tests. Although there is also a slight possibility that the *Thresher* did reach her test depth by the time of the 9:12 message, it seems unlikely. If the *Thresher* had been at her test depth she would have reported it at the 9:12 communications check.

Rather it appears that at 9:12 on the morning of April 10 the *Thresher* was approaching her test depth in what was so far a normal, safe, and seemingly routine test dive. According to Lieutenant Commander Hecker of the *Skylark*, about a minute later the *Thresher* made a report that indicated she was no longer conducting a normal or safe or routine operation. Approximately 9:13 was the beginning of the end of the *Thresher*.

The communication alluded to by those aboard the *Skylark* who were listening to the messages from the *Thresher* is somewhat uncertain. There were three parts to this message as reported: "experiencing minor problem," an allusion to "angle," and "attempting to blow."

"Experiencing minor problem." What is a minor problem in a complex nuclear-propelled submarine? For example, at 1,000 feet flooding through a six-inch pipe certainly would not be cause for a report of a minor problem. At a depth of 1,000 feet approximately 100,000 pounds of sea water would flood through a six-inch pipe in just one minute! Even flooding through a half-inch pipe would hardly be considered minor, due to the noise it would cause, the powerful spray that would cause confusion and make finding the pipe difficult, and the uncertainty as to what was happening.

Loss of control of the diving planes—provided that they were not jammed in such a way as to increase depth rapidly—might be considered minor. Even if the diving planes were jammed on "hard dive" the difficulty could still be classified as minor if the speed of the submarine through the water was not high.

The exact speed of the *Thresher* at 9:12 is not known. For positive control of the submarine, the commanding officer was probably conducting the test at a speed of five to ten knots, most likely nearer the higher speed.

Even loss of main propulsion power through an accidental reactor shutdown or other temporary failure in the main propulsion system might initially be considered minor, especially if the trim of the submarine had her on an even keel.

However, if the *Thresher* was steaming at ten knots, a loss of forward motion through the water would slowly cause a loss of buoyancy, unless the submarine was intentionally trimmed in a "positive" buoyant condition and was being "held down" by the effect of the craft's speed on her wing—like diving planes. As speed is reduced, a submarine normally and naturally acts "heavy" and "wants" to go deeper.

"Experiencing minor problem" indicates that no sudden catastrophic event befell the *Thresher*. Rather, this part of the message indicates that the initial event of a sequence took place about 9:13 A.M.

The second part of the message is less informative because it does not make sense to those familiar with submarines. Three versions of this second portion of the message were given: "have position angle," "have positive up angle," and "have position up angle."

A submariner speaks of "having an up angle" or a "down angle" to mean that the bow of the submarine is pointing up or down, respectively. The submariner pays exceedingly close attention to this angle, and instruments can measure it accurately to within one quarter to one half of a degree. A submariner does not use the term "position up angle" or "position down angle." "Have positive up angle" may have meant the bow of the submarine was pointing up and the submarine was attempting to head for the surface— if that was the wording of the message. The literal expression "have position angle" is entirely meaningless. The report of this phase of the *Thresher's* message was undoubtedly in error. Communications via underwater sound telephone are at best very poor and not unlike a long-distance, short-wave radio transmission, which is "fuzzy." Further, the sound transmission leaving the *Thresher*, in addition to traveling directly up to the *Skylark*, also traveled to the rescue ship via a bounce off the ocean floor, causing a reverberation or echo sound at the receiver. Often approximate knowledge of the message to be received assists the receiving ship in interpreting the message.

In the event, little light can be shed on the *Thresher* mystery from the second portion of the message.

The third portion of the message, "attempting to blow up," could be revealing. "Blow up" to a submariner means forcing high pressure air into the ballast tanks to expel the main ballast water, thus lightening the submarine so that she will go up.

Lieutenant Commander Harvey apparently decided, whatever the trouble and however minor it was, to shed the *Thresher's* main ballast in order to give her more buoyancy. Since the same amount or greater upward lift could also be provided by increasing speed coupled with proper use of his diving planes, it appears that he did not have the ability to control either propulsion, and hence speed, or the diving planes. For example, a simple mathematical computation shows that had the *Thresher* been able to make ten knots and obtain a 30-degree up-angle with her planes, with neutral buoyancy the submarine would have gone up at the rate of some 500 feet per minute. With complete control of speed and diving plane action the *Thresher* could—under normal circumstances—have come up to the surface even faster if necessary.

Probably this non-availability of propulsion or diving plane control was the minor difficulty the submarine announced seconds earlier.

Further, this portion of the message, as reported, did not say "am blowing up," but rather "attempting to blow up." This is disturbing because "attempting" implies the high-pressure air is not expelling water from the ballast tanks as desired or, if it is, that the submarine is still not getting the needed buoyancy. This is all the more disturbing because there is a minimum of moving parts between the high-pressure air in a submarine's storage flasks and the pipes leading this air into the main ballast tanks.

The report "attempting to blow up" has the same effect on a submariner as hearing the driver of an automobile say, "I am attempting to put on the brakes." The experienced driver knows that braking a car is a simple, almost instantaneous action. Hearing such a statement makes one imagine the brake is being applied with no noticeable effect on the car.

Was there some mishap with the high-pressure air system in the *Thresher*? According to Lieutenant Watson's testimony, he heard the message "attempting to blow up" and then, for a few seconds, he heard the sound of compressed air. Roy Mowen, boatswain's mate third class, recalled hearing the compressed air sounds in the background as the *Thresher* reported "attempting to blow." And, indeed the sound of compressed air may even have been heard before the "attempting to blow" part of the message.

If the message was received first, it would mean that, after "attempting" to blow up, the *Thresher* was finally successful, and the sound of air under pressure meant the submarine had started to blow up.

Had the message and sound been received simultaneously, the garble of the message would be understandable since the sound of compressed air flowing would seriously interfere with the sound reception (not unlike the effect of lightning on radio reception).

The estimate of hearing air under pressure for "several seconds" is very significant. If the *Thresher* wanted to blow up from near test depth, she would probably blow until she was well on the way to the surface, much longer than just a few seconds. If the message was received after the *Thresher* had started blowing air, the "attempting" would make more sense. In this case, however, the men in the *Thresher* would have begun to be concerned for their safety. Something had happened which, although at the time considered to be minor, caused Commander Harvey to want to expel his main ballast. The *Thresher* tried, and she could not.

Without control of speed and diving planes together or without high-pressure air to expel ballast, the *Thresher* could be in serious trouble at any depth—even a few feet below the surface, depending upon the trim of the submarine.

A sequence of events takes form.

For four minutes—as the *Thresher* is "attempting to blow up"—there is no communication. Then, at 9:17, the *Thresher* transmits a message ending with "test depth." It has been generally supposed that "exceeding" was one of the words preceding "test depth."

During these four minutes there was definite suspicion aboard the *Skylark* that all was not normal in the *Thresher*. Lieutenant Commander Hecker, commanding officer of the *Skylark*, personally took the *Skylark's* microphone and asked repeatedly: "Are in you control?" It is possible that Commander Hecker's attempt to communicate with *Thresher* via the UQC prevented the rescue ship from hearing messages coming the other way in much the same way communication is impaired when two people talk to each other at the same time during a telephone conversation.

The *Thresher's* failure to communicate during the four minutes—if Commander Hecker's calls were not blanking out those of the *Thresher*—could be interpreted in one of three ways:

First, it is possible that the sequence of events had quickly progressed to the point where those in the *Thresher* realized that disaster was imminent and were too busy trying to save themselves to take time out to communicate with the *Skylark*, which could not render any assistance.

Second, there is the possibility that during those four minutes the situation was static, with the *Thresher* simply hovering at about test depth, perhaps even rising at a very slow rate, but that there was not yet serious concern in the *Thresher*. In those minutes the crew was possibly busy restoring propulsion or tracing down the trouble in the high pressure air system. In this case, communication would have been postponed for a few minutes until a definite report could be transmitted.

Third—and a very definite possibility—is that the *Thresher* had lost electrical power to some or all of her lighting and electrical equipment, including her underwater telephone. Lieutenant Watson testified that seconds after the 9:17 message that ended with "test depth" he heard "the sound of a ship breaking up . . . like a compartment collapsing."

While the reported timing of all messages after the 9:12 routine communication could easily be in error by as much as a minute and quite possibly more, the timing must be assumed to be correct. Thus, about five minutes had elapsed between the initial trouble in the *Thresher* and the "sound of a ship breaking up." As the *Thresher* lost her battle to return to the surface, she began to plummet to the ocean floor, down into the depths where the tremendous pressure would destroy her.

The U.S. Navy constructs submarines to withstand one and a half times the pressure of their designed test depth. The ratio of the "test depth" to "collapse depth" of a submarine is therefore nominally two-to-three. This is a safety factor. The collapse depth is based on both mathematical calculations and model tests. The latter are not always conclusive since hydrodynamic scaling factors are difficult to calculate accurately. It is safe to assume that the collapse depth of the *Thresher* was approximately 1,950 feet.

The sequence of casualties suffered by the *Thresher* apparently caused a fateful increase of some 600 feet—from test depth to collapse depth—in five agonizing minutes.

Regardless of what the *Thresher*'s "minor problem" was, as she neared collapse depth she had major problems—fittings and pipes began to give way, admitting powerful jets of water that pushed aside men struggling to plug them and shorted out electrical equipment, making corrective action impossible. The additional weight of water thus admitted to the *Thresher* drove her still deeper at an ever-increasing speed. The submarine's hull groaned under the increasing pressure that tried to crush in her air-filled interior.

There were probably no serious personnel casualties at this point. But all men inside the submarine now sensed that they were rushing toward disaster and groped frantically for some avenue of escape or survival. Suddenly, the insulating cork that lined the submarine's interior began to crack and possibly flake off. Pipes began pulling apart as the water pressure began to "pull" the submarine's hardened steel like taffy. An instant later the hull imploded.

In a fraction of a second millions of pounds of water under tremendous pressure smashed the submarine's hull, twisting portions of it, disintegrating other parts of it along with the lighter materials inside it. Death was instantaneous and painless to all 129 men within the submarine.

The theory that water filled the plummeting *Thresher* before she could implode is generally discounted because the additional weight of the water would accelerate the downward rate and cause an implosion before the hull could fill with water. As the *Thresher* imploded and was torn apart, there could have been no air pockets to keep her "afloat" in a limbo somewhere between her collapse depth and the ocean floor. Instead, the remains of the *Thresher* rained down on the ocean floor almost a mile and a half below.

But what was the "minor" difficulty the *Thresher* encountered at about 9:13 that led to the worst submarine disaster in history? Even though the event was "minor" the *Thresher*'s commanding officer soon began to blow his main ballast tanks. Thus it appears that the minor difficulty was probably one to cause the *Thresher* to become heavy. This would most probably occur as a result of losing propulsion or taking on water. Loss of propulsion might have been a result of the latter condition.

The Navy's Court of Inquiry concluded that the "most probable" cause of the *Thresher*'s loss, with the information available, was failure of a piping system. Again, it seems doubtful that any submariner would consider flooding at or near test depth, regardless of how slight, as a "minor" difficulty. It is always possible that the report from the scene of the flooding inside of the *Thresher* could somehow have been garbled on its way to the control room, where a misinterpretation may have occurred, resulting in the report of a minor problem.

More probable, it appears that the initial minor difficulty was the loss of propulsion. With the loss of forward motion the *Thresher* began to sink deeper and deeper as a result of her heavy water ballast, which it was decided to expel. However, before the downward motion of the submarine could be halted—and before she reached her collapse depth—the increasing water pressure began to rupture some of the numerous pipes penetrating the submarine's pressure hull. This water drove the submarine still deeper and she imploded.

Following the Court of Inquiry's "most probable" cause—that the initial difficulty was a piping system failure—the flooding casualty could have been through a small (one- or two-inch) pipe or a larger opening (possibly four to six inches). Several piping systems of these diameters penetrated the *Thresher*'s engineering spaces. Again, because serious flooding would not have been reported as a minor problem, the smaller sizes seem more probable. At approximately the *Thresher*'s test depth, water entering through a one- or two-inch pipe would be shooting forth like the water shot from a high-pressure fire hose of comparable diameter. The water—possibly hitting other pipes or equipment and turning into a powerful spray—might have struck and shorted out a switchboard, causing a loss of power. Or, the force of the water might have knocked over a key member of the engine room crew. He might have been thrown against a switchboard or other control panel or, in his efforts to keep from being pushed away by the water, he might have grabbed blindly for something to hang on to and grabbed a vital control switch. Any of these actions could have occurred and led to the impending disaster.

Flooding or loss of propulsion appear to be the most probable initial incident that caused the death of the *Thresher*.

"Bearing—Mark! Down Periscope!"

BY CAPTAIN EDWARD L. BEACH, USN

(Excerpted from the novel Run Silent, Run Deep)

The scene is World War II again. In the far reaches of the vast Pacific, American submarines play the same role as the German U-boats in the Atlantic: attacking convoys. The action is narrated by the captain of the *Walrus*, out of Pearl Harbor and now moving into position off the Japanese coast to ambush passing ships.

The movie version of *Run Silent, Run Deep*, with Clark Gable and Burt Lancaster, is a personal favorite, despite the unrealistic, gin-clear underwater photography and the oversized sub compartments. Not until *The Boat* came along did filmmakers start to get those details into believable images.

We had achieved our destination. We had come over eight thousand miles to war and a few miles ahead of us lay one of the main islands of Japan—southernmost Kyushu.

Kyushu is separated from the islands to the north and east, Honshu and Shikoku, by the Japanese Inland Sea. From the Pacific side there are two entrances to this confined body of water: the Bungo Suido between Kyushu and Shikoku and the Kii Suido between Shikoku and Honshu. Since the earliest times Japan's Inland Sea has been one of the island empire's main traffic arteries between the home islands and, of course, during the war it constituted a huge sheltered harbor in which their whole battle fleet could hold maneuvers if desired.

AREA SEVEN included the eastern coast of Kyushu, beginning with the Bungo Suido on the north and extending down almost to the southern tip of the island. Our instructions were to examine the area; determine what, if anything, were the Japanese traffic patterns; estimate how often the Bungo Suido was used, whether naval units were in the habit of using that entrance. And our mission was also to sink any and all Japanese vessels we might encounter—and avoid being detected, attacked, or sunk ourselves.

We were still headed west. Up ahead, no longer in sight, was Kyushu. I stared unseeingly in that direction, then took my binoculars and made a slow sweep all the way around the horizon. It felt good to be topside, to draw in clean, wholesome air instead of the torpid atmosphere we had been breathing. My greedy senses drank in the freedom of the ocean.

There was a musty tinge to the air, an odor of wet, burned sandalwood, of unwashed foreign bodies. A seaman, near shore, can always smell the shore—it is the smell landsmen identify as the "smell of the sea." But it is not noticeable at sea—only close to shore—and it pervaded my consciousness this night. All night long we cruised aimlessly about, seeing nothing, never losing the smell of Japan. By morning we had approached close enough to Kyushu to take up a patrol station about ten miles offshore where we hoped some unwary vessel might blunder into our path, and where the first of a series of observation posts on the Bungo Suido could logically be set up.

Jim and I had studied the chart. Inshore lay a bank of moderately shallow water, hardly deep enough to shelter us in the event of a counterattack. Jim had argued for going in closer, saying that coastwise Japanese shipping would run in as shallow water as possible. I demurred, pointing out that we had the dual responsibility of watching the Bungo as well, and that we could always go closer inshore after a merchant vessel if necessary. The spot we finally selected was intended to satisfy both objectives, though Jim never did express final satisfaction.

We were finishing an austere lunch when the control room messenger appeared. "Captain," he said, "you're wanted in the conning tower. Mr. Adams says there's smoke." I dashed down the passageway, hearing the last words of his hastily muttered message over my shoulder as I ran. In a moment Hugh turned over the periscope to me. Sure enough, a thin column of smoke could be seen close inshore northwestward. I watched it carefully to see which way it was going, finally accepted the fact that it was heading away. The smoke gradually became less distinct, faded out in the distance.

Twice more we sighted smoke that day, once more to the northwest and once to the southwest. In all three cases the ships were going away, not toward; and it would have been fruitless to have pursued them.

"Do you think they are slipping by us close inshore?" Jim asked me. I shrugged. There was no way of telling. "Maybe if we went in closer, close enough to see the coast distinctly . . ."

"Too shallow," I said, but the eagerness I had noted during the fruitless attempt on the Jap submarine was now dancing in Jim's eyes, showing through the considered awareness I had become accustomed to.

"Look, skipper, why don't we go in here?" He indicated a spot on the coast where the extent of shallow water was much less than elsewhere. "They couldn't get by without our seeing them if we went in here."

To fall in with his suggestion would have meant giving up our watch position on the Bungo Suido. The position we had chosen permitted us to cover one segment of the probable traffic lines from there. Several days in this position and several days in each of three others would, we had figured, give us some idea of traffic patterns.

"Jim, we've only been here one day. Keep your shirt on," I said in small exasperation. "We've got twenty-nine days more in the area." But Jim persisted, pointing out eagerly the configuration of the coastline and the depths of water here and there to bolster his argument. On our area chart he had drawn the approximate location of the three ships we had sighted.

"Look, Captain," he said, "we already know they are going here," indicating with his finger. "We know they are running close inshore. Our main mission is to sink them. After we knock off a couple . . ." We might have argued longer had not the musical notes of the general alarm interrupted us. Startled, I jerked up, caught Jim's eye and then with one move we raced to the conning tower.

"Bong, bong, bong, bong, bong"—the doorbell chimes were still pealing out as, breathlessly, I confronted Dave Freeman. Already the reduction of oxygen was becoming noticeable.

"A ship, sir, coming this way—a big ship." The periscope was down, evidently having just been lowered. I grasped the pickle, squeezed it as Dave spoke, started it up again. In a moment I was looking through it. There in the distance, exactly like our practice approaches in New London, were the masts, stack, and bridge structure of a large vessel. I could hear the warming-up notes of the TDC. Keith was ready for business.

"Bearing—Mark! Down periscope!"

"Three-two-eight," read Dave from the azimuth ring.

Keith furiously spun one of the handles. "Angle on the bow?"

"Starboard ten."

"Estimated range?" I had not tried to get a range.

The ship was still well hull down, only her upper works showing. "Give it fifteen thousand yards," I said.

Jim had extracted the Is-Was from its stowage, was rotating the dials. Rubinoffski, garbed in his underwear with hastily thrown-on shoes and carrying his trousers, came clattering up the ladder. Off watch, he had been caught in his bunk by the call to quarters. Freeman relinquished the pickle to him, dashed below, bound for his own station. The Quartermaster hastily thrust his bony legs into his dungarees, managed to get them hooked at the top in time to grasp the periscope control button and raise it at my order. I spun the periscope around quickly, lowered it. "Nothing else in sight," I said, motioning for it to come up again. Another look, this time carefully at the sky. Clear, a few clouds, not much cover for aircraft, no airplanes in sight. Down went the periscope again. I looked around, looked at Jim. He nodded briefly.

"Conning tower manned, sir." Quin was listening on his headset, nodded also. The periscope started up with my thumb motion.

"Observation," I snapped.

"Ship is at battle stations," rapidly called out Quin.

I rose with the periscope. "Bearing—Mark!"

"Three-three-nine and a half!"

"Use forty feet. Range—Mark!"

Rubinoffski fumbled with the range dial lining up the pointers.

"One-four-oh-double-oh!" The 'scope dropped away.

"Angle on the bow still the same. Starboard ten." Keith was spinning his TDC cranks with both hands.

"Any other ships in sight, Captain?" This was Jim. "No," I said, "No escorts."

"I have the dive, Captain, depth sixty feet." Tom had climbed up two or three rungs of the ladder to the control room, had his head at the deck level.

"Very well." I turned to Keith. "What's the course to close the track with about a thirty-degree angle?" Keith looked at his dials for a moment. "We're on it now, sir. Recommend no change. What kind of a ship is it, Captain?"

Jim had finished orienting the Is-Was, now crowded between Hugh Adams at the plotting table and Keith at the TDC. He looked at me with that same look of anticipated pleasure, that eagerness for combat that I had recently noticed. "Can't tell yet. Buff superstructure, black stack, two masts. Some kind of a cargo vessel."

"Is he smoking?"

"No—no smoke at all."

"New ship then. Anyway, in good shape."

I nodded.

Up forward of the periscope hoist motors was the underwater sound receiver and control equipment for the sound heads under our bow. I leaned over alongside the earphoned sonar operator. His pointer was going around steadily and slowly. He shook his head at my inquiring glance. I indicated the area on our starboard bow as the place for him to concentrate on, stepped back to the periscope, motioned with my thumbs.

"Zig to his right," I called. The angle on the bow had changed, was now port twenty degrees, and I could see more of the enemy ship, a large new-type freighter. As I turned the periscope something else caught my eye—a discontinuity in the horizon—another mast. It would indeed have been highly improbable that a large, valuable freighter should be coming out of port unescorted. I looked closely on the other side, then back again. There were two small masts, one on either side, both apparently abeam or a little distance astern. This would not be as easy an approach as I had for a short time been hoping. "He has two escorts, Jim," I said.

"What kind?"

"Can't tell yet. They're a lot smaller and I can't see them." Quin was watching me. He picked up the telephone mouthpiece, spoke into it briefly. I could visualize everyone in the ship getting the word: "The skipper sees two destroyers up there!"

"Jim," I said, "have the ship rigged for depth charge. Shortly before we fire we will go to silent running also."

"Right," said Jim, as he squeezed by me to relay the necessary instructions to Quin.

Several observations later the situation had developed more clearly. Our target was a single large merchantman with cargo hatches forward and aft and four large goal-post type derricks. She had a single low, fat stack rising out of an amidships deckhouse evidently fitted for passenger accommodations. The ship had obviously come out of Bungo Suido and was headed south, perhaps bound for Guam or Saipan, making respectable speed and escorted by three old type destroyers. One escort rode on either beam of the target and the third one, which I had not seen until some time later, was following astern. I could feel *Walrus* tense up as the target drew steadily near her. He was zigzagging, presenting first one side and then the other. We were right on his base course and had only to maneuver for a shot as he went by. I could feel myself tense up as well, as the crucial moment approached.

We closed off the ventilation system, the air-conditioning machinery, and all other equipment not absolutely essential to the progress of the business at hand. The sweat spurted out of my pores, ran saltily down my cheeks and into the corners of my mouth. I ran my hands ceaselessly through my moist hair, wiped them off on my trousers. Hugh Adams was bothered by sweat dropping off the end of his nose onto his carefully laid-out plot.

Through the periscope I could see the whole ship now, even her red waterline heaving in and out of the sea. I had directed Tom to run several feet deeper to reduce the amount of periscope exposed, leaving me just enough height to make observations between passing waves. The range had closed to about two miles when the target made another zig.

"Angle on the bow—starboard thirty-five," I sang out, as the periscope descended. "Keith, what's the distance to the track?"

"Two thousand yards, Captain."

"Torpedo run?"

"Two-seven-double-oh." Jim, detailed to the angle solver on firing, relayed this one for me.

"Are we ready to shoot, Jim?" Jim glanced upward at his check-off list. My eyes followed his. Every item on it but one had been neatly checked off in grease pencil. "We're ready to shoot, Captain, except that outer doors are still closed."

According to the Pearl Harbor submarine base our torpedoes were prone to flood if left exposed in the torpedo tubes with the outer doors open for too long a period. It was advisable not to open them until just before firing. I turned to Quin. "Open the outer doors forward."

"Open the outer doors forward," he echoed into his telephone transmitter. Up forward at the command the torpedo-men would speedily crank open the heavy bronze torpedo tube muzzle doors. This was the last act in the preparation of torpedoes for firing.

I nodded for the periscope, crouched before it till it came up, rode it to its full extension, spun it around, lowered it. "We're inside the screen," I said. "The near escort will pass astern, well clear." I failed to mention that the rear escort, a few hundred yards astern of the target, would by no means pass clear. Within minutes after firing, he would be upon us. No point in alerting or worrying our crew at this stage over something that could not be helped.

"We'll give him three torpedoes on a ninety track, or as near to it as we can!"

"Ninety track. Three fish spread!" echoed Jim.

"The next observation will be a shooting observation! Stand by forward!" My mind racing, I studied the slowly moving dials on the face of the TDC. We could already shoot at any time. It was only a matter of waiting until the situation was most favorable. The "correct solution light," a red F, was glowing brightly on the face of the angle-solver sector of the TDC. The "torpedo run" was well within the maximum range of the torpedo. It would only be a few seconds longer.

I could feel the taut expectancy of the ship—this was to be our first kill. In the forward part of the conning tower O'Brien, the sonarman, had put the propeller beats on the loud-speaker. We could hear the "chug-a-chug, chug-a-chug, chug-a-chug, chug-a-chug," as the enemy's screws came closer and closer. Less distinct was the lighter, high-pitched beat of the nearest escort. "Thum, thum, thum, thum." The sonarman switched from one to the other, kept them both coming in. It looked about time.

"This is a shooting observation," I said again. "Up periscope!" The periscope handles met my outstretched hands. I snapped them down, put my eye to the eye guard. "No change," I said. "Bearing—Mark!"

"Three-three-six."

"Range"—I turned the range knob—"Mark!"

"One-eight-five-oh."

"Shoot," I said, snapping the handles up as the signal for the periscope to start down. Quin had turned around facing the firing panel, had turned the switch of Number One torpedo tube to "On."

"Fire!" shouted Jim. Quin leaned on the firing key. *Walrus* shuddered. Over the sonar loud-speaker I could hear the torpedo whine out of the tube. Jim made an adjustment to the face of the angle solver with his right hand, held a stop watch in his left, watched it intently. "Fire Two!" he shouted. Quin leaned on the firing key a second time.

Another adjustment by Jim, then "Fire Three!" and *Walrus* jerked for the third time. I motioned for the periscope again, took a quick look. Our torpedoes were running nicely.

"Torpedo run?" I called out, as the periscope was on the way down.

"One-six-five-oh." A quick calculation. A little over one minute to go. Up went the periscope again. I spun it around, dipped it, raised it again. One escort was passing astern. I hadn't given him much of an inspection before—he was an old type destroyer, *Momo* class as nearly as I could tell, with a well-deck forward of the bridge, and two stacks far apart. The periscope dipped again and then went back up to the target. All still serene.

"How long?"

"Thirty seconds to go." I swung around once more, then back to the target, just in time to catch sight of a white-clad figure racing out to the side of his bridge. Then a stream of vapor shot from his stack, evidently his whistle. Too late, however. There was now no chance of avoiding our torpedoes unless they were improperly aimed. I swung the periscope all the way around. The destroyer which had just crossed our stern was heeling over radically away from us, starting to turn toward with hard-over rudder. A quick look on our port beam. The rear-most destroyer was coming directly at us, showing white water all along his waterline.

There was no time to linger. "Take her down!" I shouted. There would still be a few seconds before the periscope went under, time, perhaps to see the torpedoes strike home.

I started to swing back toward the target, suddenly received a sharp blow on my head as the periscope yoke collar unexpectedly descended upon it. I reeled backward, momentarily stunned, looked up to see Rubinoffski's consternation. He was squeezing the pickle, and the periscope base with the rubber eye-pieces had already dropped out of sight into the periscope well. I could hear the rush of air in the control room as negative-tank flood valve was opened and Kohler yanked the tank vent. Negative would take in approximately nine tons of water, well forward of amidships, thus helping us to start down. I could feel *Walrus'* deck tilt forward gently. I rubbed my aching skull, opened my mouth to curse at Rubinoffski, but never got the words out. Suddenly there was a tremendous, stupifying roar.

Whrang-g-g. Our hull resounded like a tuning fork. The sensation could be likened to being inside a wash boiler and having a giant beat on the outside with a sledge hammer. My ears rang. Jim was shouting. "We've hit him! It's a hit!" He slapped me on the back. "You did it, skipper. You sunk the son-of-a-bitch!" Then he turned to Keith, pounded him on the back also.

"How about the other two fish?" I asked him.

Jim looked at his stop watch, shook his head regretfully. "No luck there . . ." As he spoke, there came clearly a tinny, high-pitched *Pwhyunng.* I glanced, startled. "That was timed for the third torpedo," Jim said, punching the winding stem of his watch, showing me its face.

Walrus' deck was tilted down even farther by now and she was clawing for the depths.

"What do you think that noise could have been?" I asked. Keith answered: "Gosh, I don't know. Maybe an air flash—have you ever heard an air flash explode, Captain?" Jim and I both shook our heads. I would have discussed it more but a shout from O'Brien started a whole new train of thought.

"He's starting a run on us!" I leaped to his side, grabbed the extra pair of earphones. The enemy destroyer's "pings" could clearly be heard, sounding just like our own destroyers'. They were coming in rapidly, too, and I could hear the "thum, thum, thum," of his propeller beats. The sonarman put his left hand on the gain control, ready to tune down the volume when the depth charges went off. I could see it shaking as he touched the knob.

"WHAM . . . WHAM . . . WHAM." The giant alongside us cut loose with three violent blows from his sledge hammer. *Walrus* quivered and shook. Dust rose from the equipment and the deck. A piece of cork bounced from nowhere, made a peculiar "plop" as it landed on Adams' chart table.

I became aware of a new sound, a click which seemed to precede each depth charge. "CLICK, WHAM . . . CLICK, WHAM . . ." two more depth charges. Then there was a prolonged swishing of water as though someone were hosing our side with a fire hose. The propeller beat, reduced in volume because of our having lowered the gain, suddenly dropped in frequency. O'Brien glanced up briefly. "He's passed overhead. That's 'Down Doppler.'" It was similar to the drop in pitch of a train going by at high speed.

"Maybe they'll go away now." This was Jim's voice. It did seem possible, for the destroyer's beat kept on without slackening or other change, toward the general direction of southeast.

"Search all around," I directed O'Brien. Obediently, he did so, holding the control handle over and causing the sound-head pointer to travel a complete circle. I still had the earphones on and something, a discontinuity in the sound as he went by it—some impulse—caused me to ask him to turn back to the northwest sector.

There it was again. A slight increase in noise level. Nothing specific, no propeller beat, just an increased sound from that bearing. *Walrus* reached her maximum designed depth and now we slowed to minimum speed in accordance with our silent-running routine. We should be difficult for someone else to hear, and, conversely, could hear better ourselves. But the noise, if such it really was, could not be resolved into identifiable components. I motioned with my finger all around the dial. Obediently O'Brien set his equipment in motion. The propeller beats of the *Momo*-class destroyer which had depth-charged us were still to be heard, more faintly than before but on the same general bearing. He was going away. There was no question of it. I could see O'Brien listen intently in its direction. Finally he looked up, uncovered one ear. "Captain," he said, "there are at least two ships over there. Two sets of high-speed propellers. Maybe more."

Jim had approached unnoticed. "Good," he said, "they've gone off."

"I'm not so sure," I muttered, half to myself. "This noise level . . ." I motioned to O'Brien, who went past the new sector again. When the sound head moved past the bearing rapidly there was no question about the increase in noise level, but when we turned directly on the bearing it was impossible to make anything out, or even to distinguish any difference.

Jim listened with me for some minutes. "What do you think it is?" he finally whispered.

"Don't know. Never heard anything like this before."

"Could it be the ship we sank?"

"Maybe."

"Maybe we should come up and take a look through the periscope."

For several more minutes we waited. Nothing more could be heard from the direction in which our *Momo*-class destroyer had disappeared. Nothing more could be heard in any direction, in fact, but the feeling of uneasiness persisted; the noise, if such it could be called, had not changed. If anything, it was a bit weaker. *Walrus* stealthily slipped through the depths, every nerve taut, unable to see, not sure of what she heard. I ordered a course change, to put the area of high-sound level nearly astern—not exactly, so as not to mask it with the quiet swishing of our own propellers.

More time passed. It was over an hour since we had fired our torpedoes. Gradually our guard relaxed. To relieve the oppressive heat and humidity I permitted the ventilation system and air-conditioning machinery to be started. It was quiet all around the sonar dial, except for our port quarter, where the faint noise level persisted.

"If there's anything up there, it's the ship we just sank! Maybe that's the sinking ship we're hearing!" Jim's sustained excitement was infectious. I could sense the approval of everyone in the conning tower. Every eye turned upon me.

Jim spoke again, eagerness flashing from every facial expression. "God, skipper! If we hurry we might be able to see him sink! We don't have to surface—just get up to periscope depth!"

The moment, after our moments of tension, was one of anticlimax. We had fired our torpedoes, heard what we had assumed was an explosion of one of them, plus another peculiar low-order explosion, and had withstood our first depth-charging. Besides, we had heard the screw noises of several ships departing from the scene of the attack, among them at least one positively identified as a destroyer. I was eager also to see the results of our first encounter with the enemy—and so I allowed myself to be convinced.

"Control! Six-four feet! Bring her up flat!" I leaned over the control-room hatch, called the order down to Tom, whose head I could see just below.

"Six-four feet, aye, aye!" Tom acknowledged, looking up. "Request more speed!"

"Nothing doing, old man," I responded, squatting on my haunches to speak to him more easily. "Bring her up easy. We've plenty of time." If Jim's evaluation was correct, there was nothing to worry about up above; there would be no reason why we should not come up with normal procedure, letting Tom have a bit more speed for better control. But more speed would mean more noise also, and more disturbance in the water. Some subconscious caution held me back, caused me to direct that the remaining torpedoes loaded forward be made ready for instant firing, though later examination of the events of the next few moments could furnish no clue as to why.

Gently *Walrus* inclined gently upward. With no more than minimum speed, it would take her a long time to plane up to periscope depth. After several minutes had passed we had only covered half the distance, and I could feel the impatience around me. As we passed the hundred-foot-depth mark the angle of inclination decreased still more; Tom was obeying my dictum to "bring her up flat." Two more minutes passed. The ship was at seventy feet, with zero inclination. Having no speed for control submerged, Tom was afraid to come right up to sixty-four feet for fear that some unexpected variation in water density or temperature might cause us to broach.

Slowly, *Walrus* swam up the few remaining feet. I now regretted not having authorized more speed, for at sixty-nine feet we were still totally blind, the periscopes still four feet short of reaching the surface. I nevertheless ordered one of our two 'scopes raised.

When it was "two-blocked"—all the way up—we were passing sixty-seven feet, and through it I could see, just overhead as though it were actually only a couple of feet above, the ripply surface of the ocean. Only two feet—as good as two hundred. As I waited, the wavy surface—which looked exactly as I had seen it many times, looking down from above—grew nearer, than farther, then nearer, as the Pacific swells passed over.

"What's the bearing of the noise now?" I spoke without taking my eyes from the periscope.

"It's shifted to the port bow, Captain!" Jim's voice.

"Put me on it!" I felt someone's hands laid on mine, felt the pressure. The periscope was twisted some considerable distance to the left, and I followed docilely.

Suddenly I was conscious of a flash of brilliant light; then it was gone, and the light through the periscope was darker than it had been before. In the split-second interval I had seen blue sky and clouds. I realized I had turned the elevation control to full elevation, was looking nearly straight up, had missed the precious chance to garner a quick look on the port bow. Hastily I turned it down to the horizontal, determined not to miss the next chance.

The periscope popped out again, for a longer interval, in the hollow of a long swell. It was possible to see only a few feet, and only for a moment at that, until the wave in front of me engulfed the periscope eye-piece. Then we were out again, in the trough of the next wave. I caught a glimpse of masts above the crest of the wave in the direction in which I was looking, but nothing more. They seemed fairly close, but the momentary impression was too fleeting to make much out about them.

I waited another second or two—I would be able to see in a moment—the periscope popped out again: there was a wave in front of it, beyond which I could see the upper section of a mast. It might be the mast of our target at some little distance away, perhaps a thousand yards, or it might be the mast of another ship considerably closer. I tried to flip the periscope handle to the low-power position, found that it was already in low power.

The wave in front of me receded, the periscope eye-piece topping it easily, and the source of the masts came clearly—and suddenly—to view.

It was a Japanese destroyer, broadside to us, and it was close, very close, nearly alongside in fact.

I snapped the handle into the high-power position, felt myself catapulted almost into his bridge. There were white-clad figure all about his topsides. A quick glimpse of activity, several arms pointed our way—we could not have been more than two hundred yards from him—a hustle on the bridge, someone battling the wheel, someone else doing something to an instrument which could have only been annunciators.

There was no time to do anything. No time to do anything at all except try to get away. We were caught—caught fair!

"FIRE!" I shouted. I banged the periscope handles up. My hair felt as though it were standing on end. The flesh crawled around my belly, "Down periscope! *Take her down! Take her down fast!*"

"What is it? What's the matter?" shouted Jim. Involuntarily my voice had risen in pitch, and my fright must have been evident. So was Jim's. Keith, Rubinoffsi, and Oregon, at the wheel, likewise turned their startled faces toward me.

"Take her down! *Take her down fast! All ahead emergency! Left full rudder!*" The urgency in my voice brought instant obedience: Oregon heaved mightily on the steering wheel, whipped both annunciators all the way to the right, banged them three times against the stops. A whoosh or released air welled up from the control room, where Tom's action in flooding negative tank had probably been equally instinctive. Through it all I felt—sensed would be more accurate—three solid jerks in *Walrus'* tough frame as three torpedoes went on their sudden way.

We could practically feel the bow and stern planes bite into the water. The increased thrust of our screws heaved us forward and downward, but the movement of two thousand tons of steel is a slow, ponderous process.

"What is it, Captain? For God's sake, tell us what's the matter!" Jim was nearly beside himself.

"Destroyer! Waiting for us! Not over two hundred yards away! He'll be on us in seconds!"

"Do you think they saw us?"

"You're Goddam right they saw us! The people on the bridge were pointing at us!" I swore without even thinking about it or meaning to. "There were at least fifty men all over his topsides on special lookout watch, and they looked as through they all—every one of them—had a big pair of binoculars!"

"Is he headed for us?"

"Hell yes! We were so close I could even see them put the rudder over and ring up full speed!"

Careless of how it might sound, I had almost been shouting. Now I recollected myself, turned to Quin, "Rig ship for depth charge! Rig ship for silent running!" The yeoman's eyes were huge as he repeated the orders over the telephone. They flickered to the conning-tower depth gauge. It read sixty-five feet. It was hardly moving.

The sounds of slamming of watertight doors and bulkhead ventilation valves came clearly into the conning tower. No need to be careful about noise right now! Our straining propellers were making more than enough anyway, and besides, our torpedoes would give us away for sure—draw an arrow to our position at the apex of their wakes. No more ventilation. The conning tower again grew stifling and humid, but no one noticed. I crossed back to the sonar gear, picked up the extra set of headphones.

"Where is he?" O'Brien indicated the pointer in the sonar dial, nearly dead ahead, moving from port bow to starboard. Our rudder was still at full left, and *Walrus* was now swinging rapidly. Turning toward had been the instinctive thing to do, and also evidently the best maneuver in the emergency. We would let her turn a bit longer, then straighten out.

"What's our depth?" I looked at Jim. "Passing eighty feet!" His face worked as he spoke, and he tapped the glass face of the gauge to make sure it was not stuck. It has only been about twenty seconds since we had started down, hardly time for *Walrus* to have gained much depth yet. We had achieved a small down angle, however, should begin to go deep rapidly now.

I put on the earphones, immediately became conscious of the high-speed screws of our enemy, and his rapid, steady pinging. Gone also, now, was any attempt to quietness or concealment on his part. The screws were becoming rapidly louder. The pings were continuous, steady, practically without interval. He was well on our starboard bow, coming in at high speed, perhaps hoping to ram.

"Rudder amidships!" Our compass card slowed its spin, steadied. This would increase our speed across the enemy track, tend to make him shoot his depth charges astern. Perhaps our torpedoes would prevent him from attacking immediately, possibly one might even, by great good fortune, hit him.

Forlorn hope! The whole inside of the submarine was resounding with the enemy destroyer's propeller beats. The pings of his echo-ranging apparatus were fast, short, continuous, implacable. I could hear the echoes rap off our hull almost as soon as transmitted, could even hear a double echo—the return bounce off him. We had reached ninety feet when the destroyer's roar attained an excruciating, violent crescendo of sound, and coherent thinking became frozen. He could not have been more than thirty feet away from where I was standing, dead overhead, roaring like an express train. My brain throbbed in the furious convulsion of noise. There was a screaming of tortured gears, the whine of high-speed turbines, the spitting, churning, tearing fury of his propellers, the blast of water—all combined into a frenzied, desperate, sudden drive to send us forever into the black depths of the sea.

"Here we are!" I remember thinking. "Here comes the granddaddy of all depth-chargings!" *Walrus* moved bodily in the water as the destroyer passed overhead. We could feel his initial pressure wave, and we also knew, by the abrupt change in the pitch of the noise, the exact instant he passed over. Just before he did so, the bearing from which the sound had been coming in widened until it encompassed the entire three hundred sixty degrees around us. Ninety-one feet the depth gauges said. It was time—it was time—here it comes—

WHAM! A prolonged, crushing, catastrophic roar! The lights went out. I was thrown to the deck, grasped the periscope hoist wires with both hands. They were tingling, alive. The deck plates were ratting likewise. There was someone lying on the deck beneath me—as I felt for him, amid the convulsive shudders of *Walrus'* great steel fabric, my feet were jerked out from under me and I was flung bodily on top of him. He felt wet, warm-wet, and he didn't move.

Scrambling to my feet, I realized the motion of the ship had changed. We were on the surface. The ship still had a large angle down by the bow, but our rocking and pitching could only be the result of being on the surface in the wash of the vessel that had just passed overhead. No doubt our stern was well out, high in view—a beautiful target. I was still holding to the periscope wires, and to my horror I saw light at the bottom of the periscope well! Then the explanation occurred: the top of the periscope, though housed, was also out of water, and light naturally streamed out of the other end. To confirm it I reached for the other 'scope, looked down into the well, saw light there also.

Still black as ink in the conning tower. On rig for depth charge the hatch between us and the control room had been dogged down, and there was no communication except by telephone—useless at the moment, of course. The whole interior of the submarine was a huge, sounding cavern, reverberating and reflecting the uproar. If only we could see!

"Turn on the emergency lights!" I shouted. I might as well have whispered. The emergency lights should have come on. Standard practice called for them to be turned on automatically—by anyone—if the main lighting went out.

No need to look at the depth gauge anyway. "All ahead emergency!" I had already ordered emergency speed, subconsciously wanted to reinforce the order after the attack. In the shattering uproar I bellowed as loud as I could. Quin might hear me, might be able to get through to the maneuvering room, or Oregon, at the other end of the conning tower, could ring for flank speed again three times. They were probably having a pretty bad time back aft, but "emergency ahead," under the circumstances existing, would cause Larto to open the main motor rheostats as far as they would go, put everything the battery could give into the propellers.

The noise was subsiding a little. I had no knowledge of how many depth charges had gone off, perhaps a dozen all almost simultaneously, and there was no telling, yet, whether *Walrus* had survived. The conning tower, we knew, was still whole. With all hatches and ventilation valves shut tightly, there could be no telltale increase in air pressure as water came rushing into another compartment. Since our stern was on the surface, a hole there might give no indication at all, or merely a loss in what slightly elevated pressure *Walrus'* atmosphere might already have. We'd find out soon enough as we drove her down.

The destroyer's rush had carried him well past. I could hear his screws again—now on our port quarter. He had passed directly overhead. Our only hope was that the depth charges had been set too deeply, that, although blown to the surface, we were not seriously damaged—but there was no time to think about damage already received. Four-inch shells would be whizzing our way within seconds. We had to get back under immediately!

There was an emergency light switch near the ladder to the bridge. I collected myself, gropingly reached for it, fumbled a moment, turned it. Dim lights came on at either end of the conning tower.

The conning tower looked as if a cyclone had struck it. Hugh Adams' chart table, shaken loose from its mountings, had fallen to the floor. Hugh himself lay still on the deck. Evidently he had been the one I had stumbled over. Keith was still at his station, frantically gripping the handles of the TDC and bracing himself with his foot on the corner of the angle solver. Jim was standing shakily beside him, white as a sheet, but apparently unhurt. But these were not the important ones at the moment. Oregon was still at his steering wheel, and there seemed to be no damage in his locality. Quin was sitting on the deck holding his left arm. There was an ugly gash in it from which blood was dripping onto his trousers. He seemed otherwise in condition to be of assistance, however.

"Quin!" I roared. "All ahead emergency!"

Painfully the yeoman reached up with his uninjured arm, gave the order into the telephone mouthpiece. Fastened to the side of the conning tower beneath the firing panel was the hand telephone for routine communication throughout the ship. I reached for it, pressed the button. "Control!" The response was immediate.

"Control; aye, aye!" It was Tom Schultz himself on the other end, and I could remember the instant feeling of relief to discover that at least part of the ship was still functioning.

"We're broached, Tom. Can you get her down?"

"Trying, sir!"

"Have you got your vents open?" Possibly some of the gases from the underwater explosions could have come up into our ballast tanks and now, having broached, we would be bound to have air in some of them.

"Yes, sir," Tom replied again.

"We're going ahead emergency speed. Drive her as deep as you can. Get on over to twenty degrees angle if you have to," I told him. The order was superfluous, since Tom knew very well the seriousness of our situation, and the ship had already attained an angle of fifteen degrees down by the bow. The slanting deck was becoming difficult to stand on.

There was nothing further I could do and no reason to hold up the telephone from other use by talking myself. I listened, however, and within a few seconds was rewarded by hearing the reports of the various compartments. All had taken some damage from the knocking about, but none, apparently, was in serious trouble except the after torpedo room. The voice from there said simply, "We have a fire back here."

"Can you handle it?" I snapped.

"Yes, sir, we're handling it." I relaxed. We couldn't go to fire quarters. The men back aft had either to get the fire out by themselves or abandon the compartment. The main problem was getting *Walrus* into the safe haven of the deep depths.

The motion of the ship felt different—less jerky. I looked at the depth gauge. We were under again! The deck tilted down even more; I had to put my left arm around a periscope barrel to retain my balance. The bubble inclinometer, similar to a curved carpenter's level, mounted beneath the depth gauge, showed eighteen degrees inclination down by the bow—more than *Walrus* had ever experienced before, or I either, even counting in *S-16* and her Polish crew. I hoped we could take it, mentally resolved to drill at steeper-than-usual angles if we ever got the chance.

Quin was struggling to his feet, still clutching his injured arm.

"Test depth, Captain?" he said through strained, bloodless lips.

This was from Tom. Our decision, made some time ago, was automatically to go to full-test submergence in situations like this. Tom would not have had to ask, unless he anticipated possibly exceeding it.

Our hull, we knew, had a large safety factor of strength. This was, if there ever was to be, the time we had to use some of it. The answer I gave Quin brought a startled look to his face before he relayed it.

Down *Walrus* plunged, the depth-gauge needle spinning rapidly. The conning-tower gauge went only to one hundred fifty feet. When it reached one hundred forty I reached over and closed the valve in the waterline for fear of breaking the delicate mechanism. We could hear the rushing sound of water streaming past us. The power we were putting into our propellers was beginning to take effect.

"Two hundred feet!" said Quin. Our down angle remained rock-steady.

"Two hundred fifty feet!" The angle was still steady. Tom was really carrying out instructions. Finally he began to ease her off, until, without slackening speed, the ship became nearly level. Her whole frame now shook and trembled as she tore through the water. Something carried away topside and I heard a rattling, banging noise for a moment. Then it stopped.

I bent over the sound receiver. O'Brien looked up, shook his head. He could hear nothing at this speed. I waited a few moments. We would run on like this for a couple of minutes, I thought, then slow down and try to creep away . . .

WHAM! Another depth charge.

WHAM! . . . WHAM! . . . WHAM! . . . Three more. Compared to our initiation these were nothing to worry about, but they did disturb the water again. Maybe, added to what had gone before, they gave us the chance we needed.

"Right full rudder!" I called to Oregon. He put his full strength into turning the wheel and the ship leaned slightly to starboard, opposite to her list during a surface turn. The gyro compass card began to spin rapidly.

"All ahead one third." This would quiet our thrashing propellers. With the speed we had already built up, the ship would coast a good distance. I picked up the telephone again.

"Tom," I called.

"Yes?"

"I didn't hear you blow negative. Is it blown?"

"It's blown!"

"Good! I want to slow down now, to as slow and quiet as you can run. We'll stay at this depth, and run as silently as we can. With the start we've had and the uproar in the water back there, this may be our chance!"

A submarine's natural habitat is the deep, silent depths of the sea. The deeper she can go, the safer she is, and with the comfortable shelter of hundreds of feet of ocean overhead the submariner can relax. Deep in the sea there is no motion, no sound, save that put there by the insane humors of man. The slow, smooth stirring of the deep ocean currents, the high-frequency snapping or popping of ocean life, even the occasional snort or burble of a porpoise are all in low key, subdued, responsive to the primordial quietness of the deep. Of life there is, of course, plenty, and of death too, for neither are strange to the ocean. But even life and death, though violent, make little or no noise in the deep sea.

So it is with the submarine, forced, for survival, to join those elemental children of nature who seek, always, for quietness. Noise means death. Quietness, in the primeval jungle of the sea, is next to slowness or stock-stillness, as a means of remaining alive. And deep in the black depths, where live only those deep-sea denizens who never see the light of the day, who never approach the surface, and for whom in reality, it does not exist, *Walrus* sought her succor. Deep below the surface, at the absolute limit of her designed depth, her sturdy hull strained and bowed under the unaccustomed compression, her steel ribs standing rigid against the fierce, implacable squeeze of millions of tons of sea water, inescapable, unyielding, *Walrus* struggled for her life. Her propellers were barely turning over, her sea valves and hull fittings were tightly shut against the deadly pressure, and no noise—no noise at all—could she make.

On the surface we could hear the sound of our adversary's screws moving about from one side to another as if with a definite plan, as if trying to cover all the possible areas we might be. But there were no more depth charges, and after a while the screws themselves quieted down, and all we could hear was the same sibilant hum, the area of higher—but undistinguishable—noise level, which had presaged the destroyer's attack upon us.

But *Walrus* was not to be fooled a second time. We remained at silent running and maximum depth the rest of the day, and it was long into the evening before we secured from depth-charge stations. The Jap destroyer apparently became satisfied with the evidence of our destruction, for he never did resume the attack. Gradually his betraying noise faded from our sonar equipment. We did not, however, trust ourselves to come back to periscope depth until long after sundown, and we did not surface until nearly midnight.

Our first day in the war zone had been long, hard, and nearly disastrous.

We took stock of our damage topside and below. Examination of the attack periscope showed the top glass cracked and the tube flooded; no hope for it. Our SJ radar, inefficient though it had been, had been a comfort in that no surface craft could get any closer than a couple of miles without alerting us. Now it, too, was gone. We had another periscope, slightly larger in diameter at the top than the attack periscope, but we had no other surface radar. Both losses were serious.

Superficial damage topside there was aplenty. All our radio antennae were gone and so were the stanchions to which they had been secured. There was a large hole in our main deck forward—approximately twenty square feet of wooden slats missing—testimony to the force and nearness of at least one depth charge. Our superstructure held a few dents, inconsequential, of course, and the three-inch gun on the main deck must have had a depth charge go off right on top of it, for the telescopic sights for both pointer and trainer were gone.

Below in the innards of the ship our four most important items of equipment were fortunately entirely undamaged. Our propellers and propeller shafts, which might have been bent or distorted by the force of the explosions were, so far as careful inspection could tell, perfectly sound. The main engines had suffered no damage whatever; the battery seemed all right, although it indicated a very low resistance to ground and had a few cracked cell tops. A hot soldering iron drawn across the cracks, melting and resealing the mastic, and a thorough washing down with fresh water afterward, brought the insulation readings—our main concern—up again. And lastly, our torpedo tubes seemed to have apparently suffered no damage. But quite a few other items had been put out of action for the rest of the patrol. The fire in the after torpedo room had been in the stern plane motor, ruining it. Until we returned to port our stern planes would have to be operated by hand power—not an easy task. The trim pump, cracked right across the heavy steel housing and knocked off its foundation, was beyond repair; we would have to cross-connect the drain pump to the trim line and make shift with it as well as we might. One air compressor was also cracked across one of its foundation frames and could not be used. The other was still intact; if we were careful it would provide us with enough compressed air to remain operational.

There were also several persons slightly injured, among them Quin and Hugh Adams, and we had one case of smoke inhalation from the after torpedo room. None of the injuries was serious, however, and all the men were soon back to duty. And after thoroughly looking the ship over, it was apparent we could stay on patrol.

During the remainder of that first night, from midnight to dawn, we worked feverishly against time to get things back in shape enough for *Walrus* to dive. The radar and the stern plane motor were probably our two most serious losses, and we wasted hours on both of them before admitting defeat.

But the ship as a whole was undamaged. We searched for evidence of cracks in her hull or dents where a too-close depth charge might have caved in her skin. There were none of any kind, despite plenty of mute evidence of the closeness of the explosions. I wrote in our patrol report:

Thorough inspection of the vessel indicates no further structural damage. The hull appears to have stood up very well. Our fervent thanks to the workers at Electric Boat who built this wonderful ship for us.

I meant every word of it.

"An Audacious Plan"

(Excerpted from the book *Shadow Divers*)

In writing about deep-wreck divers, who descend one to three hundred feet to explore sunken ships like the *Andrea Doria* for both adventure and profit, Robert Kurson focuses on the obsession some divers have for finding sunken U-boats. Kurson reports that of 859 U-boats known to have left base for frontline patrol, 648 were sunk or captured. Of these, 65 disappeared without explanation, and their final locations were never known or entered into German records.

For experienced wreck divers John Chatterton and Richie Kohler out of Brielle, New Jersey, the fall of 1991 brought an unexpected but welcome treasure: a fishing charter boat captain's tip gave them the GPS numbers to reach a secret sunken-vessel site he had been fishing sixty miles off the Jersey coast. The tip came with a serious caveat: "This site I found is a bad place. This part of the ocean is a bad place; it's a dangerous place. It's in a little depression, there's an edge there, with a huge current coming up and over the continent shelf, lots of moving water—"

At that time, Chatterton and Kohler did not know what kind of vessel rested on the bottom, but they were thinking U-boat all the way. They had become fascinated by U-boat history and lore and the many mysteries that surrounded the subs never accounted for. The jacket copy of *Shadow Divers* tells us what happened next:

". . . not even these courageous divers were prepared for what they found 230 feet below the surface in the frigid Atlantic waters . . . a World War II German U-boat, its ruined interior a macabre wasteland of twisted metal, tangled wires, and human bodies—all buried under decades of accumulated sediment.

"No identifying marks were visible on the submarine or the few artifacts that Chatterton and Kohler brought to the surface. No historian, expert, or government had a clue as to which U-boat the men had found. In fact, the official records all agreed that there simply could not be a sunken U-boat at that location."

Over the next six years, men died at the U-boat site trying to investigate the dangerous, tangled, and ruined interior compartments of the sub. Chatterton and Kohler were among the divers who failed in their efforts. Eventually, they obtained some reliable information that the identity of what they had begun to call "*U-Who*" probably rested in wooden spare parts boxes, about the size of a shoe box. There would be tags in these boxes with the name of the U-boat listed. Unfortunately, the boxes were normally kept in the electric motor room. On *U-Who* a massive steel obstruction of fallen metal blocked access to part of the diesel motor room and the adjoining electric motor room.

Still Chatterton and Kohler would not be deterred. They formed a plan to attack the problem, and in August, 1997, put it into motion with an audacious dive. Here, Robert Kurson takes us below the depths on their strange journey—but first he plots the mysterious course of one of Germany's missing U-boats.

Aweek and a half after leaving Germany, Commander [Helmuth] Neuerburg and *U-869* arrived in the southern Norwegian port town of Kristiansand, where they took on fuel and supplies. Brimming with provisions, the U-boat could now wage war anywhere in the Atlantic. Neuerburg's first assignment was to crawl northward along the Norwegian coast, then break into the open Atlantic via the Iceland-Faeroes gap. He would receive further orders—war orders—when the submarine reached the open seas. Radio traffic between the U-boat and Control would be kept to a minimum; by this time in the war, even the slightest chatter from a U-boat could be intercepted by the Allies.

On December 8, the U-boat's diesels belched to life and it pushed away from the Norwegian U-boat base. For three weeks, it crawled along

Norway's coast and then onward into the Atlantic, submerged virtually nonstop to avoid Allied air patrols and ships. On December 29, Control radioed its next order. *U-869* was to head for naval grid CA 53, the center of which was about 110 miles southeast of New York. Neuerburg had been issued perhaps the most prestigious assignment a U-boat could receive: *U-869* had seen sent to wage war against America.

The U-boat pushed westward. Protocol required Neuerburg to radio a brief passage report to Control once *U-869* broke into the open Atlantic. Control, which had been plotting *U-869's* presumed progress, had expected such a report no later than December 29. None was received. On December 30, Control requested a passage report. Again, it received none. Control became "concerned," its officers reported in the diary, though they did not yet take the silence to mean that *U-869* had been lost. On January 1, 1945, Control requested a position report from *U-869*, this time in strong language. It received no reply. It repeated its requests. Still it heard nothing from the submarine. Now Control was worried.

Control did not know why it had not heard from *U-869*. Four possible explanations must have been considered. The first was that Neuerburg simply refused to use his radio for fear of Allied detection. That, however, must have seemed unlikely, as commanders would have been loath to ignore such urgent requests from Control. The second was that *U-869's* radio equipment was malfunctioning, making reception and/or transmission impossible. The third was that atmospheric problems—known to be an issue in that area of the Atlantic—were wreaking havoc with the radios. The fourth was that the boat was no more.

For the next several days, and probably using increasingly urgent terms, Control demanded position reports from *U-869*. On January 3, Control noted its "considerable anxiety" at *U-869's* silence. At around the same time, Allied intelligence studied its radio intercepts and made this assessment: "A U/Boat (*U-869*) now estimated in the central North Atlantic has been ordered to head for a point about 70 miles southeast of the New York approaches."

By January 6, Control was likely mourning for *U-869*. In almost every case in which a U-boat was five days late in reporting to Control, that U-boat was lost. Still, Control beseeched *U-869* to answer. That day, in a broadcast that must have seemed a miracle inside Control, *U-869* radioed her position. Even as Control officials celebrated they scratched their heads. *U-869* was in naval grid AK 63, about six hundred miles southwest of Iceland. The U-boat, they wrote in their diary, "should have been considerably further southwest." It was then that Control likely realized that Neuerburg had made a big and bold decision, one with which they probably were not pleased. Rather than use the Iceland-Faeroes gap—the most direct route from Norway into the open Atlantic—he had diverted much farther north, making a loop over Iceland before heading southwestward through the Denmark Strait. There could be no doubt as to why Neuerburg had spent the extra days and fuel going the long way: the Denmark Strait was less heavily patrolled by Allied airplanes and ships. Though a commander was allowed such discretion, Control never liked the move; every extra day spent in transit was an extra day spent away from the war. Neuerburg's crew, on the other hand, was likely grateful to their commanding officer. He had made his first major war move, and it had been in the name of protecting his men. What no one knew—not Neuerburg, his crew, or Control—was that Allied code breakers had intercepted their broadcast and knew where they were.

Neuerburg's decision to use the circuitous Denmark Strait sent Control strategists scrambling. They likely determined that he must have burned at least five extra days' fuel going the long way, meaning that it would cost the boat one hundred days to stay perhaps fourteen days off New York, an unacceptable ratio. Control requested a fuel-status report. Again, it received no reply from *U-869* "in spite of continuous queries." As Neuerburg had showed himself willing to use the radio, and as the radios appeared at least sometimes to be working, Control probably blamed atmospheric conditions for the lack of communication from *U-869*. Unwilling to wait any longer for a fuel-status report, Control radioed a new order to Neuerburg: *U-869* was to change course and head to Gibraltar, to patrol the African coast. By rerouting the submarine away from New York and to this closer operating area, Control could expect a longer patrol from *U-869*.

Control would not have expected *U-869* to acknowledge receipt of this new order—it would have been too dangerous for Neuerburg to use his radio simply to confirm the directive. Control therefore presumed Neuerburg to have received the order and began plotting *U-869* to Gibraltar, calculating that the submarine should arrive there around February 1. Had Neuerburg received the order, it is certain that he would have followed it—while a commander had discretion in choosing his routes, he had no such option when receiving a direct order. Whether because of equipment or atmospheric problems, it is virtually certain that *U-869* never received the new order to Gibraltar. Neuerburg kept heading for New York.

The Allies, however, were interrupting almost everything. On January 17, their intelligence wrote, "The U/Boat heading for the New York approaches, *U-869* (Neuerburg), is presently estimated about 180 miles SSE of Flemish Cap. . . . She is expected to arrive in the New York area at the beginning of February."

On January 25, American intelligence pegged the situation: "One U/Boat may be south of Newfoundland heading for New York approaches, although her location is uncertain due to a mix up in orders and Control assumes she is heading for Gibraltar."

Then, in the chillingly matter-of-fact language of war, American intelligence announced its plans for *U-869*: "The *CORE* will begin sweeping for this U/Boat shortly prior to proceeding against the U/Boats reporting weather in the North Atlantic."

The Americans would be sending a hunter-killer group to destroy *U-869*. They knew where the submarine was going.

All the while, Neuerburg and his crew continued their long push toward New York. U-boats went largely unmolested during travel in the open Atlantic—hunter-killer groups often waited for them to arrive in shallower waters closer to shore, where the U-boats could less easily run and hide. To pass the time, perhaps the crewmen organized a checkers tournament or a limerick contest or a lying competition, as had occurred on other U-boat patrols; a man could lose a day's rations for overconfidence in such matters. Or perhaps they adopted a mascot—one U-boat had selected a fly for this purpose, which they named Emma and whose daily routines they followed with keen interest.

U-869 likely approached American coastal waters in early February. From that point forward, Neuerburg certainly would have kept the submarine submerged full-time, using the snorkel for the fresh-air intake necessary to run the diesel engines underwater. By now, the American hunter-killer group had begun its search for *U-869*. Neuerburg, who knew well the Allies' ability to track and stalk a U-boat, must have navigated with extreme stealth—the hunter-killer group found only fathoms of empty sea.

Now *U-869* was in American waters and bearing down on the New York approaches. Neuerburg's targets would be whatever enemy vessels he could find. The crew's nerves must have been stretched taught against their knowledge of the odds against them. Perhaps a day passed, perhaps several days. Then, through the crosshairs of the U-boat's periscope, Neuerburg must have spotted an enemy ship. At that point, he would have ordered his men to their battle stations. The men would have remained silent. From this point forward, every order would have been whispered.

As *U-869* crept forward at a speed of perhaps two knots, the crew likely heard the sound of water outside the submarine, the hum of the electric engines, and perhaps even the faint revolutions of the enemy target's propellers in the distance. All else would have been quiet. Now *U-869* was ready to attack. At this moment, Neuerburg, Brandt, and the rest of the crew knew certain things. They knew that the war was being lost. They knew U-boats were not returning home. They knew that it was up to Neuerburg, not Control, to decide when *U-869's* patrol had concluded.

No one knows what Neuerburg thought then. He kept the periscope raised. The men remained at their battle stations. Seconds later, Neuerburg whispered this kind of order inside the steel, cigar-shaped hull of *U-869*:

"Tube one ready—fire."

★ ★ ★

Chatterton's final plan for the *U-Who* was audacious and lethal. He would swim into the diesel motor room with just a single tank on his back, not the customary two. He would then remove that tank and hold it in front of him—much as a child holds a kickboard when learning to swim—and push it through the narrow opening between the fallen fuel tank and the U-boat's ceiling. Once on the other side of the diesel motor room, he would reattach the tank to his back and swim into the adjoining electric motor room, where he hoped to find identifying tags attached to boxes of spare parts. After recovering the bounty, he would swim back into the diesel motor room, pass it over the top to Kohler, again remove his single trimix tank, and slither back out the way he had come in. Only by carrying a single tank of trimix—and then taking it off—did Chatterton believe a diver could pass over the fuel tank that blocked nearly every inch of space between the electric motor room and the rest of the *U-Who*.

The plan's dangers were encyclopedic, a textbook on how to get killed inside a shipwreck. With a just a single tank to breathe, Chatterton would have only twenty minutes on the other side of the obstruction.

"Forget it," Kohler said by phone on the evening Chatterton revealed the plan. "That is the single most insane plan I have ever heard in my life. I'm not watching you die. I'm not participating in your suicide."

"This is vision," Chatterton said. "This can work."

"This is lunacy," Kohler said.

Kohler found a notebook and began scribbling a list of risks. Most of them ended with the phrase "then John runs out of gas and drowns." The list read like this:

- Chatterton could become entangled—in wire, pipes, fittings, fixtures, bent metal, anything.
- Chatterton could be pinned under falling debris.
- A piece of machinery could fall and block Chatterton's exit.
- Relying on a single gas supply eliminates the safety of redundancy—if a high-pressure hose or O-ring fails, Chatterton loses his sole breathing source.
- The dive's high risk will almost certainly cause Chatterton to breathe harder than usual, meaning he will burn through his already limited gas supply even faster.
- The electric motor room will be packed with cables, wires, and machinery no diver has seen before, meaning that Chatterton will not have his usual chance to mentally diagram the room's layout.
- There is no way out the other end of the electric motor room, as its aft end has been crushed downward.
- The water inside the electric motor room, undisturbed by divers or the ocean, has been stagnant for fifty years. Chatterton's activity inside the compartment will disturb the dusty brown silt and reduce the visibility to zero.
- Chatterton's bubbles could disturb fuel or lubrication oil floating on the compartment's ceiling, clouding his mask, blinding him, and seeping into his mouth.

"Any one of these can kill you," Kohler said. "But you'll be lucky if only one of them happens. More likely a bunch of them will gang up on you and kill you even faster. And don't forget maybe the biggest danger, John."

"What's that?"

"You will be alone inside that compartment. Even if I agreed to this outrageous plan, even if I waited for you on the other side of that obstruction. I can't help you once you get into trouble. I can't take my tanks off. I've got kids. I have mouths to feed. The most I can do is peer over that fuel tank and watch you drown."

"We can't stop now," Chatterton said. "I have a plan. This is why I dive, Richie. This is the art."

"It's too goddamned dangerous."

"I need you with me."

"I'm bailing on this, John. I'm out."

The divers hung up. Word spread throughout the local diving community about Chatterton's plan. There were two schools of thought. Chatterton's friends, including John Yurga and Danny Crowell, pronounced Chatterton "out of his fucking mind." Those who knew him only in passing were more liberal: "If he wants to kill himself, let him," they said.

For three days, Chatterton and Kohler did not speak. Kohler envisioned the dive from a thousand angles and it always ended up the same— with Chatterton slumped over drowned or pinned under some piece of fallen steel, Kohler helpless to move through the crack to save him. But he also found himself imagining another scene, this one of his first dive to the *U-Who*. While hanging underwater, he had been overcome with joy at the sight of Chatterton's mesh bag filled with china, and had reached instinctively to take a closer look. Chatterton had snatched the bag away—the men did not like each other then, did not like what the other represented. For a moment there had been a standoff. Then Chatterton had seemed to look into Kohler's heart. A few seconds later he'd offered his bag to Kohler.

Kohler called Chatterton.

"John, I'm scared to death for you," Kohler said. "But we're partners. I'm not going to bail on you now."

"We are partners, Richie," Chatterton replied. "Let's do this."

The first attempt was scheduled for August 17, 1997. Chatterton spent the weeks leading up to the mission rehearsing his moves in his office, in his garage, in line at the grocery store, a combination mime and ballerina practicing for a recital in which a single misstep would mean death. By this time, his divorce was nearly final. In 1991, when he'd discovered the *U-Who*, he had believed his marriage would last forever. Now Kathy did not even know of this daring plan for the U-boat. Some nights, he mourned the marriage so deeply he found himself unable to move. At those times, he told himself, "I must put everything out of my mind for this dive. I must focus absolutely. If I don't, if I'm the slightest bit distracted, I won't come back."

On August 17, Chatterton, Kohler, and five other top wreck divers boarded the *Seeker* and set sail for the *U-Who*. No one said much during the trip. In the morning, Chatterton reviewed his plan with Kohler. He would use the first dive as a trial run to get a feel for taking off his tank, investigating the accessibility of the electric motor room, and learning the layout of the compartment. Kohler would hover near the top of the fallen fuel-tank obstruction, shining his flashlight as a beacon and waiting to take any artifacts Chatterton might pass through.

"Let's make a three-of-anything plan," Chatterton told Kohler as he pulled on his fins. "If I bang my hammer three times or flash my light three times or do anything three times, it means I'm in trouble."

"Okay, it means you're in trouble," Kohler replied. "I still can't squeeze through that crack in the top to help you. So three of anything basically means you're dead."

"Yeah, you're right. Forget it."

A few minutes later, Chatterton and Kohler were in the water. In total Chatterton carried three gas tanks—the one he would breathe inside the electric motor room, plus two stage bottles for his trip down to the wreck and back. As the divers reached the *U-Who*, Chatterton placed his stage bottles on top of the wreck and began breathing from his primary tank.

The divers swam toward the fallen fuel tank that blocked much of the diesel motor room and the adjoining electric motor room. Chatterton removed the tank from his back and held it in front of him. Kohler ascended toward the gap between the fuel tank and the ceiling, through which Chatterton would pass. Chatterton kicked his fins and began gliding up and forward. He was now just a few feet away from pushing his tank through the gap and igniting this crazy plan, but he still had a moment to dip his shoulder and turn back, to U-turn on this mystery he had all but solved already. He never stopped kicking. A few seconds later, he pushed his tank through the gap—vigilant not to let it slip—and then sardined through himself. On the other side of the diesel motor room, he slung the tank onto his back. No diver had ever been in this part of the *U-Who*. He began to explore.

The path to the electric motor room was clear. Chatterton swam to the rectangular hatch that led into the compartment and passed through it. He was now floating inside the electric motor room, the place he and Kohler believed held proof of the wreck's identity. Chatterton felt six years of mystery pushing him farther inside. He talked that instinct down. He had done well enough on this trial run. He had ten minutes of gas remaining. He would use it to become accustomed to leaving these compartments. He swam back up to the fallen fuel tank in the diesel motor room and again removed his tank. A few seconds later, he pushed the tank and himself back through the opening near the ceiling and landed on the other side. From there, he reattached the

tank, glided to where his stage bottles lay atop the wreck, and switched regula-
tors. He now had plenty of gas with which to do his decompression. Kohler
shook his head in amazement. Chatterton had made a near-perfect trial run.

Bad weather blew out the day's second dive. The next trip was scheduled for August 24, 1997. Kohler's nerves settled a bit in the intervening
week. If Chatterton could replicate his trial dive, he thought, the S.O.B.
might just be able to pull off this so-called vision.

The plan would be the same as on the first trip, with a single excep-
tion: Kohler would pass Chatterton a video camera once he got past the obstruction and reaffixed his tank. Chatterton would thus be able to videotape
the compartments for future study, if necessary.

As before, Chatterton's tank maneuvering was seamless. The video
camera he had taken from Kohler, however, would not work. Frustrated, he
swam to the top of the compartment to hand it back through the gap to
Kohler. By now, however, he had reaffixed the tank to his back, and he found
that the equipment made him slightly too bulky to reach the gap. Chatterton
spotted a massive steel beam near the ceiling, a piece he could use to pull himself closer to Kohler. He grabbed the beam and pulled. The steel shook for a
moment, then gave way, crashing into Chatterton's lap and hurling him against
one of the diesel engines. His heart pounded. He ordered himself to control his
breathing. He looked at the beam—its ends had lodged in the surrounding machinery. Chatterton slowly reached to remove the steel from his lap. Its weight
was enormous, at least two hundred pounds out of water. Still, he managed to
begin lifting it. His breathing rate increased. His gas supply dropped. He lifted
harder. The beam moved just an inch before stopping cold, the mirror image of
an amusement-park roller coaster restraint. Chatterton pushed harder. The
gauges on his tank moved lower. The beam would not budge. Chatterton
pushed with his legs to get free. He could not move. He was trapped.

Chatterton began to talk to himself.

"Panic is how guys die," he thought. "Take thirty seconds. Take a little break. Collect yourself."

Kohler looked into the gap. Silt had billowed everywhere. He could
see nothing. He presumed Chatterton was going about his dive.

"Deal with this problem," Chatterton told himself. "Guys die because they don't take care of the first problem. Don't let the snowball roll."

Chatterton's gas gauge crept downward.

"This thing got onto me," he thought. "It's just a matter of figuring
the way it landed on me, then reversing the process. Stay calm. Don't make
more problems. Just reverse the process."

Chatterton used his mind's eye to replay the collapse of the beam. For five minutes, he gently tried to push the steel in the opposite direction. The object would not move. He continued to concentrate, replaying the accident in his mind over and over. Another five minutes passed. The object would not budge. Primal instincts raged in Chatterton's head, begging him to thrash and flail and scream and lunge. He ordered his instincts to wait. He had five minutes of gas to breathe. He would watch more film.

With just a few minutes of gas remaining, Chatterton again reached to move the beam. There would be no more time for movies if this attempt failed. He pushed up and felt one end clank free. He pushed on the other end. The beam collapsed forward and pivoted away from his lap. Chatterton pushed himself off the diesel engine and swam swiftly but not wildly toward the gap near the ceiling. His gauge needle dipped farther into red. He removed his tank and pushed it through, then kicked his fins and wriggled out of the compartment. Kohler moved to join his partner, but he backed off when he saw Chatterton head directly for the tanks he had left on top of the wreck. A moment later, Chatterton had switched to one of his stage bottles. The gauge on his primary tank was near empty. He likely had exited the diesel motor room with less than a minute of air remaining.

Topside, Chatterton told the story. Danny Crowell, who had captained the boat that day, shook his head and turned to another diver.

"Any other diver in the world and we're calling the Coast Guard for a body recovery," he said.

Kohler turned white. He'd had no idea that Chatterton had experienced any trouble.

"Forget it," Kohler said. "This is too dangerous. This whole plan was a big mistake. John, you gotta reconsider. This is really bad."

"Let's get that video camera working," Chatterton said, reaching inside the cooler for a soda. "I'll want to shoot lots of film on my second dive today."

Kohler walked away.

"Crazy bastard," he muttered.

A few hours later, Chatterton was back inside the diesel motor room, Kohler hovering outside and waiting again to be helpless. This time, the camera worked. Chatterton moved through the rectangular hatch that led into the electric motor room. A half century of silt exploded in clouds around him. Chatterton pointed the camera to where his research indicated the spare-parts boxes and their identifying tags should be—the camera could always see better than the human eye underwater. When the visibility fell to zero, Chatterton exited the electric motor room and swam back up toward Kohler, then passed him the camera. He removed his tank—a move with which he was becoming comfortable—and made his way out of the diesel motor room. He had not recovered any artifacts. He had almost lost his life on the first dive. But now he had video. Topside, as the divers undressed and the boat headed back to shore, he thanked Kohler for his support.

"Next trip and I haul the boxes," Chatterton said. "I feel it. The next trip is the one."

The next charter to the *U-Who* was scheduled for a week later, on August 31, 1997. Chatterton spent the intervening days studying the videotape he had shot. In one of the spots he saw what appeared to be a stack of three or four boxes. Now he really knew the next dive would be the one.

At home, Kohler went to war with himself. His friend and partner had come within a minute of drowning. Worse, on Sunday Chatterton planned to go back in and recover the spare-parts boxes. Kohler knew that the electric motor room was jungled in the worst, most ravenous scream of wires, tubes, jagged metal, and silt. He also knew Chatterton's heart. His friend would breathe his tank dry on Sunday before he would exit without his answer. His friend would die inside that wreck on Sunday.

Kohler decided to quit. Whatever satisfaction he might derive from delivering an answer to the crewmen's families and to history would be smothered by his helpless proximity to a drowning friend.

Yet whenever he picked up the phone to deliver his resignation, he ended up putting the receiver back on its cradle. There might be, he thought, one scenario worse than watching his friend die in the wreck, and as Sunday drew near he knew that worst scenario to be allowing his friend to die while he stayed home and waited for the news.

On Saturday evening, August 30, 1997, the *Seeker* jockeyed away from her dock and pointed toward the *U-Who*. Chatterton and Kohler spoke little; each knew that today was the day.

The next morning's weather was perfect and calm. Over a bowl of cereal, Chatterton asked Kohler if he was ready to receive the spare-parts boxes he expected to recover and pass over the top of the fallen fuel tank. Kohler nodded. An hour later, they were on the wreck. Chatterton took off his tank, extended it in front of him, and, stretched horizontally like Superman, moved through the crack between the obstruction and the ceiling. Kohler turned on his flashlight and lifted it to the space, a beacon for Chatterton's return.

Visibility was good inside the diesel motor room. Chatterton re-attached his tank and glided through the rectangular hatch that led into the electric motor room. The scene was just as his videotape had depicted it. He looked to the right. There, stacked in a free-standing pyramid, were four increasingly large boxes of spare parts, each fused to the next by decades of marine encrustation and rust. The smallest of them was slightly larger than a shoe box. They were exactly what Chatterton had come for.

Chatterton inched toward the boxes. Lying at a thirty-degree angle against the top box was what appeared to be a five-foot-tall section of pipe, one that had likely broken from the room's machinery and fallen atop the box. Chatterton pushed gently against the boxes. The pipe was wedged hard against them, and nothing moved. He thrust his palms, football lineman-style, into the stack. Nothing. The pipe, he could now see, had pinned the boxes in place. He reached for his knife and tried prying the pipe away. It did not budge. Silt billowed overhead, reducing the visibility to near zero. Chatterton turned back and exited the compartment. He now understood the final element of his plan. He would have to take drastic action.

Topside, Chatterton briefed Kohler.

"The boxes are fused together and pinned down by this huge pipe," Chatterton said. "But those are the boxes, Richie. If there are identifying tags on this wreck, they're in those boxes."

"That's great," Kohler said. "But if nothing's moving, what can you do?"

"A sledgehammer. I'm taking a short-handled sledgehammer down there. The boxes are mine."

Slinging a sledgehammer at 230 feet was perhaps the best way for a diver to blow through his gas supply. Kohler did not bother to object. Chatterton was on a mission being directed from somewhere deeper than good advice.

"I'll find you the sledgehammer," Kohler said.

Chatterton and Kohler splashed four hours later. Like pulling off a T-shirt, Chatterton removed his single tank and pushed it, the sledgehammer, and himself through the crack between the fallen fuel tank and the ceiling. Inside, he reattached his tank and swam for the electric motor room. Kohler noted the time on his watch. He grumbled a half prayer. Several of the words were *please*.

Chatterton moved swiftly into the electric motor room. The compartment remained brown and cloudy from his earlier dive, but he could still see the boxes and the pipe through the silt. His approach would be simple: he would use the sledgehammer to knock the pipe loose, then pry the boxes free from one another with a crowbar.

Chatterton crept to within two feet of the pipe. He spread his hands wide across the sledgehammer's handle—using the tool in the water required a different technique from on land, one in which the diver pushed from the chest rather than swung with the arms. He anchored his left knee on the ground in front of the boxes and his right foot across the aisle on solid machinery. Then, in a short, violent forward explosion, he thrust the sledgehammer's head into the section of pipe fused to the boxes. The compartment thundered with the impact as pieces of encrustation flew from the pipe and hailstormed the room in rust. Chatterton stayed motionless. When the pieces settled to the bottom, he stood, amazed at the sight. The pipe had not moved. And the pipe was not a pipe. Naked and shiny without its encrustation, the object flashed its true identity to Chatterton. This was a five-foot-tall pressurized oxygen tank. This was the colossal big brother to the miniature version that had destroyed Chatterton's garage. It was a miracle that the tank had not just exploded.

"I need to make a decision," Chatterton said to himself.

He flashed through his options; they numbered exactly two. He could turn and leave the compartment. Or he could take another swing at the giant oxygen tank, which he would have to strike on the cap—its most dangerous spot—in order to shake it loose.

"If the thing blows, I won't hear anything," Chatterton thought. "I'll be dead and in a billion pieces."

"If I leave now, I can leave in one piece."

He stepped forward and found purchase with his feet.

When things are easy a person doesn't really learn about himself.

He spread his hands across the sledgehammer's smooth, long handle.

It's what a person does at the moment of his greatest struggle that shows him who he really is.

He lifted the sledgehammer against his chest.

Some people never get that moment.

He breathed deeper than he had ever breathed.

The U-Who *is my moment.*

He thrust the head of the sledgehammer toward the cap of the oxygen tank.

What I do now is what I am . . .

The sledgehammer bashed into the tank. The room thundered. Silt flew everywhere. Chatterton waited for the sound of a million sticks of dynamite. He heard only the whoosh of his bubbles leaving his regulator and the clank of falling metal. He peered through the silt. The tank had dropped away from the boxes. He was alive.

"Oh, Christ," he said aloud.

Chatterton moved toward the boxes, pulled the smallest one free, and stuffed it into his mesh bag. He checked his watch—he had five minutes remaining. He swam out of the electric motor room and up toward Kohler's flashlight beam. Though the box was heavy, he managed to hoist it through the gap to Kohler, who passed it to another diver to take to the surface and inspect for tags. By all rights, Chatterton should have exited the diesel motor room then, while he still had three minutes of time remaining. He could not. It was possible that the first box did not contain a tag. There were other boxes inside the electric motor room. He needed to retrieve a second box. Kohler desperately flashed his light. Chatterton turned around.

A minute later, Chatterton found the second box. This one, however, was even heavier than the first and could not be picked up and swum to Kohler. Instead. Chatterton began to roll it end over end out of the electric motor room. The visibility dropped to zero. Chatterton shined his flashlight on his gauges but could see nothing—the room had gone entirely black. He pushed the box farther, huffing and puffing just to move it another foot closer to Kohler. He pressed his watch against his face mask. He could make out only the vague outline of his timer. He had already stayed longer than planned. He abandoned the box.

"I've gotta get my ass out of here," he thought.

Chatterton swam to the top of the electric motor room so that he could use the ceiling topography to feel his way out of the pitch-black compartment. His navigation was perfect, delivering him to the hatchway that led to the diesel motor room. He was now just a few kicks away from Kohler. He swam forward. Suddenly, his head jerked back. A wire noose had caught around his neck. Chatterton was being strangled.

He tried swimming backward gently. He could not move. In that small bit of motion, the equipment on his back had become tangled on dangling electrical cables. He was now fully sewn into the wreck. Chatterton knew he did not have time to relax and reverse the process, as was necessary in such a predicament. He knew he would have to fight. From his waiting post, Kohler checked his watch. Chatterton was not just late. He was crazy late.

Chatterton pulled at the wire noose around his throat and managed to muscle it off his neck. His breathing quickened even more. He reached up and clawed at the cables that had snared his equipment. Nothing gave. He could not move. He tore harder at the restraints. They hissed in protest and would not loosen. He pulled at them with all he had. Finally, they dropped away. Now free, he dug hard for Kohler, knowing that the slightest additional entanglement would kill him. A moment later he was there. All that remained was for Chatterton to remove his tank and swim through the gap. He took a breath as he reached for the tank. Only the tiniest trickle of gas came through the regulator. Chatterton knew this sensation. He was a breath away from going empty.

Chatterton ripped off his tank and shoved it through the crack near the ceiling, then lunged through the space himself. As he reached the other side, he inhaled, but nothing came from his tank. He was entirely out of gas.

Chatterton spit the regulator from his mouth. His only remaining hope lay in reaching his stage bottles. But they were outside the compartment and on top of the wreck, a swim of at least fifty feet. He dared not risk buddy-breathing with Kohler, as even a slight delay or mix-up in communication could be deadly. Chatterton, his mouth now totally exposed to the ocean, kicked with force and equanimity. He had seen guys die flailing. He was near death. He would not flail.

Chatterton torpedoed out of the diesel motor room and up toward the top of the wreck. Kohler, stunned by the sight of his friend without a regulator, gave chase behind him. Chatterton's lungs screamed as his stage bottles came into sight. He kicked harder. Every cell in his body shrieked for oxygen and pulled at his jaws to breathe. He clenched his mouth shut. He reached the stage bottles. In a single motion, he grabbed a regulator from one of the bottles, stuck it in his mouth, and turned the valve. Fresh gas flooded into his lungs. Chatterton had come down to his final breath.

A few seconds later, Kohler arrived at his side. He looked Chatterton in the eye, then pointed to his chest, sign language for "You just gave me a heart attack—now I'm the one who's going to die instead of you." The divers began their long decompression hang. For nearly two hours, Chatterton thought only of the terrible risks he had taken during the dive. Often, he said aloud, "I can't ever let that happen again." He had long since forgotten the spare-parts box he had recovered, which Kohler had passed to another diver for tag inspection topside.

Near the end of their decompressions, Chatterton and Kohler saw another diver, Will McBeth, swim down the anchor line. McBeth handed

Chatterton a slate just like the one on which Chatterton had written "'SUB" during the discovery trip six years earlier. This time, however, the slate said something different. This time, it read:

The *U-Who* now has a name—it is *U-869*. Congratulations.

In his younger days, Kohler might have jumped for joy and slapped Chatterton on the back. Chatterton might have pumped his fists in triumph. Today, they looked into each other's eyes. Then, simultaneously, neither one before the other, each extended his hand. The divers shook. Today, they had found something important. Today, they had their answers.

★ ★ ★

Chatterton and Kohler identified *U-869* in 1997. To this day, mysteries remain. Why did *U-869* continue to New York after being rerouted to Gibraltar? How did *U-869* meet her end? How did the crew die?

The answers to these questions will probably never be known; the U-boat sank with all hands and without witnesses. It is possible, however, to construct a most-likely-case scenario. That scenario looks like this:

The cataclysmic damage to *U-869*'s control room was almost certainly caused by a strike from its own torpedo. U-boats such as *U-869* carried two types of torpedoes in 1945. Normal "pattern" torpedoes were programmed to run a specific course toward their targets and used a gyroscopic steering mechanism to get there. Acoustic torpedoes were more advanced, homing in on the sound of an enemy ship's propellers. Both types of torpedoes, however, occasionally turned back on their own U-boats. These torpedoes became known as circle-runners. U-boats recorded several instances in which circle-runners passed beneath or above them. An acoustic circle-runner could be especially dangerous, as it chased the sounds of its own submarine's electric motors, pumps, and generators. To avoid being hit, U-boat commanders were ordered to crash-dive immediately after firing an acoustic torpedo.

Commanders often had advance warning of circle-runners. Torpedo propellers spun at several hundred revolutions per minute and produced a distinct, high-pitched whir-whine audible at great distances to the U-boat's radioman, and then to the entire crew as the weapon drew closer. When a commander got such a warning, he was often able to dive or otherwise change course to avoid the circle-runner. History will likely never know how many of the sixty-five still-missing U-boats met their ends by circle-runners. By its nature, a circle-runner gives little warning and bears no witness.

Under ideal conditions—calm seas, good underwater sound propagation, early detection, and fast reporting—Neuerburg might have had thirty seconds or more to respond to the circle-runner. In worse conditions or if the radioman hesitated (or both), he would have had less time.

The torpedo would not have blown up instantly upon striking *U-869*. Instead, there would have been perhaps a one-second delay between contact and detonation as the pistol on the weapon's nose clicked and triggered the explosion. That click—an unmistakable sound to submariners—could be heard even when a torpedo struck a distant target. It would have sounded just long enough before detonation to register in the awarenesses of the crewmen.

Most German torpedoes carried between 620 and 780 pounds of high explosives. Based on damage to the wreck, the circle-runner likely impacted just below the conning tower, in the center of the submarine. Men located in the boat's control-room area—including Neuerburg and Brandt—would have been blown apart and nearly vaporized by the explosion. Men in adjoining rooms likely also died immediately from the concussion or from being hurricaned into machinery. Rippling sheets of air pressure would have rampaged toward both ends of the 252-foot-long submarine, probably slingshotting some crewmen off ceilings and walls and one another, crumpling others like marionettes. Steel doors were blown open. So strong was the blast that it bowed the steel hatch leading into the diesel motor room and blew the steel hatch off the torpedo-loading tube in the forward torpedo room, the compartment farthest from the blast's epicenter. The force of the explosion was easily strong enough to blow open the overhead hatches—hatches Chatterton and Kohler once speculated had been opened by crewmen attempting to escape the sinking sub.

With the U-boat now open to the ocean, torrents of icy water would have rushed inside. A merciless process of replacing air with water in the sub would have begun, and it would have happened with great sound and violence. Bodies would have been rag-dolled off machinery and other structures. Rushing air would have sounded and impacted like a tornado to anyone still alive. Machinery and parts and clothes and tools would have flown at right angles in the furious columns of air rushing from the sub, some of which would have been expelled as ocean debris. No one could have held on.

Corpses—some of them likely missing heads or limbs—would have begun a crooked float to the surface.

It probably took the U-boat less than thirty seconds to fill with water. The submarine would have sunk to the ocean bottom in less than a minute. If anyone had survived the explosion and somehow made it out of the boat and to the surface, he likely would not have lasted more than an hour in the icy waters. The enemy target ship, now as far as ten minutes away, its own engines running, wind and water lapping at its sides, would almost certainly have never heard or seen a thing.

The most likely explanation for the communications problems between *U-869* and Control involves atmospheric conditions, though it is possible that the boat also experienced mechanical problems with its radios. Though Neuerburg might have been hesitant to broadcast for fear of exposing his position to Allied eavesdroppers, the submarine placed itself in no danger by receiving messages from Control. That *U-869* continued to New York after Control ordered her to Gibraltar makes it virtually certain that Neuerburg never got the rerouting orders.

The fate of *U-857*—the submarine that had been hunting targets on the American East Coast in April 1945 and was believed for months by Chatterton and Kohler to be the *U-Who*—remains a mystery. It is still thought lost to unknown causes.

Editor's postscript: Author Robert Kurson and Richie Kohler went to Germany in 2002 and met with several survivors of U-869 *officers and crew, including the son of Helmuth Neuerburg, 869's commander; Neuerburg's eighty-six-year-old brother; and the radioman, Herbert Guschewski, who was to have been aboard 869 but missed the voyage after coming down with pneumonia hours before departure. He had been visited in the hospital by Commander Neuerburg and members of the crew before they left on the final journey of* U-869.

"*Jack* the Pack"

BY JAMES F. CALVERT, VICE ADMIRAL, USN (RET.)

(Excerpted from the book *Silent Running*)

How can a single submarine attack a Japanese convoy with such speed and effectiveness that the sinking ships radio command headquarters that they have been hit by a wolf pack of subs? Incredible as it seems, it really happened—and now you will be aboard as the event is recalled.

This true story is taken from the pages of one of my favorite books describing submarine warfare against the Japanese during World War II. Recalling his days as a lieutenant aboard the USS *Jack*, Admiral Calvert's engaging prose delivers the kind of "you are there" spirit I long to find on the pages of books like this.

Built in great haste at Electric Boat at Groton, Connecticut, the *Jack* took to the sea with Calvert aboard in January 1943. Calvert was the youngest and most junior officer on board, fresh out of the Naval Academy at Annapolis and the New London Submarine School. The *Jack* would go on to become one of the most successful submarines to operate in the Pacific in World War II, due in no small part to Lt. Calvert's performance as the operator of the torpedo data computer (TDC). In the foreword to *Silent Running*, the noted author Captain Edward L. Beach (USN, Ret.) relates, "In submarine doctrine, shooting a torpedo was like firing a rifle. We took big risks to aim them individually and carefully, and we fired them at close range. . . . Aiming a torpedo involved a combination of talents: accurate periscope observation, which was the skipper's responsibility, and meticulously accurate operation of the torpedo data computer, the TDC."

The skipper of the *Jack* is Lieutenant Commander Tommy Dykers (Annapolis, 1927). Also aboard, handling navigation duties, is Commander Frederick Laing, assigned to this mission to qualify for a future command.

On January 16, 1944, we departed Pearl Harbor for our patrol area, which we were told would probably be in the South China Sea but would be confirmed for us when we reported to Commander Submarines Southwest Pacific. That would happen about the time we crossed the international date line.

We had more foul weather on the eleven-hundred-mile passage to Midway, and when we arrived on the twentieth, it was too rough for us to enter. This was not left up to us: the Base commander told us to lay off the entrance at a safe distance until told we could enter.

Our new engines were running like Swiss watches. It is hard for me to tell you what this confidence in our ability to stay at sea without engineering disasters meant to us. It was a whole new ball game.

Finally, on the morning of the twenty-first, we were cleared to enter. Not long after leaving Pearl, we had developed difficulty with the new SJ radar training mechanism, the motorized device that made the radar antenna search around automatically rather than by hand (as the old set had made us do). The repairs took longer than expected, and it was the twenty-fourth before we could leave.

Even then, luck was not with us. We had more radar trouble. In addition to the surface search SJ, we were equipped with an air search radar—by and large, relatively primitive—designated the *SD*; it didn't orient you to the direction of the airplane, but it told you how far away it was. About eight hours out of Midway, the SD's main transformer shorted out. This was not a spare we carried; we had no choice except to go back to Midway. On the way back, the SJ training mechanism jammed again. What kind of a start was this?

The next morning, January 25, we were again told that it was too rough to enter. So once more here we were laying off Midway Island, impatient to get in, get repaired, and get going. This was getting to be a habit. On the morning of the twenty-sixth, the sea calmed a bit, and we were able to reenter Midway.

The repair folks at Midway put in a new SD transformer and an entirely new gear train for the SJ training mechanism. Satisfied that we finally had everything right, we departed again on January 28, eight days later than we had hoped to say good-bye to this desolate home of the gooney birds.

About a week later, the SD earned its salt. It was a heavily overcast day with many low-lying clouds. We were passing Marcus Island, a known base for Japanese patrol planes. We had an SD contact at four miles and did not wait to try to see him. As we passed about sixty feet, *WHAM!*

The SD had seen something, all right, and the patrol plane must have seen us diving. We leveled off at 150 feet.

WHAM! . . .WHAM! Two more bombs, much closer.

"Let's hope that three is all he carries," said Dykers, who by now had come to the conning tower. Apparently it was, for we heard no more. About a half hour later, we surfaced. Although visibility was still poor, we had no sign of anyone on the SD. This all-around primitive radar had until then been looked on as a sort of poor cousin of the SJ, not really needed with our faultless lookout system. Suddenly the SD took on a new status. No lookout had seen that plane, and if we had stayed up until we *had* seen him, I might not be writing this now.

All day that day, February 5, we were plagued with aircraft from Marcus obviously looking for the submarine that had been bombed. They combed the area pretty thoroughly. We had to dive four times. Each time the airplane was detected by the SD. Twice the lookouts sighted the planes about the same time; they were proud of the fact that even in such thick weather they could match the SD in performance.

On the eighth we reached the boundary between ComSubPac's area of responsibility and that of Commander Submarines Southwest Pacific (ComSubSouWestPac) and reported by radio to Admiral Cristie for operational control. We were given a large area in the South China Sea covering much of the route used by the tankers going between the Empire (the name we used for Japan all through the war) and the oil fields in southeast Asia (formerly the Dutch East Indies).

The South China Sea is big. It stretches some fifteen hundred miles, more or less north and south, from Formosa (Taiwan) at its northern end to Singapore at its southern. Its western side is bounded by China in the north, Vietnam in the central part, and Malaysia in the south. Its eastern boundary is formed by the Philippines on the north and Borneo on the south. The sea narrows to about five hundred miles between Vietnam and the northern tip of Borneo. This, coupled with the fact that much of the oil for the Empire was coming from huge refineries along the north coast of Borneo, made the South China Sea a good hunting ground.

In early 1944 the Pacific war was reaching the point where the supply of petroleum for the Japanese homeland was becoming critical. Just before we reached our area, Admiral Christie changed the top priority for submarine targets from Japanese combatant ships to oil tankers. We were primed to look for tankers.

After a few days of trying to patrol this huge sea by periscope during the day, we realized this was a vain effort. By running on the surface and setting a watch on the high periscope, we achieved significant increase in our coverage. In this condition we had an effective height of eye of about fifty feet. This meant that in the clear weather characteristic of the South China Sea, we could see the top of a ship at fifteen miles, her smoke maybe even farther. Thus we were covering an area of more than seven hundred square miles with the high periscope watch, as compared to a maximum of fifty square miles with the submerged periscope watch.

Of course, patrolling on the surface in the daytime made us vulnerable to detection and bombing by patrol aircraft, but we had to take that risk. Although we were not far from the major Japanese base at Cam Ranh Bay, we believed our lookouts were up to the job of spotting its patrol planes before they saw us.

Even with this new patrolling technique (which resulted in at least two or three dives a day to avoid aircraft), we were not spotting any tanker traffic. The crew was beginning to wonder if the South China Sea was just plain empty of everything except Japanese patrol aircraft. Where were these tankers we had heard so much about?

Then, about 3:30 in the morning on February 19, Charley Caw, our battle stations radar operator, picked up a group of ships at about thirteen miles. They were northbound. We were about halfway between Cam Ranh Bay and Manila, a little north of the narrowest point of the Vietnam-Borneo passage. Caw reported the contact to Kent, who had the deck.

GONG-GONG-GONG went the incessant call of the battle stations alarm. I woke up and, after a moment of wondering what was going on, crawled hastily out of my bunk and padded to the conning tower in a pair of khaki trousers, an undershirt, and bare feet. Speed was more important than formality at this point. When I got there, Alec and Kent already had the plot going and were trying to figure out the formation.

Before long they had it doped out pretty well. To the east of us and up-moon were four large ships. They looked like tankers in the dim light,

moving in a column with three other, smaller ships on the side of the formation away from us. At least two of the smaller ships looked as though they
might be escorts, but we couldn't be sure. The convoy was running a fairly
standard zig plan, turning the formation twenty to thirty-five degrees about
every five minutes, on the average. There did not seem to be any escort ships
on our side. This seemed hard to believe, but we could not see any on the
radar or visually from the bridge.

Before long we could see for certain that these were tankers, and we realized we were going to get a crack at these top-priority targets. All of us felt that
the big chance the *Jack* had been looking for ever since she had been built was
right here, staring us in the face. All the hard work in training, all the disappoint-
ments, all the worry over HOR engines and torpedoes that didn't work—all of
these could be put in the background forever if we could just do properly the
work that was sitting before us. Our training on night surface attack procedures
was also going to pay off, for this was a situation made to order for that tactic.

The night surface attack required the skipper to be on the bridge,
where he could make the tough decisions about just how to come in on the
convoy, how close to come to the escorts, when to dive if necessary, and
when to shoot. Dykers wanted to have Freddy Laing on the bridge with him
because there Laing could learn the most about night surface attacks. So
Miles Refo and I were joined in the conning tower only by Kent and Alec on
the plot and Charley Caw on the radar. It was a bit of a lonely feeling.

I also worried about Dykers being on the bridge with no TDC or
plot to help him get the picture. He was used to standing about three feet
from the TDC, where he could easily see, continuously updated, the target's
range and bearing, course and speed—everything he needed to know, there
at a glance. Up on the bridge, he had nothing on the tactical picture other
than what he could visualize in his head. We did have a talkback system between the TDC and the bridge, so I could keep him posted on how the situation looked on the TDC; but it wasn't easy. In our drills at Pearl Harbor, we
had worked over and over on this new arrangement, and we had slowly gotten more used to it. Now it was going to get a real test.

We had a senior signalman, Stacey Bennett, whose night vision was
extraordinarily good, and Dykers wanted him on the bridge at battle stations.
Bennett could see at night, all right, but he had another habit that gave the
whole bridge gang, from Dykers down to the lookouts, the willies. He had a
good singing voice, and when a situation got tight—as it certainly was now, as

we closed in on the near column of tankers—he would start to sing. Bennett's favorite, "Nearer, My God, to Thee," may have been great for him, but it had a distinctly unsettling effect on everyone else.

"Dammit, Bennett, can't you sing something else?" from the skipper.

"I guess so, Captain, but this just seems to be so comforting."

Moments later Bennett saw and reported something about the formation that no on else had seen. Even when specifically pointed out by Bennett, it remained invisible to others. This was priceless information, so the skipper just shrugged. "Nearer, My God, to Thee" kept on—at a slightly lower volume.

We were getting in close enough so that when they zigged the next time, we should get a good shot.

"We'll shoot six torpedoes. Make ready all six tubes forward. Set depth ten feet," came from Dykers. "Jim, we'll shoot at the second and third tankers on this side of the formation."

"Aye aye, sir, but they're about due to zig."

"OK, I can hold off a bit longer, but they're getting pretty close."

Conscious of how visible our bow wake could be, Dykers decided to slow: "All ahead one-third."

"There comes the zig—they're going away." I reported on the intercom.

"Yeah, I can see it from up here. Dammit, they're going farther away than I wanted. Let me know when they've settled down."

It turned out to be a forty-degree zig away, the biggest one they had made since we started tracking them. This made the torpedo runs longer than we wanted, but there was nothing to do but shoot now. It would only get worse. The memory of that miss on the Akikaze was still plaguing me.

One of the key things in shooting torpedoes was to get the exact bearing of the target set in the TDC just before you shot. With the periscope three feet away from the TDC in a daytime periscope attack, this was no problem. At night it was a different matter. Someone had to look over the gyro repeater on the bridge with a thing called a *pelorus* and while looking at the target read the bearing from the illuminated dial underneath. Freddy Laing had been assigned this job.

"Jim, as soon as you get the bearing from us, shoot the first three. We'll give you a new bearing on the second target for the next three."

"Aye aye, sir."

"Bearing two four," from Laing.

"Fire one!" I said as our first surface-fired torpedo lurched from the bow of the submarine.

"Fire two! . . . Fire three!" The next two went out at eight-second intervals.

"First three are gone," I reported to Dykers.

"Here's the second ship—bearing one three," from Laing.

"Fire four! . . . Fire five! . . . Fire six!" The last three went out as scheduled.

Just as I turned to the quartermaster with the stopwatch to ask how much more time was left for the first fish: Ker-*WHOOM*!

This was no torpedo explosion. I had never heard any explosion so loud or so paralyzing. Then two *WHAMS* as the second and third torpedoes hit.

"Holy suh-*moly*," from the bridge. "After the first fish hit, flames ran back and forth across his deck, and then in about two seconds the whole ship exploded. "He's gone—there's nothing left of him."

A moment later there were two more loud *WHAMS* as the second salvo began to hit. The bridge could see the flashes at the water line as these torpedoes hit a ship in the far column. No ship explosion there, however. No flames. But two unmistakable hits.

"Right full rudder, all ahead flank," from Dykers as he prepared to pull out.

"One of the ships in the far column is a well-decked destroyer, and he's shooting at us—I can see the big, orange flashes!" reported Dykers, still cool but obviously concerned.

"Pour it on, maneuvering. Don't spare the horses," from the skipper as he simultaneously gave orders to the helm to start weaving twenty degrees either side of our course to make us a harder target.

I gave a short prayer of thanks that we had those sturdy Wintons back there instead of four HOR cripples. I also thought of Sandy Sanderlin and Bob Craig, our battle station controller operators, back there coaxing everything they could out of that propulsion plant without making the fatal mistake of tripping something out.

"He's got the range, all right. Some of these splashes are getting damn close," from Dykers.

From the bridge, down the hatch, I could now hear the strong, clear tones of "Nearer, My God, to Thee." Bennett was in full voice now, with no holding back.

We were all thinking the same thought—Is the skipper going to have to dive? Are we in for another five hours of depth charging?

No order was given for diving, but the skipper did send everyone down from the bridge except Bennett. As Freddy Laing came down to the conning tower, he said, "Either the skipper likes the singing, or he wants to keep that night vision up there." I think we all knew which it was.

"All stop. Steady as she goes. Make ready all four tubes aft," from Dykers.

What was up? I couldn't figure this one out.

"I think all he sees is our wake. If he continues to close, we'll try to shoot him before we dive. Get him up on the TDC," from Dykers.

"He already is. We've got him locked in," I replied.

Then I remembered our night training experience with the other submarine at Pearl. The wake was all we could see. Dykers was trying to make us disappear. But if this Japanese destroyer had radar . . .

The next shot from the destroyer went way over. Then off to the right. We could hear Bennett and the skipper talking about it on the bridge, their voices drifting down through the conning tower hatch. We didn't need the intercom.

I was getting continual ranges and bearings from Charley Caw on the radar. "He's slowing down and turning to his right," I reported.

"I don't think he can see us any more—most of these shots are going wild out to starboard," from Dykers.

A minute or two passed uneventfully.

"I think he has stopped shooting. No shots for quite a while now," from the bridge.

"The destroyer is echo ranging now," came the report from the sonar room. "And he has slowed down."

Good! I thought. He thinks we've submerged.

The ruse had worked.

I reported all this to the bridge. "Great, but we can't see him any more. I don't know what he's doing," from Dykers.

Then, distantly, one of the sweetest sounds I had ever heard: click . . . bang! . . . click . . . bang! Depth charges. But not the bone-rattling noise that we had gotten to know all too well. Instead, this was a sort of benevolent, distant confirmation of the fact that we had given him the slip.

We were still up, and he thought we were down.

"Come right twenty degrees. All ahead two-thirds," from the bridge. We were slipping away.

Little by little, Dykers eased away from the destroyer and came to the same course as the convoy, which had now reformed and was fleeing to the north. We slowly worked up to flank speed, twenty knots.

Dykers came down from the bridge, looked at the TDC and plot, and said, "I'm going to pull out far enough from them so that when it gets light, they won't see us. We'll make an end-around and then dive on their track so we can get another shot at them."

By daylight on the twentieth, we had pulled out so far that we could no longer see the convoy except through the high periscope. It was a clear, calm day, and from time to time we would check the convoy on the radar. We were just seeing their tops at a range of more than fifteen miles. There was little or no chance they could see us since all we had above the horizon, as they saw it, was our high, thin attack periscope. Not much to see.

During the day Dykers secured the battle stations so people could get some rest, but he asked me to stay on the TDC. Nading and Lukingbeal took turns keeping the plot up-to-date. I was still dressed only in my undershirt, so I asked Domingo, our senior steward, to bring me a regular shirt, a sandwich, and some coffee.

During the morning Dykers and Laing came up for a bit of a postmortem with me.

"The tanker must have been loaded with high octane gasoline. When he exploded, the flames shot hundreds of feet in the air. Within less than a minute, he was gone. We could see clearly because the sea was covered with burning gasoline," explained Dykers.

"I don't see how anyone on board could have lived more than a few seconds. It was an enormous explosion," added Laing.

"How come you gave us a bearing on a ship in the far column for the second salvo? I thought we were going to take two of the tankers in the close column," I asked. "I know we had their course and speed nailed right to the mast."

"My fault," said Laing. "In the excitement I gave you the bearing on one of the ships in the far column. We were so close I got them mixed up."

"I don't think he was a tanker. I still don't know why only one destroyer came after us. Maybe we hit an escort of some kind in the far column," said Dykers. "Whatever he was, you sure had the dope on these guys. Five hits out of six isn't bad."

"You really had us guessing when you came to all stop and got those after tubes ready," I said.

"There was no way we could outrun him. We were making twenty knots, and he was still closing us. I decided to find out if he could see us—or just our wake."

"It sure worked," I grinned.

"Yeah, but not everyone on the bridge thought it was a great idea. When I came to all stop, Bennett groaned and muttered under his breath. 'Oh no . . . oh, no.' He's a real morale booster, that boy. But he can see like a nighthawk. I'll take him any day," said Dykers.

"He's a great singer, too," added Freddy Laing.

All that day we worked ahead of the convoy. Twice we had to dive for patrol planes. But we stayed down only about twenty minutes, then were back up again. After last night's action, we couldn't see why there were not more planes out, but we just accepted what was happening without worrying too much about the shortcomings of the Japanese ASW effort. The convoy was zigging much more radically than the night before, and all this back-and-forth made their advance substantially slower. Of course, it also made it easier for us to pull ahead of them.

The performance of the new SJ radar was superb, but we didn't want to use it unless we had to. There was a chance the convoy had a radar detector on board, and we were just as happy to have them think we were still back at the scene of last night's attack. So we tracked the convoy on the high periscope, staying at the extreme range we could see them, playing it as safe as possible. Every once in a while, they would zig far away and we would lose them on the periscope. Cutting in the radar, we could hold them out as far as eighteen miles and thus had no trouble closing enough to get their tops in sight once again.

What a difference this all was from our first two patrols, when we had been struggling with a balky radar set and worrying continually about those undependable HORs. The *Jack* was really flexing her muscles now.

I could not help but think, also, about how much the Pacific submarines had progressed since those early days of the war when some skippers were so fearful of being detected that they tried to shoot on sonar bearings alone. The night surface attack was a far cry from that.

In the afternoon we began to close their track to get dead ahead of them. By about three o'clock, we submerged on what we estimated from the daylong plot was their intended track.

There was a considerable period after we dove when we could not see them, had no sonar contact, and of course lacked radar information. We were betting on the accuracy of our plot and the hope that the convoy com-modore would not decide to make a significant change of base course. We knew we would find ourselves hopelessly out in left field if he did.

Somehow, though, I believed this was our day. We had been training this ship more than a year to be ready for just this kind of opportunity, and I could not believe it was going to get away from us. All of our equipment was working beautifully, and all of our people were right at the top of their game. Whether on the surface or at periscope depth, we were, I believed, going to get some more shots at these guys.

About an hour after submerging, sonar reported faint echo ranging dead ahead. Once again that practice of echo ranging as they proceeded was betraying them.

Before long Dykers had their tops in sight through the periscope. Alec Nading and Kent Lukingbeal had worked out an overall speed of ad-vance for the convoy based on its zig plan, and I had just set that in the TDC rather than trying to estimate the convoy's many zigs and zags.

As the ships got closer, Dykers was able to get a periscope range; it was only five hundred yards out from the estimate we had from the plot and the TDC. We were really hitting on all cylinders.

"There are still four tankers left, two in each column. One escort far out on the other side," from the skipper.

Because they were west of us, proceeding north, they were silhouet-ted against the lowering sun. We were working in close. Dykers had to be very careful of the scope since the sea was almost mirror smooth.

"Make ready all six bow tubes. Set depth ten feet."

The echo ranging from the escorts was loud now. But sonar kept reporting that they were on the long search scale—no sign of their having detected us.

We were in very tight, waiting for the zig. It came, but it was small. We were too tight for a bow shot.

"Left full rudder. Make ready all four stern tubes," snapped the skipper.

Once again the part-luck, part-skill Dykers formula worked. We were going to be in beautiful position for a stern shot.

"We'll shoot two at the first and two at the second . . . stand by."

"Bearing, mark."

"One six five," from Laing.

"Fire seven! . . . Fire eight! . . . Fire nine! . . . Fire ten!"

All four torpedoes went out on time and spread just as planned.

WHAM! . . . *WHAM!* . . . *WHAM!* Three hits, all right on time.

Then, a few seconds later, Ker-*WHOOM!* . . . and then Ker-*WHOOM!* These ships were exploding!

"Up scope."

"They must all be high-octane gasoline tankers. Our targets are almost gone, and the sea is covered with burning gasoline. What a sight." After our near-disaster on the first patrol, however, we had agreed that there would be no more sight-seeing through the periscope.

Apparently the escort on the far side was confused since he started off in the wrong direction, dropping depth charges as he went. They were too far away to be dangerous, but still, I liked the sound of them better when we were on the surface.

It looked as though the convoy commodore, whichever ship he was in, did not want his escort to stay around looking for submarines while he went north without any protection. All the remaining ships took off in a northerly direction without much delay. When the generated range of the TDC made it look as though it would be safe to surface, we came up and started to chase them at flank speed.

On the word "Prepare to surface," we got a question from the forward torpedo room: "Shall we blow down the forward tubes?" in the excitement of the attack, we had all forgotten that those tubes were being left flooded for a long time. Not good for the torpedoes, but probably OK.

When we got to the surface and got the radar going, we could see that the Japanese commodore had split his convoy. There now remained two tankers and apparently only one escort. One tanker was going to the north alone while the other was diverging to the north-northwest with the escort.

We prepared for another night surface attack, this time on the unescorted tanker. We made our end-around him, and as we tracked him, it became apparent that he had taken the wildest zig plan in the book. He was zigging every two or three minutes, with course changes up to fifty degrees each time.

We made ready the bow tubes as we completed our end-around and began to close in for the attack. We were in good position and were firing from about eighteen hundred yards. I didn't see how he could fail to see us, but there was no sign that he had.

We used our regular procedure of Freddy giving me a bearing from the pelorus on the bridge.

"One six," from Laing.

"Fire one! . . . Fire two! . . . Fire three!" I snapped. Everything went as arranged.

"No noise from the first torpedo, sir. Sounds like a cold run," came from the sonar room.

Oh no, I thought, remembering that these fish had been flooded a long time on the late-afternoon periscope attack.

"The second fish sound OK, but I think it's running too far ahead of the target," from sonar.

I reported all this to the bridge as Dykers gave the orders to turn and pull away from the target.

"I never saw any torpedo tracks from up here," said the skipper. This was unusual for a night surface attack.

"The last torpedo is erratic. It is running away off to the right and doesn't sound right," came the next depressing report from sonar.

Our lone tanker friend had dodged the bullet.

"I'm afraid we've missed him," I said to the bridge.

"That's OK. We'll get him yet. He's shooting at us now. From the flash it looks like a pretty big gun. Five-incher, I would guess. Big orange flashes," came the calm report from the bridge. Bennett will be singing now, I thought.

"Tell the forward torpedo room to pull those other three fish that were flooded so long and load fresh ones. We'll check the flooded ones later."

Suddenly we felt the whole ship shudder as though from a collision. Had we been hit?

"Wow! That shot was close," said the skipper. "It passed right over the forward deck below the bridge level. It sounded like a freight train going by. The splash from it was close as hell!"

If it had been three feet lower, that would have been the end of the *Jack*.

We started weaving again and went to twenty knots. We knew we had the speed advantage of this guy in a big way. The highest speed at which we had tracked him was ten knots.

There were a couple more shudders from close shots, but none as close as the one that crossed over below the bridge level. The sounds of "Nearer, My God, to Thee" were coming down the conning tower hatch loud and clear now.

But as we pulled away from our slow target, we all began to breathe a little easier and to make plans for the next attack.

The tanker continued his frantic zigging, and although we had no trouble catching him, it was extremely difficult to get into a good position. We did not want to give him another chance to use that five-inch gun on us.

Finally, at about eleven at night, we got into the right spot and fired four torpedoes from up forward.

WHAM! ... *WHAM!* ... *WHAM!* Three hits!

The tanker disappeared in a burst of high-octane white flame. Tojo was losing of lot of valuable aviation gasoline in this series of attacks.

It had taken so long to finish off this lone wolf that we had lost the other tanker and escort on the radar. We took off after them at flank speed, but long after midnight, we had to admit defeat. We broke off the chase.

I had been at the TDC for nearly twenty-four hours and now noticed for the first time that I was still in my bare feet. I had been out of the conning tower only a couple of times, to go to the head, and I had had nothing to eat but that one sandwich. I suddenly realized that I was ravenously hungry and awfully tired.

Alec had the watch on the bridge, but the rest of us convened in the wardroom for a review.

We had fired seventeen torpedoes for eleven hits—and two of those torpedoes had malfunctioned because of the long flooding. If we counted just the good torpedoes, we had eleven hits out of fifteen. That was good in any league.

We had sunk four tankers loaded with gasoline and clearly had sunk a fifth ship in the first night attack. We could not be certain whether the fifth was a tanker or an escort, but we were sure the other four were tankers. Not many submariners had seen such spectacular fireworks from each target. Every one had been a high-octane bomb.

After about four ham sandwiches and three cups of hot cocoa, I was beginning to feel revived.

"Shouldn't we say something to the crew?" asked Freddy Laing.

"Good idea," said Dykers.

All fleet submarines had an announcing system that led to each compartment and was loud enough to be heard even over the noise in the engine rooms.

"This is the captain speaking. We have lost contact with the convoy, but we have sunk four of the five tankers and probably one of the two escorts. It has been quite a day's work—one that any submarine in this Navy could be proud of.

"This was a team effort. We all worked together, and I am proud of every one of you."

I had the eight-to-twelve watch coming up in the morning, now only about three hours away. They were three of the soundest hours of sleep I ever had. I was exhausted.

After pulling about sixty miles south from the scene of the attacks, the morning of February 21, we spent the next week patrolling on the surface with the high periscope—without results. Many dives for patrol planes, but no ship contacts.

By this point in the war American submarines were getting extremely valuable help from the code breakers at Pearl. These were the same men who had given Admiral Nimitz the information that helped win the Battle of Midway against such tremendous odds.

As the months went by after Midway, it became more and more apparent, even to the nonbelievers in Washington, that the code breakers were consistently getting good, solid information.* It also became apparent that much of this information could be of great value to submarines on patrol.

Very important in the development of this information for submarines was a former submarine skipper named Jasper Holmes, who had been retired because of a physical disability. After retirement he became well-known as the author of submarine adventure stories for the *Saturday Evening Post*, written under the pen name Alec Hudson.

When the war came, he asked to come back to active duty. He was assigned to duty with the ultra-top-secret code-breaking group at Pearl Harbor. Naturally he had no trouble putting himself in the place of the submarine skippers on patrol, and he realized how valuable to them some of the intercepted information on Japanese ship movements could be.

Holmes had been a good friend of Tommy Dykers during their S-boat days. Dykers had had the *S-35*, Jasper the *S-30*. After Holmes retired, they had remained in touch. Dykers was a big fan of the Alec Hudson stories in the *Saturday Evening Post*. So was I. They were great.

Working with ComSubPac staff, Holmes was able to develop a series of messages, called *Ultras*, that gave submarines good information on the projected tracks both of convoys and of combatant ships.

---

*The first significant tactical use of code-break information had been at the Battle of the Coral Sea, about one month before Midway. Its use there, however, had not been as decisive as at Midway.

Needless to say, the security surrounding these Ultra messages was severe. We would have lost a priceless advantage in the war had the Japanese gotten any clear indication that we were reading their mail. Messages containing such information had a special symbol indicating that they could be decoded only by an officer cleared for Ultra.

The Ultra messages did not yield any concrete results for us on the first two patrols, but the five-tanker convoy contact had been developed with the help of an Ultra. Then on February 29, ten days after our tanker sweep, we received an Ultra telling us of the approach of a Nachi-class heavy cruiser. He was believed to be unescorted and traveling north at high speed.

We closed the projected track at high speed on the surface. After a few hours, his tops came plainly into view, and we dove. If he had sighted us, he would have diverted and our opportunity would have been lost.

We had not had any stars that morning and thus were not absolutely sure of our position. Either our navigation or his was a bit off, for we were never able to close him to less than nine thousand yards, far too great for even a desperation torpedo shot. He was making twenty-five knots, so it was all over in a hurry.

The tremendous handicaps under which a submerged submarine operates were driven home to us vividly by this experience. Once again I realized that a battery-powered submarine operating submerged was no more than a slightly mobile minefield. With the submarine on the surface . . . well, that was different.

The big cruiser was a tough one to lose. Things had been going so well that we believed we could do anything. This showed us that we could not. If we could have gotten him, this would have been the best patrol of the war to date.

We had seven torpedoes left, four after and three forward. The forward torpedoes were suspect since they had been in flooded tubes for so long during the tanker convoy attack. They had, however, been worked over carefully, and the torpedomen were confident they were OK.

That evening (February 29) we received another Ultra giving us information on a southbound convoy that would pass fairly close. We cranked up our faithful Wintons and got over to the projected track. About one in the morning on March 1, we had radar contact with a convoy of four large ships, in a box formation, and two escorts, each out on the forward wing about a thousand yards. Because we had four torpedoes aft and only three forward, we tried hard to get into position for a stern shot. This is much harder to do on the surface than submerged.

We tried for more than an hour to get a stern shot but could not do it. The moon had set and it was pitch dark, but those escorts seemed to know that something was up. Every time we tried to work into position for firing, one of them would start over in our direction. Did they have radar?

After another half hour or so, we were getting into final position. I was waiting for the pelorus bearing from Freddy.

"Uh-oh. Tracer fire coming in our direction—long yellow arcs," came the alarmed report from the skipper.

This was a new experience for us. We pulled out again, armed with the information that they almost certainly knew, or strongly suspected, that there was a surfaced submarine about.

We gave up the stern shot idea and began carefully to work in for a bow shot. We came in well abaft the escort on our side. This convoy was tracking at fourteen knots, making it much more difficult to work in and around it than had been the case with the tanker convoy at ten knots.

Try as we might, we could not get a torpedo run of much less than twenty-five hundred yards. This didn't leave much room for error, but I believed we had them about right and told Dykers so.

We fired the three remaining bow tube torpedoes at this long range and, right on time, *WHAM! . . . WHAM! . . .* Two hits.

The target exploded violently and issued a lot of smoke amidships. He wasn't a tanker, but he was clearly carrying something explosive. He was sinking fast. The convoy was scattering in all directions, and the near escort was heading for us with a zero angle on the bow and a large bone in his teeth.

Dykers turned away at flank speed and gave him a small, weaving target. Two bursts of tracer fire came our way, but there was no large gunfire. It seen became clear that sixteen knots was the escort's top speed. Before long he gave up the chase and turned back to the convoy. So did we. We were determined to use those last four torpedoes on this convoy.

There were now three heavies left, along with the two escorts. Everyone was obviously fully alerted. The zig plan became even more frantic. But once again Dykers worked his way in astern of the close escort and then, in a quick maneuver at high speed, turned the submarine to bring the stern tubes to bear. Fortunately, this leg turned out to be long enough for us to complete the turn. We had a good setup, though once again the torpedo run was much longer than we wanted. Nevertheless, we fired four torpedoes at the regular intervals. As soon as Dykers heard the last torpedo go, he began to pour on the speed to get out of there. We were headed in the right direction—there was no delay.

WHAM! ... WHAM! ... WHAM! ... Three hits out of four!

There was no big explosion from the target this time, but it was apparent to all on the bridge that he was mortally wounded. He sagged in the middle, clearly broken in two. Shortly we saw him go under the waves.

The escort, however, was not out of action, and he came for us like a wolf in the fold. We poured on the coal and weaved.

"Here come the tracers again. Pretty close—he has us spotted," from the bridge. We could hear Bennett singing.

Once again Dykers got everyone off the bridge except himself and Bennett.

How fast was this escort? Could he catch us? Soon we knew that he could not; sixteen knots was his best speed. After a few more tracer bursts, the escort turned away and rejoined the convoy, which now had only two heavies remaining.

We were out of torpedoes. That was disappointing, but this was the *right* way to end a patrol instead of with howling propeller shafts or disabled engines as we had before.

We got off a message to Admiral Christie giving him the results of our patrol and telling him we were proceeding to Fremantle. We set our course for the Mindoro Strait to pass from the South China Sea into the Sulu Sea.

En route we picked up another convoy, consisting of two large ships and two escorts. They came right over us, but there was nothing we could do except go deep, let them pass over, and then watch them disappear over the horizon.

"We sit on station for days with twenty-four torpedoes and no targets, and then when the fish are all gone, we run into a convoy we can't avoid even when we try," said Dykers ruefully as we talked it over in the wardroom.

There were lots of planes out looking for us this time. We dove again and again but tried to come up each time so that we could make some time. In the afternoon one spotted us for sure and, as we passed one hundred feet on the way down, *BANG! ... BANG!*

Two bombs—not too close, but they sure got our attention.

A half hour later, just as we were getting ready to come to periscope depth, *BANG!*

"Well," said Dykers, "I think we'll stay down a little longer."

We surfaced at dark and proceeded to pass through the Mindoro Strait. We couldn't forget about enemy submarines. These guys were probably not as tough as the U-boats, but they might well have been advised of our presence and be watching for us. We kept up a pretty vigorous zig plan as we traveled.

That evening as we cruised on the surface past the islands of Mindoro and Panay, I could see long strings of fire on the sides of the island mountains. Because I did not know what they were, I reported them to the captain.

"I'll come up and see them," he replied.

"Those are Filipinos burning out their sugarcane fields. They always do it about this time of the year." Dykers had served out here on the Asia station as a younger officer and had seen the burning fields many times.

This seemed totally strange to me. "You mean, these guys are out here farming their sugarcane as though nothing was going on?"

"Not everyone takes this war as seriously as we do. They are living in an occupied land, and they have to feed their families. So they work." With that, after a careful look around, Dykers went below.

But for the rest of the watch, I looked at those strings of golden lights and reflected on how differently war affects different nations. Here we were, twelve thousand miles from home, fighting a vicious war in the Filipino's backyards, and they were up in the hills, quietly burning their sugarcane. I concluded that this disparity was the price of power—at least, that was the best explanation I could come up with at the time.

It was quiet, but all through the night the breeze came slowly to us from the land, carrying with it the sweet scent of the burning cane.

Soon we passed through the Sibutu Passage, near the northeastern tip of Borneo, and entered the Celebes Sea. Each day brought more patrol planes and more emergency dives, but we had to stay up as much as we could during the day if we wanted to get to Australia within the month.

Next was the Makassar Strait, between Borneo and Celebes. This strait is wide, and we were able to make most of the passage on the surface, thus entering the Java Sea. As we spent day after day cruising through these huge islands, so rich in resources, we realized how much the Japanese had taken from the Dutch. The value of it all was staggering to contemplate.

The Lombok Strait, between the islands of Bali and Lombok, is only about ten miles wide; we knew it had given many of our submarines trouble in the past. The currents were so swift that we thought it risky to make the transit submerged. Dykers decided to do it on the surface.

Radar showed at least two patrol boats in the strait—maybe more. They were small and hard to see. The night was dark and the sea as smooth as a mirror. There was so much phosphorescence in the water that both our bow wave and our wake looked like neon signs. Should we use high speed and hang the phosphorescence or creep along and take much longer getting through? We decided to compromise by moving through at about ten knots, making some wake but not too much.

It was an eerie sight with the huge, cone-shaped mountain of Bali looming to the right and the more distant mountain of Lombok to the left. Choosing a time when the patrol boats were mostly to the east, we moved along the Bali shore at our sedate ten knots.

It worked. Within an hour or two, we were clear of the strait and going back to four-engine speed to put distance between ourselves and this southernmost boundary of Japanese control.

★ ★ ★

After clearing the Lombok Strait, we were still some seventeen hundred miles from our new home in Fremantle, Australia. Through day after day of balmy weather and smooth seas, we plowed southward, with the Southern Cross hanging high in the clear night skies. As we got into the part of the Indian Ocean bordering Western Australia, we knew that any patrol planes we saw would be friendly and well briefed on our presence. Still, we kept our two-letter recognition signals at hand. The sea began to take on a Caribbean blue look, and even the flying fish were back. We were more relaxed than we had been for weeks.

Our landfall on Fremantle was to be in the early morning, and although it was not my watch, I was on the bridge to catch the first glimpse of the huge light perched on Rottnest Island outside Fremantle harbor. We were told it would be burning, and since it would be the fist navigational light we would have seen since leaving Midway, it was going to be a welcome sight in more ways than one.

We had had beautiful stars all the way down from Lombok; we knew just about when we would see the light. But even before it was due to appear over the horizon, we sighted the loom of the powerful light in the clear night sky. We checked its characteristics—it was Rottnest Light for certain. It is difficult to convey what seeing that light meant to me. It was safety; it was respite from the eternal vigilance for Japanese planes; it promised relaxation and letters from home; and it welcomed us to a place that would, we knew, be our home away from home for some time to come.

As dawn was breaking, we sighted and exchanged recognition signals with the Australian Navy ASW ship sent to escort us into Fremantle. It was March 13, 1944, a month and a half since we had left Midway on that stormy, gray afternoon. What a difference those six weeks had made. We had crossed the Western Pacific, spent almost a month in the South China Sea, then come home through the Celebes Sea, the Makassar Strait, the Lombok Strait, and the Indian Ocean, a total of more than twelve thousand miles—more than halfway around the world—without a single worry about our engines. The Wintons smoked a bit when suddenly loaded heavily, but that was a shortcoming we could easily forgive. The change in the whole outlook of the engine room team was phenomenal. They knew now that they had reliable horses.

More important, we had proved ourselves. The attack on the tanker convoy had been brilliantly conducted and was certainly one of the finest single-submarine actions of the war to that date. We were entering Fremantle with all of our torpedoes expended and all of our machinery working. What a contrast from our second patrol, when we came home having accomplished nothing and with our engines falling apart.

We came up the Swan River to the small submarine base at Fremantle with the welcome sight of our old tender, the *Griffin*, moored there. Appropriately, the weather was beautiful, a Navy band was playing on the dock, and Admiral Christie was there to meet us. As soon as the brow, or gangway, was in place, he came on board with a big grin on his face.

"Tommy that was a *great* patrol. We're all proud of you and the *Jack*."

And with what he pinned a Navy Cross on our skipper's chest. This was most unusual. Combat awards had to be recommended, then approved by the Fleet Commander (Admiral Nimitz), a process that usually took at least two or three weeks, sometimes longer. We learned later that some of the higher-ups were not pleased with this short-circuiting of the regular procedures. For one thing, it seemed to reveal that Admiral Christie had used the code breaker's work, because he knew exactly the results of our patrol. At the time, however, none of that worried us. We were just proud of our ship and our skipper.

While Admiral Christie was not free to discuss code-break material with us, he was free to tell us that in the midst of our night-and-day attack on the tankers, the convoy commodore had sent an uncoded message to his superiors in Tokyo stating that he was under attack by a wolf pack of submarines. You can imagine how the crew felt about that. From then on we were "*Jack* the Pack" to all of them. It was truly frosting on the cake.

To top off the recognition that Dykers was receiving, all of the *Jack* officers were invited to have lunch at The Bend of the Road, Admiral Christie's handsome house on the outskirts of Perth. We knew that this was a privilege extended only to those submarines considered to have made a particularly outstanding patrol.

"Red Route One"

BY TOM CLANCY

(Excerpted from the novel *The Hunt for* Red October)

During the Cold War, U.S. and Russian nuclear missile-bearing attack submarines played a deadly serious game of hide-and-seek in the depths of the Atlantic. The American subs tried to monitor and track the maneuvers and courses of the entire Soviet sub fleet. In his best-selling novel and the popular film, Tom Clancy builds high drama around a Russian commander's attempt to defect to the U.S. in the pride of the Russian navy, a new submarine called *Red October*. While Russian subs seek to destroy *Red October* before it can fall into U.S. hands, American subs try to track *Red October* and lead it to safety. The task is difficult, for *Red October* is armed with a new super-silent propulsion system. In this excerpt, the U.S. submarine *Dallas*, under Commander Bart Mancuso, is monitoring the underwater highway called "Red Route One." In the interplay between Mancuso and Sonarman Ronald Jones, Tom Clancy presents a superb portrait of the high-tech nuclear submarine warfare in the Cold War.

Sonarman Second Class Ronald Jones, his division officer noted, was in his usual trance. The young college dropout was hunched over his instrument table, body limp, eyes closed, face locked into the same neutral expression he wore when listening to one of the many Bach tapes on his expensive personal cassette player. Jones was the sort who categorized his tapes by their flaws, a ragged piano tempo, a botched flute, a wavering French horn. He listened to sea sounds with the same discriminating intensity. In all the navies of the world, submariners were regarded as a curious breed, and submariners themselves looked upon sonar operators as odd. Their eccentricities, however, were among the most tolerated in the military service. The executive officer liked to tell a story about a sonar chief he'd served with for two years, a man who had patrolled the same areas in missile submarines for virtually his whole career. He became so familiar with the humpback whales that summered in the area that he took to calling them by name. On retiring, he went to work for the Woods Hole Oceanographic Institute, where his talent was regarded not so much with amusement as awe.

Three years earlier, Jones had been asked to leave the California Institute of Technology in the middle of his junior year. He had pulled one of the ingenious pranks for which Cal Tech students were justly famous, only it hadn't worked. Now he was serving his time in the navy to finance his return. It was his announced intention to get a doctorate in cybernetics and signal processing. In return for an early out, after receiving his degree he would go to work for the Naval Research Laboratory. Lieutenant Thompson believed it. On joining the *Dallas* six months earlier, he had read the files of all his men. Jones' IQ was 158, the highest on the boat by a fair margin. He had a placid face and sad brown eyes that women found irresistible. On the beach Jones had enough action to wear down a squad of marines. It didn't make much sense to the lieutenant. He'd been the football hero at Annapolis. Jones was a skinny kid who listened to Bach. It didn't figure.

The USS *Dallas*, a 688-class attack submarine, was forty miles from the coast of Iceland, approaching her patrol station, code-named Toll Booth. She was two days late getting there. A week earlier, she had participated in the NATO war game NIFTY DOLPHIN, which had been postponed several days because the worst North Atlantic weather in twenty years had delayed other ships detailed to it. In that exercise the *Dallas*, teamed with HMS *Swiftsure*, had used the foul weather to penetrate and ravage the simulated enemy formation. It was yet another four-oh performance for the *Dallas* and her skipper, Commander Bart Mancuso, one of the youngest submarine commanders in the U.S. Navy. The mission had been followed by a courtesy call at the *Swiftsure*'s Royal Navy base in Scotland, and the American sailors were still shaking off hangovers from the celebration . . . Now they had a different mission, a new development in the Atlantic submarine game. For three weeks, the *Dallas* was to report on traffic in and out of Red Route One.

Over the past fourteen months, newer Soviet submarines had been using a strange, effective tactic for shedding their American and British shadowers. Southwest of Iceland the Russian boats would race down the Reykjanes Ridge, a finger of underwater highlands pointing to the deep Atlantic basin. Spaced at intervals from five miles to half a mile, these mountains with their knife-edged ridges of brittle igneous rock rivaled the Alps in size. Their peaks were about a thousand feet beneath the stormy surface of the North Atlantic. Before the late sixties submarines could barely approach the peaks, much less probe their myriad valleys. Throughout the seventies Soviet naval survey vessels had been seen patrolling the ridge—in all seasons, in all weather, quartering and requartering the area in thousands of cruises. Then, fourteen months before the *Dallas'* present patrol, the USS *Los Angeles* had been tracking a Soviet *Victor II*–class attack submarine. The *Victor* had skirted the Icelandic coast and gone deep as she approached the ridge. The *Los Angeles* had followed. The *Victor* proceeded at eight knots until she passed between the first pair of seamounts, informally known as Thor's Twins. All at once she went to full speed and moved southwest. The skipper of the *Los Angeles* made a determined effort to track the *Victor* and came away from it badly shaken. Although the 688-class submarines were faster than the older *Victors*, the Russian submarine had simply not slowed down—for fifteen hours, it was later determined.

At first it had not been all that dangerous. Submarines had highly accurate inertial navigation systems able to fix their positions to within a few hundred yards from one second to another. But the *Victor* was skirting cliffs as though her skipper could see them, like a fighter dodging down a canyon to avoid surface-to-air missile fire. The *Los Angeles* could not keep track of the cliffs. At any speed over twenty knots both her passive and active sonar, including the echofathometer, became almost useless. The *Los Angeles* thus found herself navigating completely blind. It was, the skipper later reported, like driving a car with the windows painted over, steering with a map and a stopwatch. This was theoretically possible, but the captain quickly realized that the inertial navigation system had a built-in error factor of several hundred yards; this was aggravated by gravitational disturbances, which affected the "local vertical," which in turn affected the inertial fix. Worst of all, his charts were made for surface ships. Objects below a few hundred feet had been known to be misplaced by miles—something that mattered to no one until recently. The interval between mountains had quickly become less than his cumulative navigational error—sooner or later his submarine would drive into a mountainside at over thirty knots. The captain backed off. The *Victor* got away.

Initially it was theorized that the Soviets had somehow staked out one particular route, that their submarines were able to follow it at high speed. Russian skippers were known to pull some crazy stunts, and perhaps they were trusting to a combination of inertial systems, magnetic and gyro compasses attuned to a specific track. This theory had never developed much of a following, and in a few weeks it was known for certain that the Soviet submarines speeding through the ridge were following a multiplicity of tracks. The only thing American and British subs could do was stop periodically to get a sonar fix of their positions, then race to catch up. But the Soviet subs never slowed, and the 688s and *Trafalgars* kept falling behind.

The *Dallas* was on Toll Booth station to monitor passing Russian subs, to watch the entrance to the passage the U.S. Navy was now calling Red Route One, and to listen for any external evidence of a new gadget that might enable the Soviets to run the ridge so boldly. Until the Americans could copy it, there were three unsavory alternatives: they could continue losing contact with the Russians; they could station valuable attack subs at the known exits from the route; or they could set up a whole new SOSUS line.

Jones' trance lasted ten minutes—longer than usual. He ordinarily had a contact figured out in far less time. The sailor leaned back and lit a cigarette.

"Got something, Mr. Thompson."

"What is it?" Thompson leaned against the bulkhead.

"I don't know." Jones picked up a spare set of phones and handed them to his officer. "Listen up, sir."

Thompson himself was a masters candidate in electrical engineering, an expert in sonar system design. His eyes screwed shut as he concentrated on the sound. It was a very faint low-frequency rumble—or swish. He couldn't decide. He listened for several minutes before setting the headphones down, then shook his head.

"I got it a half hour ago on the lateral array," Jones said. He referred to a subsystem of the BQQ-5 multifunction submarine sonar. Its main component was an eighteen-foot-diameter dome located in the bow. The dome was used for both active and passive operations. A new part of the system was a gang of passive sensors which extended two hundred feet down both sides of the hull. This was a mechanical analog to the sensory organs on the body of a shark. "Lost it, got it back, lost it, got it back," Jones went on. "It's not screw sounds, not whales or fish. More like water going through a pipe, except for that funny rumble that comes and goes. Anyway, the bearing is about two-five-zero. That puts it between us and Iceland, so it can't be too far away."

"Let's see what it looks like. Maybe that'll tell us something."

Jones took a double-plugged wire from a hook. One plug went into a socket on his sonar panel, the other into the jack on a nearby oscilloscope. The two men spent several minutes working with the sonar controls to isolate the signal. They ended up with an irregular sine wave which they were only able to hold a few seconds at a time.

"Irregular," Thompson said.

"Yeah, it's funny. It sounds regular, but it doesn't look regular. Know what I mean, Mr. Thompson?"

"No, you've got better ears."

"That's cause I listen to better music, sir. That rock stuff'll kill your ears."

Thompson knew he was right, but an Annapolis graduate doesn't need to hear that from an enlisted man. His vintage Janis Joplin tapes were his own business. "Next step."

"Yessir." Jones took the plug from the oscilloscope and moved it into a panel to the left of the sonar board, next to a computer terminal.

During her last overhaul, the *Dallas* had received a very special toy to go along with her BQQ-5 sonar system. Called the BC-10, it was the most powerful computer yet installed aboard a submarine. Though only about the size of a business desk, it cost over five million dollars and ran at eighty million operations per second. It used newly developed sixty-four-bit chips and made use of the latest processing architecture. Its bubble memory could easily accommodate the computing needs of a whole squadron of submarines. In five years every attack sub in the fleet would have one. Its purpose, much like that of the far larger SOSUS system, was to process and analyze sonar signals; the BC-10 stripped away ambient noise and other naturally produced sea sounds to classify and identify man-made noise. It could identify ships by name from their individual acoustical signatures, much as one could identify the finger or voice prints of a human.

As important as the computer was its programming software. Four years before, a PhD candidate in geophysics who was working at Cal Tech's geophysical laboratory had completed a program of six hundred thousand steps designed to predict earthquakes. The problem the program addressed was one of signal versus noise. It overcame the difficulty seismologists had discriminating between random noise that is constantly monitored on seismographs and genuinely unusual signals that foretell a seismic event.

The first Defense Department use of the program was in the Air Force Technical Applications Command (AFTAC), which found it entirely satisfactory for its mission of monitoring nuclear events throughout the world in accordance with arms control treaties. The Navy Research Laboratory also redrafted it for its own purposes. Though inadequate for seismic predictions, it worked very well indeed in analyzing sonar signals. The program was known in the navy as the signal algorythmic processing system (SAPS).

"SAPS SIGNAL INPUT," Jones typed into the video display terminal (VDT).

"READY," the BC-10 responded at once.

"RUN."

"WORKING."

For all the fantastic speed of the BC-10, the six hundred thousand steps of the program, punctuated by numerous GOTO loops took time to run as the machine eliminated natural sounds with its random profile criteria and then locked into the anomalous signal. It took twenty seconds, an eternity in computer time. The answer came up on the VDT. Jones pressed a key to generate a copy on the adjacent matrix printer.

"Hmph." Jones tore off the page. " 'ANOMALOUS SIGNAL EVALUATED AS MAGMA DISPLACEMENT.' That's SAPS' way of saying take two aspirin and call me at the end of the watch."

Thompson chuckled. For all the ballyhoo that had accompanied the new system, it was not all that popular in the fleet. "Remember what the papers said when we were in England? Something about seismic activity around Iceland, like when that island poked up back in the sixties."

Jones lit another cigarette. He knew the student who had originally drafted this abortion they called SAPS. One problem was that it had a nasty habit of analyzing the wrong signal—and you couldn't tell it was wrong from the result. Besides, since it had been originally designed to look for seismic events, Jones suspected it of a tendency to interpret anomalies as seismic events. He didn't like the built-in bias, which he felt the research laboratory had not entirely removed. It was one thing to use computers as a tool, quite another to let them do your thinking for you. Besides, they were always discovering new sea sounds that nobody had ever heard before, much less classified.

"Sir, the frequency is all wrong for one thing—nowhere near low enough. How 'bout I try an' track in on this signal with the R–15?" Jones referred to the towed array of passive sensors that the *Dallas* was trailing behind her at low speed.

Commander Mancuso came in just then, the usual mug of coffee in his hand. If there was one frightening thing about the captain, Thompson thought, it was his talent for showing up when something was going on. Did he have the whole boat wired?

"Just wandering by," he said casually. "What's happening this fine day?" The captain leaned against the bulkhead. He was a small man, only five eight, who had fought a battle against his waistline all his life and was now losing because of the good food and lack of exercise on a submarine. His dark eyes were surrounded by laugh lines that were always deeper when he was playing a trick on another ship.

Was it day, Thompson wondered? The six-hour one-in-three rotating watch cycle made for a convenient work schedule, but after a few changes you had to press the button on your watch to figure out what day it was, else you couldn't make the proper entry in the log.

"Skipper, Jones picked up a funny signal on the lateral. The computer says it's magma displacement."

"And Jonesy doesn't agree with that." Mancuso didn't have to make it a question.

"No, sir, Captain, I don't. I don't know what it is, but for sure it ain't that."

"You against the machine again?"

"Skipper, SAPS works pretty well most of the time, but sometime it's a real *kludge*." Jones' epithet was the most pejorative curse of electronics people. "For one thing, the frequency is all wrong."

"Okay, what do you think?"

"I don't know, Captain. It isn't screw sounds, and it isn't any naturally produced sound that I've heard. Beyond that . . ." Jones was struck by the informality of the discussion with his commanding officer, even after three years on nuclear subs. The crew of the *Dallas* was like one big family, albeit one of the old frontier families, since everybody worked pretty damned hard. The captain was the father. The executive officer, everyone would readily agree, was the mother. The officers were the older kids, and the enlisted men were the younger kids. The important thing was, if you had something to say, the captain would listen to you. To Jones, this counted for a lot.

Mancuso nodded thoughtfully. "Well, keep at it. No sense letting all this expensive gear go to waste."

Jones grinned. Once he had told the captain in precise detail how he could convert this equipment into the world's finest stereo rig. Mancuso had pointed out that it would not be a major feat, since the sonar gear in this room alone cost over twenty million dollars.

"Christ!" The junior technician bolted upright in his chair. "Somebody just stomped on the gas."

Jones was the sonar watch supervisor. The other two watchstanders noted the new signal, and Jones switched his phones to the towed array jack while the two officers kept out of the way. He took a scratch pad and noted the time before working on his individual controls. The BQR-15 was the most sensitive sonar rig on the boat, but its sensitivity was not needed for this contact.

"Damn," Jones muttered quietly.

"*Charlie*," said the junior technician.

Jones shook his head. "*Victor. Victor* class for sure. Doing turns for thirty knots—big burst of cavitation noise, he's digging big holes in the water, and he doesn't care who knows it. Bearing zero-five-zero. Skipper, we got good water around us, and the signal is real faint. He's not close." It was the closest thing to a range estimate Jones could come up with. Not close meant anything over ten miles. He went back to working his controls. "I think we know this guy. This is the one with a bent blade on his screw, sounds like he's got a chain wrapped around it."

"Put it on speaker," Mancuso told Thompson. He didn't want to disturb the operators. The lieutenant was already keying the signal into the BC-10.

The bulkhead-mounted speaker would have commanded a four-figure price in any stereo shop for its clarity and dynamic perfection; like everything else on the 688-class sub, it was the very best that money could buy. As Jones worked on the sound controls they heard the whining chirp of propeller cavitation, the thin screech associated with a bent propeller blade, and the deeper rumble of a *Victor's* reactor plant at full power. The next thing Mancuso heard was the printer.

"*Victor I*–class, number six," Thompson announced.

"Right," Jones nodded. "*Vic*-six, bearing still zero-five-zero." He plugged the mouthpiece into his headphones. "Conn, sonar, we have a contact. A *Victor* class, bearing zero-five-zero, estimated target speed thirty knots."

Mancuso leaned out into the passageway to address Lieutenant Pat Mannion, officer of the deck. "Pat, man the fire-control tracking party."

"Aye, Cap'n."

"Wait a minute!" Jones' hand went up. "Got another one!" he twiddled some knobs. "This one's a *Charlie* class. Damned if he ain't digging holes, too. More easterly, bearing zero-seven-three, doing turns for about twenty-eight knots. We know this guy, too. Yeah, *Charlie II*, number eleven." Jones slipped a phone off one ear and looked at Mancuso. "Skipper, the Russkies have sub races scheduled for today?"

"Not that they told me about. Of course, we don't get the sports page out here," Mancuso chuckled, swirling the coffee around in his cup and hiding his real thoughts. What the hell was going on? "I suppose I'll go forward and take a look at this. Good work, guys."

He went a few steps forward into the attack center. The normal steaming watch was set. Mannion had the conn, with a junior officer of the deck and seven enlisted men. A first-class firecontrolman was entering data from the target motion analyzer into the Mark 117 fire control computer. Another officer was entering control to take charge of the tracking exercise. There was nothing unusual about this. The whole watch went about its work alertly but with the relaxed demeanor that came with years of training and experience. While the other armed services routinely had their components run exercises against allies or themselves in emulation of Eastern Block tactics, the navy had its attack submarines play their games against the real thing—and constantly. Submariners typically operated on what was effectively an at-war footing.

"So we have company," Mannion observed.

"Not that close," Lieutenant Charles Goodman noted. "These bearings haven't changed a whisker."

"Conn, sonar." It was Jones' voice. Mancuso took it.

"Conn, aye. What is it, Jonesy?"

"We got another one, sir. *Alfa 3*, bearing zero-five-five. Running flat out. Sounds like an earthquake, but faint, sir."

"*Alfa 3*? Our old friend the *Politovskiy*. Haven't run across her in a while. Anything else you can tell me?"

"A guess, sir. The sound on this one warbled, then settled down, like she was making a turn. I think she's heading this way—that's a little shaky.

And we have some more noise to the northeast. Too confused to make any sense of just now. We're working on it."

"Okay, nice work, Jonesy. Keep at it."

"Sure thing, Captain."

Mancuso smiled as he set the phone down, looking over at Mannion. "You know, Pat, sometimes I wonder if Jonesy isn't part witch."

Mannion looked at the paper tracks that Goodman was drawing to back up the computerized targeting process. "He's pretty good. Problem is, he thinks we work for him."

"Right now we are working for him." Jones was their eyes and ears, and Mancuso was damned glad to have him.

"Chuck?" Mancuso asked Lieutenant Goodman.

"Bearing still constant on all three contacts, sir." Which probably meant they were heading for the *Dallas*. It also meant that they could not develop the range data necessary for a fire control solution. Not that anyone wanted to shoot, but this was the point of the exercise.

"Pat, let's get some sea room. Move us about ten miles east," Mancuso ordered casually. There were two reasons for this. First, it would establish a base line from which to compute probable target range. Second, the deeper water would make for better acoustical conditions, opening up to them the distant sonar convergence zones. The captain studied the chart as his navigator gave the necessary orders, evaluating the tactical situation.

Bartolomeo Mancuso was the son of a barber who closed his shop in Cicero, Illinois, every fall to hunt deer on Michigan's Upper Peninsula. Bart had accompanied his father on these hunts, shot his first deer at the age of twelve and every year thereafter until entering the Naval Academy. He had never bothered after that. Since becoming an officer on nuclear submarines he had learned a much more diverting game. Now he hunted people.

Two hours later an alarm bell went off on the ELF radio in the sub's communications room. Like all nuclear submarines, the *Dallas* was trailing a lengthy wire antenna attuned to the extremely low-frequency transmitter in the central United States. The channel had a frustratingly narrow data band width. Unlike a TV channel, which transmitted thousands of bits of data per frame, thirty frames per second, the ELF radio passed on data slowly, about one character every thirty seconds. The duty radioman waited patiently while the information was recorded on tape. When the message was finished, he ran the tape at high speed and transcribed the message, handing it to the communications officer who was waiting with his code book.

The signal was actually not a code but a "one-time-pad" cipher. A book, published every six months and distributed to every nuclear submarine, was filled with randomly generated transpositions for each letter of the signal. Each scrambled three-letter group in this book corresponded to a pre-selected word or phrase in another book. Deciphering the message by hand took under three minutes, and when that was completed it was carried to the captain in the attack center.

NHG	JPR	YTR
FROM COMSUBLANT	TO LANTSUBS AT SEA	STANDBY
OPY TBD	QEQ	GER
POSSIBLE MAJOR	REDEPLOYMENT ORDER	LARGE-SCALE
MAL	ASF	NME
UNEXPECTED	REDFLEET OPERATION	IN PROGRESS
TYQ	ORV	
NATURE UNKNOWN	NEXT ELF MESSAGE	
HWZ		
COMMUNICATE SSIX		

COMSUBLANT—commander of the Submarine Force in the Atlantic—was Mancuso's big boss, Vice Admiral Vincent Gallery. The old man was evidently contemplating a reshuffling of his entire force, no minor affair. The next wake-up signal, AAA—encrypted, of course—would alert them to go to periscope-antenna depth to get more detailed instructions from SSIX, the submarine satellite information exchange, a geosynchronous communications satellite used exclusively by submarines.

The tactical situation was becoming clearer, though its strategic implications were beyond his ability to judge. The ten-mile move eastward had given them adequate range information for their initial three contacts and another *Alfa* which had turned up a few minutes later. The first of the contacts, *Vic 6*, was now within torpedo range. A Mark 48 was locked in on her, and there was no way that her skipper could know the *Dallas* was here. *Vic 6* was a deer in his sights—but it wasn't hunting season.

Though not much faster than the *Victors* and *Charlies*, and ten knots slower than the smaller *Alfas*, the *Dallas* and her sisters could move almost silently at nearly twenty knots. This was a triumph of engineering and design, the product of decades of work. But moving without being detected was useful only if the hunter could at the same time detect his quarry. Sonars lost effectiveness as their carrier platform increased speed. The *Dallas'* BQQ-5 retained twenty percent effectiveness at twenty knots, nothing to cheer about. Submarines running at high speed from one point to another were blind and unable to harm anyone. As a result, the operating pattern of an attack submarine was much like that of a combat infantryman. With a rifleman it was called dash-and-cover; with a sub, sprint-and-drift. After detecting a target, a sub would race to a more advantageous position, stop to reacquire her prey, then dash again until a firing position had been achieved. The sub's quarry would be moving too, and if the submarine could gain position in front of it, she had then only to lie in wait like a great hunting cat to strike.

The submariner's trade required more than skill. It required instinct, and an artist's touch; monomaniacal confidence, and the aggressiveness of a professional boxer. Mancuso had all of these things. He had spent fifteen years learning his craft, watching a generation of commanders as a junior officer, listening carefully at the frequent round-table discussions which made submarining a very human profession, its lessons passed on by verbal tradition. Time on shore had been spent training in a variety of computerized simulators, attending seminars, comparing notes and ideas with his peers. Aboard surface ships and ASW aircraft he learned how the "enemy"—the surface sailors—played his own hunting game.

Submariners lived by a simple motto: There are two kinds of ships, submarines . . . and targets. What would *Dallas* be hunting? Mancuso wondered. Russian subs? Well, if that was the game and the Russians kept racing around like this, it ought to be easy enough. He and the *Swiftsure* had just bested a team of NATO ASW experts, men whose countries depended on their ability to keep the sea-lanes open. His boat and his crew were performing as well as any man could ask. In Jones he had one of the ten best sonar operators in the fleet. Mancuso was ready, whatever the game might be. As on the opening day of hunting season, outside considerations were dwindling away. He was becoming a weapon.

★ ★ ★

Bart Mancuso had been on duty in the attack center for more than twenty hours. Only a few hours of sleep separated this stretch from the previous one. He had been eating sandwiches and drinking coffee, and two cups of soup had been thrown in by his cooks for variety's sake. He examined his latest cup of freeze-dried without affection.

"Cap'n?" He turned. It was Roger Thompson, his sonar officer.

"Yes, what is it?" Mancuso pulled himself away from the tactical display that had occupied his attention for several days. Thompson was standing at the rear of the compartment. Jones was standing beside him holding a clipboard and what looked like a tape machine.

"Sir, Jonesy has something I think you ought to look at."

Mancuso didn't want to be bothered—extended time on duty always taxed his patience. But Jones looked eager and excited. "Okay, come on over to the chart table."

The *Dallas'* chart table was a new gadget wired into the BC-10 and projected onto a TV-type glass screen four feet square. The display moved as the *Dallas* moved. This made paper charts obsolete, though they were kept anyway. Charts can't break.

"Thanks, Skipper," Jones said, more humbly than usual. "I know you're kinda busy, but I think I got something here. That anomalous contact we had the other day's been bothering me. I had to leave it after the ruckus the other Russkie subs kicked up, but I was able to come back to it three times to make sure it was still there. The fourth time it was gone, faded out. I want to show you what I worked up. Can you punch up our course track for back then on this baby, sir?"

The chart table was interfaced through the BC-10 into the ship's inertial navigation system, SINS. Mancuso punched the command in himself. It was getting so that you couldn't flush the head without a computer command . . . The *Dallas'* course track showed up as a convoluted red line, with tick marks displayed at fifteen-minute intervals.

"Great!" Jones commented. "I've never seen it do that before. That's all right. Okay." Jones pulled a handful of pencils from his back pocket. "Now, I got the contact first at 0915 or so, and the bearing was about two-six-nine." He set a pencil down, eraser at *Dallas'* position, point directed west towards the target. "Then at 0930 it was bearing two-six-zero. At 0948, it was two-five-zero. There's some error built into these, Cap'n. It was a tough signal to lock in on, but the errors should average out. Right about then we got all this other activity, and I had to go after them, but I came back to it about 1000, and the bearing was two-four-two." Jones set down another pencil on the due-east line traced when the *Dallas* had moved away from the Icelandic coast. "At 1015 it was two-three-four, and at 1030 it was two-two-seven. These last two are shaky, sir. The signal was real faint, and I didn't have a very good lock on it." Jones looked up. He appeared nervous.

"So far, so good. Relax, Jonesy. Light up if you want."

"Thanks, Cap'n." Jones fished out a cigarette and lit it with a butane lighter. He had never approached the captain quite this way. He knew Mancuso to be a tolerant, easygoing commander—if you had something to say. He was not a man who liked his time wasted, and it was sure as hell he wouldn't want it wasted now. "Okay, sir, we gotta figure he couldn't be too far away from us, right? I mean, he had to be between us and Iceland. So let's say he was about halfway between. That gives him a course about like this." Jones set down some more pencils.

"Hold it, Jonesy. Where does the course come from?"

"Oh, yeah." Jones flipped open his clipboard. "Yesterday morning, night, whatever it was, after I got off watch, it started bothering me, so I used the move we made offshore as a baseline to do a little course track for him. I know how, Skipper. I read the manual. It's easy, just like we used to do at Cal Tech to chart star motion. I took an astronomy course in my freshman year."

Mancuso stifled a groan. It was the first time he had ever heard this called easy, but on looking at Jones' figures and diagrams, it appeared that he had done it right. "Go on."

Jones pulled a Hewlett Packard scientific calculator from his pocket and what looked like a National Geographic map liberally coated with pencil marks and scribblings. "You want to check my figures, sir?"

"We will, but I'll trust you for now. What's the map?"

"Skipper, I know it's against the rules an' all, but I keep this as a personal record of the tracks the bad guys use. It doesn't leave the boat, sir, honest. I may be a little off, but all this translates to a course of about two-two-zero and a speed of ten knots. And that aims him right at the entrance of Route One. Okay?"

"Go on." Mancuso had already figured that one. Jonesy was on to something.

"Well, I couldn't sleep after that, so I skipped back to sonar and pulled the tape on the contact. I had to run it through the computer a few times to filter out all the crap—sea sounds, the other subs, you know—then I rerecorded it at ten times normal speed." He set his cassette recorder on the chart table. "Listen to this, Skipper."

The tape was scratchy, but every few seconds there was a thrum. Two minutes of listening seemed to indicate a regular interval of about five seconds. By this time Lieutenant Mannion was looking over Thompson's shoulder, listening, and nodding speculatively.

"Skipper, that's gotta be a man-made sound. It's just too regular for anything else. At normal speed it didn't make much sense, but once I speeded it up, I had the sucker."

"Okay, Jonesy, finish it," Mancuso said.

"Captain, what you just heard was the acoustical signature of a Russian submarine. He was heading for Route One, taking the inshore track off the Icelandic cost. You can bet money on that, Skipper."

"Roger?"

"He sold me, Captain," Thompson replied.

Mancuso took another look at the course track, trying to figure an alternative. There wasn't any. "Me, too. Roger, Jonesy makes sonarman first class today. I want to see the paper work done by the turn of the next watch, along with a nice letter of commendation for my signature. Ron," he poked the sonarman in the shoulder, "that's all right. Damned well done!"

"Thanks, Skipper." Jones' smile stretched from ear to ear.

"Pat, please call Lieutenant Butler to the attack center."

Mannion went to the phone to call the boat's chief engineer.

"Any idea of what it is, Jonesy?" Mancuso turned back.

The sonarman shook his head. "It isn't screw sounds. I've never heard anything like it." He ran the tape back and played it again.

Two minutes later, Lieutenant Earl Butler came into the attack center. "You rang, Skipper?"

"Listen to this, Earl." Mancuso rewound the tape and played it a third time.

Butler was a graduate of the University of Texas and every school the navy had for submarines and their engine systems. "What's that supposed to be?"

"Jonesy says it's a Russian sub. I think he's right."

"Tell me about the tape," Butler said to Jones.

"Sir, it's speeded up ten times, and I washed it through the BC-10 five times. At normal speed it doesn't sound like much of anything." With uncharacteristic modesty, Jones did not point out that it had sounded like something to him.

"Some sort of harmonic? I mean, if it was a propeller, it'd have to be a hundred feet across, and we'd be hearing one blade at a time. The regular interval suggests some sort of harmonic." Butler's face screwed up. "But a harmonic what?"

"Whatever it was, it was headed right here." Mancuso tapped Thor's Twins with his pencil.

"That makes him a Russian, all right," Butler agreed. "Then they're using something new. Again."

"Mr. Butler's right," Jones said. "It does sound like a harmonic rumble. The other funny thing is, well, there was this background noise, kinda like water going through a pipe. I don't know, it didn't pick up on this. I guess the computer filtered it off. It was real faint to start with—anyway, that's outside my field."

"That's all right. You've done enough for one day. How do you feel?" Mancuso asked.

"A little tired, Skipper. I've been working on this for a while."

"If we get close to this guy again, you think you can track him down?" Mancuso knew the answer.

"You bet, Cap'n. Now that we know what to listen for, you bet I'll bag the sucker!"

Mancuso looked at the chart table. "Okay, if he was heading for the Twins, and then ran the route at, say twenty-eight or thirty knots, and then settled down to his base course and speed of about ten or so . . . that puts him about here now. Long ways off. Now, if we run at top speed . . . forty-eight hours will put us here, and that'll put us in front of him. Pat?"

"That's about right, sir," Lieutenant Mannion concurred. "You're figuring he ran the route at full speed and then settled down—makes sense. He wouldn't need the quiet drive in that damned maze. It gives him a free shot for four or five hundred miles, so why not uncrank his engines? That's what I'd do."

"That's what we'll try and do, then. We'll radio in for permission to leave Toll Booth station and track this character down. Jonesy, running at max speed means you sonarmen will be out of work for a while. Set up the contact tape on the simulator and make sure the operators all know what this guy sounds like, but get some rest. All of you. I want you at a hundred percent when we try to reacquire this guy. Have yourself a shower. Make that a Hollywood shower—you've earned it—and rack out. When we do go after this character, it'll be a long, tough hunt."

"No sweat, Captain. We'll get him for you. Bet on it. You want to keep my tape, sir?"

"Yeah." Mancuso ejected the tape and looked up in surprise. "You sacrificed a Bach for this?"

"Not a good one, sir. I have a Christopher Hogwood of this piece that's much better."

Mancuso pocketed the tape. "Dismissed, Jonesy. Nice work."

"A pleasure, Cap'n." Jones left the attack center counting the extra money for jumping a rate.

"Roger, make sure your people are well rested over the next two days. When we do go after this guy, it's going to be a bastard."

"Aye, Captain."

"Pat, get us up to periscope depth. We're going to call this one into Norfolk right now. Earl, I want you thinking about what's making that noise."

"Right, Captain."

While Mancuso drafted his message, Lieutenant Mannion brought the *Dallas* to periscope-antenna depth with an upward angle on the diving planes. It took five minutes to get from five hundred feet to just below the stormy surface. The submarine was subject to wave action, and while it was very gentle by surface ship standards, the crew noted her rocking. Mannion raised the periscope and ESM (electronic support measures) antenna, the latter used for the broad-band receiver designed to detect possible radar emissions. There was nothing in view—he could see about five miles—and the ESM instruments showed nothing except for aircraft sets, which were too far away to matter. Next Mannion raised two more masts. One was a reedlike UHF (ultrahigh frequency) receiving antenna. The other was new, a laser transmitter. This rotated and locked onto the carrier wave signal of the Atlantic SSIX, the communications satellite used exclusively by submarines. With the laser, they could send high-density transmissions without giving away the sub's position.

"All ready, sir," the duty radioman reported.

"Transmit."

The radioman pressed a button. The signal, sent in a fraction of a second, was received by photovoltaic cells, read over to a UHF transmitter, and shot back down by a parabolic dish antenna towards Atlantic Fleet Communications headquarters. At Norfolk another radioman noted the reception and pressed a button that transmitted the same signal up to the satellite and back to the *Dallas*. It was a simple way to identify garbles.

The *Dallas* operator compared the received signal with the one he'd just sent. "Good copy, sir."

Mancuso ordered Mannion to lower everything but the ESM and UHF antennae.

Atlantic Fleet Communications
In Norfolk the first line of the dispatch revealed the page and line of the one-time-pad cipher sequence, which was recorded on computer tape in the maximum security section of the communications complex. An officer typed

the proper numbers into his computer terminal, and an instant later the machine generated a clear text. The officer checked it again for garbles. Satisfied there were none, he took the printout to the other side of the room where a yeoman was seated at a telex. The officer handed him the dispatch.

The yeoman keyed up the proper addressee and transmitted the message by dedicated landline to COMSUBLANT Operations, half a mile away. The landline was fiber optic, located in a steel conduit under a paved street. It was checked three times a week for security purposes. Not even the secrets of nuclear weapons performance were as closely guarded as day-to-day tactical communications.

COMSUBLANT *Operations*
A bell went off in the operations room as the message came up on the "hot" printer. It bore a Z prefix, which indicated FLASH-priority status.

> Z090414ZDEC
> TOP SECRET THEO
> FM: USS DALLAS
> TO: COMSUBLANT
> INFO: CINCLANTFLT
> //NOOOOO//
> REDFLEET SUBOPS
> 1. REPORT ANOMALOUS SONAR CONTACT ABOUT 0900Z 7DEC AND LOST AFTER INCREASE IN REDFLEET SUB ACTIVITY. CONTACT SUBSEQUENTLY EVALUATED AS REDFLEET SSN/SSBN TRANSITING ICELAND INSHORE TRACK TOWARDS ROUTE ONE. COURSE SOUTHWEST SPEED TEN DEPTH UNKNOWN.
> 2. CONTACT EVIDENCED UNUSUAL REPEAT UNUSUAL ACOUSTICAL CHARACTERISTICS. SIGNATURE UNLIKE ANY KNOWN REDFLEET SUBMARINE.
> 3. REQUEST PERMISSION TO LEAVE TOLL BOOTH TO PURSUE AND INVESTIGATE. BELIEVE A NEW DRIVE SYSTEM WITH UNUSUAL SOUND CHARACTERISTICS BEING USED THIS SUB. BELIEVE GOOD PROBABILITY CAN LOCATE AND IDENTIFY.

A lieutenant junior grade took the dispatch to the office of Vice Admiral Vincent Gallery. COMSUBLANT had been on duty since the Soviet subs had started moving. He was in an evil mood.

"A FLASH priority from *Dallas*, sir."

"Uh-huh." Gallery took the yellow form and read it twice. "What do you supposed this means?"

"No telling, sir. Looks like he heard something, took his time figuring it out, and wants another crack at it. He seems to think he's onto something unusual."

"Okay, what do I tell him? Come on, mister. You might be an admiral yourself someday and have to make decisions." An unlikely prospect, Gallery thought.

"Sir, *Dallas* is in an ideal position to shadow their surface force when it gets to Iceland. We need her where she is."

"Good textbook answer." Gallery smiled up at the youngster, preparing to cut him off at the knees. "On the other hand, *Dallas* is commanded by a fairly competent man who wouldn't be bothering us unless he really thought he had something. He doesn't go into specifics, probably because it's too complicated for a tactical FLASH dispatch, and also because he thinks that we know his judgment is good enough to take his word on something. 'New drive system with unusual sound characteristics.' That may be a crock, but he's the man on the scene, and he wants an answer. We tell him yes."

"Aye aye, sir," the lieutenant said, wondering if the skinny old bastard made decisions by flipping a coin when his back was turned.

The Dallas

Z090432ZDEC
TOP SECRET
FM: COMSUBLANT
TO: USS DALLAS
A. USS DALLAS Z090414ZDEC
B. COMSUBLANT INST 2000.5
OPAREA ASSIGNMENT //N04220//
1. REQUEST REF A GRANTED.
2. AREAS BRAVO ECHO GOLF REF B ASSIGNED FOR UNRESTRICTED OPS 090500Z TO 140001Z. REPORT AS NECESSARY.   VADM GALLERY SENDS.

"Hot damn!" Mancuso chuckled. That was one nice thing about Gallery. When you asked him a question, by God, you got answer, yes or no, before you could rig your antenna in. Of course, he reflected, if it turned out that Jonesy was wrong and this was a wild-goose chase, he's have some explaining to do. Gallery had handed more than one sub skipper his head in a bag and set him on the beach.

Which was where he was headed regardless, Mancuso knew. Since his first year at Annapolis all he had ever wanted was command of his own attack boat. He had that now, and he knew that the rest of his career would be downhill. In the rest of the navy your first command was just that, a first command. You could move up the ladder and command a fleet at sea eventually, if you were lucky and had the right stuff. Not submariners, though. Whether he did well with the *Dallas* or poorly, he'd lose her soon enough. He had this one and only chance. And afterwards, what? The best he could hope for was command of a missile boat. He'd served on those before and was sure that commanding one, even a new *Ohio*, was about as exciting as watching paint dry. The boomer's job was to stay hidden. Mancuso wanted to be the hunter, that was the exciting end of the business. And after commanding a missile boat? He could get a "major surface command," perhaps a nice oiler— it would be like switching mounts from Secretariat to Elsie the Cow. Or he could get a squadron command and sit in an office onboard a tender, pushing paper. At best in that position he'd go to sea once a month, his main purpose being to bother sub skippers who didn't want him there. Or he could get a desk job in the Pentagon—what fun! Mancuso understood why some of the astronauts had cracked up after coming back from the moon. He, too, had worked many years for this command, and in another year his boat would be gone. He'd have to give the *Dallas* to someone else. But he did have her now.

"Pat, let's lower all masts and take her down to twelve hundred feet."

"Aye aye, sir. Lower the masts," Mannion ordered. A petty officer pulled on the hydraulic control levers.

"ESM and UHF masts lowered, sir," the duty electrician reported.

"Very well. Diving officer, make your depth twelve hundred feet."

"Twelve hundred feet, aye," the diving officer responded. "Fifteen degrees down-angle on the planes."

"Fifteen degrees down, aye,"

"Let's move her, Pat."

"Aye, Skipper. All ahead full."

"All ahead full, aye." The helmsman reached up to turn the annunciator.

Mancuso watched his crew at work. They did their jobs with mechanistic precision. But they were not machines. They were men. His.

In the reactor spaces aft, Lieutenant Butler had his enginemen acknowledge the command and gave the necessary orders. The reactor coolant pumps went to fast speed. An increased amount of hot, pressurized water entered the exchanger, where its heat was transferred to the steam on the outside loop. When the coolant returned to the reactor it was cooler than it had been and therefore denser. Being denser, it trapped more neutrons in the reactor pile, increasing the ferocity of the fission reaction and giving off yet more power. Farther aft, saturated steam in the "outside" or nonradioactive loop of the heat exchange system emerged through clusters of control valves to strike the blades of the high-pressure turbine. The *Dallas'* huge bronze screw began to turn more quickly, driving her forward and down.

The engineers went about their duties calmly. The noise in the engine spaces rose noticeably as the systems began to put out more power, and the technicians kept track of this by continuously monitoring the banks of instruments under their hands. The routine was quiet and exact. There was no extraneous conversation, no distraction. Compared to a submarine's reactor spaces, a hospital operating room was a den of libertines.

Forward, Mannion watched the depth gauge go below six hundred feet. The diving officer would wait until they got to nine hundred feet before starting to level off, the object being to zero the dive out exactly at the ordered depth. Commander Mancuso wanted the *Dallas* below the thermocline. This was the border between differing temperatures. Water settled in isothermal layers of uniform stratification. The relatively flat boundary where warmer surface water met colder deep water was a semipermeable barrier which tended to reflect sound waves. Those waves that did manage to penetrate the thermocline were mostly trapped below it. Thus, though the *Dallas* was now running below the thermocline at over thirty knots and making as much noise as she was capable of, she would still be difficult to detect with surface sonar. She would also be largely blind, but then, there was not much down there to run into.

Mancuso lifted the microphone for the PA system. "This is the captain speaking. We have just started a speed run that will last forty-eight hours. We are heading towards a point where we hope to locate a Russian sub that went past us two days ago. This Russkie is evidently using a new and rather quiet propulsion system that nobody's run across before. We're going to try and get ahead of him and track on him as he passes us again. This time we know what to listen for, and we'll get a nice clear picture of him. Okay, I want everyone on this boat to be well rested. When we get there, it'll be a long, tough hunt. I want everybody at a hundred percent. This one will probably be interesting." He switched off the microphone. "What's the movie tonight?"

The diving officer watched the depth gauge stop moving before answering. As chief of the boat, he was also manager of the *Dallas'* cable TV system, three video-cassette recorders in the mess room which led to televisions in the wardroom, and various other crew accommodations. "Skipper, you got a choice. *Return of the Jedi* or two football tapes: Oklahoma-Nebraska and Miami-Dallas. Both those games were played while we were on the exercise sir. It'll be like watching them live." He laughed. "Commercials and all. The cooks are already making the popcorn."

"Good. I want everybody nice and loose." Why couldn't they ever get Navy tapes, Mancuso wondered. Of course, Army had creamed them this year . . .

"Morning, Skipper." Wally Chambers, the executive officer, came into the attack center. "What gives?"

"Come on back to the wardroom, Wally. I want you to listen to something." Mancuso took the cassette from his shirt pocket and led Chambers aft.

"The South Pole"

BY JULES VERNE

(Excerpted from the novel *20,000 Leagues Under the Sea*)

Welcome aboard the granddaddy of all submarine stories—the Jules Verne
sci-fi epic first published in 1869. Does the prose still hold the reader, or has
it become mellow and quaint? For this reader and editor, the thrill is still
there. Not only in the action passages, but in his observations of the natural
world about him, Jules Verne still ranks as a superb storyteller. *20,000 Leagues*
is a classic, deserving every page we have given it in this collection. In this excerpt, the story's narrator, Professor Pierre Aronnax is a virtual prisoner
aboard the colossal undersea vessel *Nautilus*, commanded by the mysterious
genius Captain Nemo. As the excerpt begins, *Nautilus* is nearing the latest of
its fantastic oceanic objectives—the South Pole.

I rushed on to the platform. Yes! the open sea, with but a few scattered
pieces of ice and moving icebergs;—a long stretch of sea; a world of
birds in the air, and myriads of fishes under those waters, which varied
from intense blue to olive green, according to the bottom. The thermometer marked three degrees centigrade above zero. It was comparatively
spring, shut up as we were behind this iceberg, whose lengthened mass was
dimly seen on our northern horizon.

    "Are we at the pole?" I asked the Captain, with a beating heart.

    "I do not know," he replied. "At noon I will take our bearings."

"But will the sun show himself through this fog?" said I, looking at the leaden sky.

"However little it shows, it will be enough," replied the Captain.

About ten miles south, a solitary island rose to a height of one hundred and four yards. We made for it, but carefully, for the sea might be strewn with banks. One hour afterwards we had reached it, two hours later we had made the round of it. It measured four or five miles in circumference. A narrow canal separated it from a considerable stretch of land, perhaps a continent, for we could not see its limits. The existence of this land seemed to give some colour to Maury's hypothesis. The ingenious American has remarked, that between the south pole and the sixtieth parallel, the sea is covered with floating ice of enormous size, which is never met with in the North Atlantic. From this fact he has drawn the conclusion that the antarctic circle encloses considerable continents, as icebergs cannot form in open sea, but only on the coasts. According to these calculations, the mass of ice surrounding the southern pole forms a vast cap, the circumference of which must be, at least, 2500 miles. But the *Nautilus*, for fear of running aground, had stopped about three cables' length from a strand over which reared a superb heap of rocks. The boat was launched; the Captain, two of his men bearing instruments, Conseil, and myself, were in it. It was ten in the morning. I had not seen Ned Land. Doubtless the Canadian did not wish to admit the presence of the south pole. A few strokes of the oar brought us to the sand, where we ran ashore. Conseil was going to jump on to the land, when I held him back.

"Sir," said I to Captain Nemo, "to you belongs the honour of first setting foot on this land."

"Yes, sir," said the Captain; "and if I do not hesitate to tread this south pole, it is because, up to this time, no human being has left a trace there."

Saying this he jumped lightly on to the sand. His heart beat with emotion. He climbed a rock, sloping to a little promontory, and there, with his arms crossed, mute and motionless, and with an eager look, he seemed to take possession of these southern regions. After five minutes passed in this ecstasy he turned to us.

"When you like, sir."

I landed, followed by Conseil, leaving the two men in the boat. For a long way the soil was composed of a reddish, sandy stone, something like crushed brick, scoriae, streams of lava, and pumice stones. One could not mistake its volcanic origin. In some parts, slight curls of smoke emitted a sulphurous smell, proving that the internal fires had lost nothing of their expansive powers, though, having climbed a high acclivity, I could see no volcano for a radius of several miles. We know that in those antarctic countries, James Ross found two craters, the Erebus and Terror, in full activity, on the 167th meridian, latitude 77°32'. The vegetation of this desolate continent seemed to me much restricted. Some lichens of the species unsnea melanoxantha lay upon the black rocks; some microscopic plants, rudimentary diatomas, a kind of cells, placed between two quartz shells; long purple and scarlet fucus, supported on little swimming bladders, which the breaking of the waves brought to the shore. These constituted the meagre flora of this region. The shore was strewn with molluscs, little mussels, limpets, smooth bucards in the shape of a heart, and particularly some clios, with oblong membranous bodies, the head of which was formed of two rounded lobes. I also saw myriads of northern clios, one and a quarter inches long, of which a whale would swallow a whole world at a mouthful; and some charming pteropods, perfect sea-butterflies, animating the waters on the skirts of the shore.

Amongst other zoophytes, there appeared on the high bottoms some coral shrubs, of that kind which, according to James Ross, live in the antarctic seas to the depth of more than 1000 yards. Then there were little kingfishers, belonging to the species procellaria pelagica, as well as a large number of asteriads, peculiar to these climates, and starfish studding the soil. But where life abounded most was in the air. There, thousands of birds fluttered and flew of all kinds, deafening us with their cries; others crowded the rocks, looking at us as we passed by without fear, and pressing familiarly close by our feet. There were penguins, so agile in the water, that they have been taken for the rapid bonitos, heavy and awkward as they are on the ground; they were uttering harsh cries, a large assembly, sober in gesture, but extravagant in clamour. Amongst the birds I noticed the chionis, of the long-legged family, as large as pigeons, white, with a short conical beak, and the eye framed in a red circle. Conseil laid in a stock of them, for these winged creatures, properly prepared, make an agreeable meat. Albatrosses passed in the air (the expanse of their wings being at least four yards and a half), and justly called the vultures of the ocean; some gigantic petrels, and some damiers, a kind of small duck, the under part of whose body is black and white; then there were a whole series of petrels, some whitish, with brown-bordered wings, other blue, peculiar to the antarctic seas, and so oily, as I told Conseil, that the inhabitants of the Ferroe Islands had nothing to do before lighting them, but to put a wick in.

"A little more," said Conseil, "and they would be perfect lamps! after that, we cannot expect Nature to have previously furnished them with wicks!"

About half a mile further on, the soil was riddled with ruffs' nests, a sort of laying ground, out of which many birds were issuing. Captain Nemo had some hundreds hunted. They uttered a cry like the braying of an ass, were about the size of a goose, slate colour on the body, white beneath, with a yellow line round their throats; they allowed themselves to be killed with a stone, never trying to escape. But the fog did not lift, and at eleven the sun had not yet shown itself. Its absence made me uneasy. Without it no observations were possible. How, then, could we decide whether we had reached the pole? When I rejoined Captain Nemo, I found him leaning on a piece of rock, silently watching the sky. He seemed impatient and vexed. But what was to be done? This rash and powerful man could not command the sun as he did the sea. Noon arrived without the orb of day showing itself for an instant. We could not even tell its position behind the curtain of fog; and soon the fog turned to snow.

"Till to-morrow," said the Captain, quietly, and we returned to the *Nautilus* amid these atmospheric disturbances.

The tempest of snow continued till the next day. It was impossible to remain on the platform. From the saloon, where I was taking notes of incidents happening during this excursion to the polar continent, I could hear the cries of petrels and albatrosses sporting in the midst of this violent storm. The *Nautilus* did not remain motionless, but skirted the coast, advancing ten miles more to the south in the half light left by the sun as it skirted the edge of the horizon. The next day, the 20th of March, the snow had ceased. The cold was a little greater, the thermometer showing two degrees below zero. The fog was rising, and I hoped that that day our observations might be taken. Captain Nemo not having yet appeared, the boat took Conseil and myself to land. The soil was still of the same volcanic nature; everywhere were traces of lava, scoriae, and basalt; but the crater which had vomited them I could not see. Here, as lower down, this continent was alive with myriads of birds. But their rule was now divided with large troops of sea-mammals, looking at us with their soft eyes. There were several kinds of seals, some stretched on the earth, some on flakes of ice, many going in and out of the sea. They did not flee at our approach, never having had anything to do with man; and I reckoned that there were provisions there for hundreds of vessels.

"Sir," said Conseil, "will you tell me the names of these creatures?"

"They are seals and morses."

It was now eight in the morning. Four hours remained to us before the sun could be observed with advantage. I directed our steps towards a vast bay cut in the steep granite shore. There, I can aver that earth and ice were lost to sight by the numbers of sea-mammals covering them, and I involuntarily sought for old Proteus, the mythological shepherd who watched these immense flocks of Neptune. There were more seals than anything else, forming distinct groups, male and female, the father watching over his family, the mother suckling her little ones, some already strong enough to go a few steps. When they wished to change their place, they took little jumps, made by the contraction of their bodies, and helped awkwardly enough by their imperfect fin, which, as with the lamantin, their congener, forms a perfect forearm. I should say that, in the water, which is their element—the spine of these creatures is flexible—with smooth and close skin, and webbed feet, they swim admirably. In resting on the earth they take the most graceful attitudes. Thus the ancients, observing their soft and expressive looks, which cannot be surpassed by the most beautiful look a women can give, their clear voluptuous eyes, their charming positions, and the poetry of their manners, metamorphosed them, the male into a triton and the female into a mermaid. I made Conseil notice the considerable development of the lobes of the brain in these interesting cetaceans. No mammal, except man, has such a quantity of cerebral matter; they are also capable of receiving a certain amount of education, are easily domesticated, and I think, with other naturalists, that, if properly taught, they would be of great service as fishing-dogs. The greater part of them slept on the rocks or on the sand. Amongst these seals, properly so called, which have no external ears (in which they differ from the otter, whose ears are prominent), I noticed several varieties of stenorhynchi about three yards long, with a white coat, bulldog heads, armed with teeth in both jaws, four incisors at the top and four at the bottom, and two large canine teeth in the shape of a "fleur-de-lis." Amongst them glided sea-elephants, a kind of seal, with short flexible trunks. The giants of this species measured twenty feet round, and ten yards and a half in length; but they did not move as we approached.

"These creatures are not dangerous?" asked Conseil.

"No; not unless you attack them. When they have to defend their young, their rage is terrible, and it is not uncommon for them to break the fishing-boats to pieces."

"They are quite right," said Conseil.

"I do not say they are not."

Two miles further on we were stopped by the promontory which shelters the bay from the southerly winds. Beyond it we heard loud bellowings such as a troop of ruminants would produce.

"Good!" said Conseil; "a concert of bulls!"

"No; a concert of walruses."

"They are fighting!"

"They are either fighting or playing."

We now began to climb the blackish rocks, amid unforeseen stumbles, and over stones which the ice made slippery. More than once I rolled over at the expense of my loins. Conseil, more prudent or more steady, did not stumble, and helped me up, saying—

"If, sir, you would have the kindness to take wider steps, you would preserve your equilibrium better."

Arrived at the upper ridge of the promontory, I saw a vast white plain covered with walruses. They were playing amongst themselves, and what we heard were bellowings of pleasure, not of anger.

As I passed near these curious animals, I could examine them leisurely, for they did not move. Their skins were thick and rugged, of a yellowish tint, approaching to red; their hair was short and scant. Some of them were four yards and a quarter long. Quieter, and less timid than those of the north, they did not, like them, place sentinels round the outskirts of their encampment. After examining this city of walruses, I began to think of returning. It was eleven o'clock, and if Captain Nemo found the conditions favourable for observations, I wished to be present at the operation. We followed a narrow pathway running along the summit of the steep shore. At half-past eleven we had reached the place where we landed. The boat had run aground, bringing the Captain. I saw him standing on a block of basalt, his instruments near him, his eyes fixed on the northern horizon, near which the sun was then describing a lengthened curve. I took my place beside him, and waited without speaking. Noon arrived, and, as before, the sun did not appear. It was a fatality. Observations were still wanting. If not accomplished tomorrow, we must give up all idea of taking any. We were indeed exactly at the 20th of March. Tomorrow, the 21st, would be the equinox; the sun would disappear behind the horizon for six months, and with its disappearance the long polar night would begin. Since the September equinox it had emerged from the northern horizon, rising by lengthened spirals up to the 21st of December. At this period, the summer solstice of the northern regions, it had begun to descend; and tomorrow was to shed its last rays upon them. I communicated my fears and observations to Captain Nemo.

"You are right, M. Aronnax," said he; "if tomorrow I cannot take the altitude of the sun, I shall not be able to do it for six months. But precisely because chance has led me into these seas on the 21st of March, my bearings will be easy to take, if at twelve we can see the sun."

"Why, Captain?"

"Because then the orb of day describes such lengthened curves, that it is difficult to measure exactly its height above the horizon, and grave errors may be made with instruments."

"What will you do then?"

"I shall only use my chronometer," replied Captain Nemo. "If tomorrow, the 21st of March, the disc of the sun, allowing for refraction is exactly cut by the northern horizon, it will show that I am at the south pole."

"Just so," said I. "But this statement is not mathematically correct, because the equinox does not necessarily begin at noon."

"Very likely, sir; but the error will not be a hundred yards, and we do not want more. Till tomorrow then!"

Captain Nemo returned on board. Conseil and I remained to survey the shore, observing and studying until five o'clock. Then I went to bed, not, however, without invoking, like the Indian, the favour of the radiant orb. The next day, the 21st of March, at five in the morning, I mounted the platform. I found Captain Nemo there.

"The weather is lightening a little," said he. "I have some hope. After breakfast we will go on shore, and choose a post for observation."

That point settled, I sought Ned Land. I wanted to take him with me. But the obstinate Canadian refused, and I saw that his taciturnity and his bad humour grew day by day. After all I was not sorry for his obstinacy under the circumstances. Indeed, there were too many seals on shore, and we ought not to lay such temptations in his unreflecting fisherman's way. Breakfast over, we went on shore. The *Nautilus* had gone some miles further up in the night. It was a whole league from the coast, above which reared a sharp peak about five hundred yards high. The boat took with me Captain Nemo, two men of the crew, and the instruments, which consisted of a chronometer, a telescope, and a barometer. While crossing, I saw numerous whales belonging to the three kinds peculiar to the southern seas; the whale, or the English "right whale," which has no dorsal fin; the "humpback," or balaenopteron, with reeved chest, and large whitish fins which, in spite of its name, do not form wings; and the fin-back, of a yellowish brown, the liveliest of all the cetacea. This powerful creature is heard a long way off when he throws to a great height columns of air and vapour, which look like whirlwinds of smoke. These different mammals were disporting themselves in troops in the quiet waters; and I could see that this basin of the antarctic pole served as a place of refuge to the cetacea too closely tracked by the hunters. I also noticed long whitish lines of salpae, a kind of gregarious mollusc, and large medusae floating between the reeds.

At nine we landed; the sky was brightening, the clouds were flying to the south, and the fog seemed to be leaving the cold surface of the waters. Captain Nemo went towards the peak, which he doubtless meant to be his observatory. It was a painful ascent over the sharp lava and the pumice stones, in atmosphere often impregnated with a sulphurous smell from the smoking cracks. For a man unaccustomed to walk on land, the Captain climbed the steep slopes with an agility I never saw equalled, and which a hunter would have envied. We were two hours getting to the summit of this peak, which was half porphyry and half basalt. From thence we looked upon a vast sea, which, towards the north, distinctly traced its boundary line upon the sky. At our feet lay fields of dazzling whiteness. Over our heads a pale azure, free from fog. To the north the disc of the sun seemed like a ball of fire, already horned by the cutting of the horizon. From the bosom of the water rose sheaves of liquid jets by hundreds. In the distance lay the *Nautilus* like a whale asleep on the water.

Behind us, to the south and east, an immense country, and a chaotic heap of rocks and ice, the limits of which were not visible. On arriving at the summit, Captain Nemo carefully took the mean height of the barometer, for he would have to consider that in taking his observations. At a quarter to twelve, the sun, then seen only by reflection, looked like a golden disc shedding its last rays upon this deserted continent, and seas which never man had yet ploughed. Captain Nemo, furnished with a lenticular glass, which, by means of a mirror, corrected the refraction, watched the orb sinking below the horizon by degrees, following a lengthened diagonal. I held the chronometer. My heart beat fast. If the disappearance of the half-disc of the sun coincided with twelve o'clock on the chronometer, we were at the pole itself.

"Twelve!" I exclaimed.

"The South Pole!" replied Captain Nemo, in a grave voice, handing me the glass, which showed the orb cut in exactly equal parts by the horizon.

I looked at the last rays crowning the peak, and the shadows mounting by degrees up its slopes. At that moment Captain Nemo, resting with his hand on my shoulder, said—

"I Captain Nemo, on this 21st day of March, 1868, have reached the south pole on the ninetieth degree; and I take possession of this part of the globe, equal to one-sixth of the known continents."

"In whose name, Captain?"

"In my own, sir!"

Saying which, Captain Nemo unfurled a black banner, bearing an N in gold quartered on its bunting. Then turning towards the orb of day, whose last rays lapped the horizon of the sea, he exclaimed—

"Adieu, sun! Disappear, thou radiant orb! rest beneath this open sea, and let a night of six months spread in shadows over my new domains!"

★ ★ ★

The next day, the 22d of March, at six in the morning, preparations for departure were begun. The last gleams of twilight were melting into night. The cold was great; the constellations shone with wonderful intensity. In the zenith glittered that wondrous Southern Cross—the polar bear of antarctic regions. The thermometer showed twelve degrees below zero, and when the wind freshened, it was most biting. Flakes of ice increased on the open water. The sea seemed everywhere alike. Numerous blackish patches spread on the surface, showing the formation of fresh ice. Evidently the southern basin, frozen during the six winter months, was absolutely inaccessible. What became of the whales in that time? Doubtless they went beneath the icebergs, seeking more practicable seas. As to the seals and morses, accustomed to live in a hard climate, they remained on these icy shores. These creatures have the instinct to break holes in the ice-fields, and to keep them open. To these holes they come for breath; when the birds, driven away by the cold, have emigrated to the north, these sea-mammals remain sole masters of the polar continent. But the reservoirs were filling with water, and the *Nautilus* was slowly descending. At 1000 feet deep it stopped; its screw beat the waves, and it advanced straight towards the north, at a speed of fifteen miles an hour. Towards night it was already floating under the immense body of the iceberg. At three in the morning I was awakened by a violent shock. I sat up in my bed and listened in the darkness, when I was thrown into the middle of the room. The *Nautilus*, after having struck, had rebounded violently. I groped along the partition, and by the staircase to the saloon, which was lit by the luminous ceiling. The furniture was upset. Fortunately the windows were firmly set, and had held fast. The pictures on the starboard-side, from being no longer vertical, were clinging to the paper, whilst those of the port-side were hanging at least a foot from the wall. The *Nautilus* was lying on its starboard side perfectly motionless. I heard footsteps, and a confusion of voices; but Captain Nemo did not appear. As I was leaving the saloon, Ned Land and Conseil entered.

"What is the matter?" said I, at once.

"I came to ask you, sir," replied Conseil.

"Confound it!" exclaimed the Canadian, "I know well enough! The *Nautilus* has struck; and judging by the way she lies, I do not think she will right herself as she did the first time in Torres Straits."

"But," I asked, "has she at least come to the surface of the sea?"

"We do not know," said Conseil.

"It is easy to decide," I answered. I consulted the manometer. To my great surprise it showed a depth of more than 180 fathoms. "What does that mean?" I exclaimed.

"We must ask Captain Nemo," said Conseil.

"But where shall we find him?" said Ned Land.

"Follow me," said I, to my companions.

We left the saloon. There was no one in the library. At the centre staircase, by the berths of the ship's crew, there was no one. I thought that Captain Nemo must be in the pilot's cage. It was best to wait. We all returned to the saloon. For twenty minutes we remained thus, trying to hear the slightest noise which might be made on board the *Nautilus*, when Captain Nemo entered. He seemed not to see us; his face, generally so impassive, showed signs of uneasiness. He watched the compass silently, then the manometer; and going to the planisphere, placed his finger on a spot representing the southern seas. I would not interrupt him; but some minutes later, when he turned towards me, I said, using one of his own expressions in the Torres Straits—

"An incident, Captain?"

"No, sir; an accident this time."

"Serious?"

"Perhaps."

"Is the danger immediate?"

"No."

"The *Nautilus* has stranded?"

"Yes."

"And this has happened—how?"

"From a caprice of nature, not from the ignorance of man. Not a mistake has been made in the working. But we cannot prevent equilibrium from producing its effects. We may brave human laws, but we cannot resist natural ones."

Captain Nemo had chosen a strange moment for uttering this philosophical reflection. On the whole, his answer helped me little.

"May I ask sir, the cause of this accident?"

"An enormous block of ice, a whole mountain, has turned over," he replied. "When icebergs are undermined at their base by warmer water or re-iterated shocks, their centre of gravity rises, and the whole thing turns over. This is what has happened; one of these blocks, as it fell, struck the *Nautilus*, then, gliding under its hull, raised it with irresistible force, bringing it into beds which are not so thick, where it is lying on its side."

"But can we not get the *Nautilus* off by emptying its reservoirs, that it may regain its equilibrium?"

"That, sir, is being done at this moment. You can hear the pump working. Look at the needle of the manometer; it shows that the *Nautilus* is rising, but the block of ice is rising with it; and, until some obstacle stops its ascending motion, our position cannot be altered."

Indeed, the *Nautilus* still held the same position to starboard; doubt-less it would right itself when the block stopped. But at this moment who knows if we may not be frightfully crushed between the two glassy surfaces? I reflected on all the consequences of our position.

Captain Nemo never took his eyes off the manometer. Since the fall of the iceberg, the *Nautilus* had risen about a hundred and fifty feet, but it still made the same angle with the perpendicular. Suddenly a slight movement was felt in the hold. Evidently it was righting a little. Things hanging in the saloon were sensibly returning to their normal position. The partitions were nearing the upright. No one spoke. With beating hearts we watched and felt the straightening. The boards became horizontal under our feet. Ten minutes passed.

"At last we have righted!" I exclaimed.

"Yes," said Captain Nemo, going to the door of the saloon.

"But are we floating?" I asked.

"Certainly," he replied; "since the reservoirs are not empty; and, when empty, the *Nautilus* must rise to the surface of the sea."

We were in open sea; but at a distance of about ten yards, on either side of the *Nautilus*, rose a dazzling wall of ice. Above and beneath the same wall. Above, because the lower surface of the iceberg stretched over us like an immense ceiling. Beneath, because the overturned block, having slid by degrees, had found a resting place on the lateral walls, which kept it in that position. The *Nautilus* was really imprisoned in a perfect tunnel of ice more than twenty yards in breadth, filled with quiet water. It was easy to get out of it by going either forward or backward, and then make a free passage under the iceberg, some hundreds of yards deeper. The luminous ceiling had been extinguished, but the saloon was still resplendent with intense light. It was the powerful reflection from the glass partition sent violently back to the sheets of the lantern. I cannot describe the effect of the voltaic rays upon the great blocks so capriciously cut; upon every angle, every ridge, every facet was thrown a different light, according to the nature of the veins running through the ice; a dazzling mine of gems, particularly of sapphires, their blue rays crossing with the green of the emerald. Here and there were opal shades of wonderful softness, running through bright spots like diamonds of fire, the brilliancy of which the eye could not bear. The power of the lantern seemed increased a hundredfold, like a lamp through the lenticular plates of a first-class lighthouse.

"How beautiful! how beautiful!" cried Conseil.

"Yes," I said, "it is a wonderful sight. Is it not, Ned?"

"Yes, confound it! Yes," answered Ned Land, "it is superb! I am made at being obliged to admit it. No one has ever seen anything like it; but the sight may cost us dear. And if I must say all, I think we are seeing here things which God never intended man to see."

Ned was right, it was too beautiful. Suddenly a cry from Conseil made me turn.

"What is it?" I asked.

"Shut your eyes, sir! do not look, sir!" Saying which, Conseil clapped his hands over his eyes.

"But what is the matter, my boy?"

"I am dazzled, blinded."

My eyes turned involuntarily towards the glass, but I could not stand the fire which seemed to devour them. I understood what had happened. The *Nautilus* had put on full speed. All the quiet lustre of the ice-walls was at once changed into flashes of lightning. The fire from these myriads of diamonds was blinding. It required some time to calm our troubled looks. At last the hands were taken down.

"Faith, I should never have believed it," said Conseil.

It was then five in the morning; and at that moment a shock was felt at the bows of the *Nautilus*. I knew that its spur had struck a block of ice. It must have been a false manoeuvre, for this submarine tunnel, obstructed by blocks, was not very easy navigation. I thought that Captain Nemo, by changing his course, would turn these obstacles, or else follow the windings of the tunnel. In any case, the road before us could not be entirely blocked. But, contrary to my expectations, the *Nautilus* took a decided retrograde motion.

"We are going backwards?" said Conseil.

"Yes," I replied. "This end of the tunnel can have no egress."

"And then?"

"Then," said I, "the working is easy. We must go back again, and go out at the southern opening. That is all."

In speaking thus, I wished to appear more confident than I really was. But the retrograde motion of the *Nautilus* was increasing; and, reversing the screw it carried us at great speed.

"It will be a hindrance," said Ned.

"What does it matter, some hours more or less, provided we get out at last!"

"Yes," repeated Ned Land, "provided we do get out at last!"

For a short time I walked from the saloon to the library. My companions were silent. I soon threw myself on an ottoman and took a book which my eyes overran mechanically. A quarter of an hour after, Conseil, approaching me, said, "Is what you are reading very interesting, sir?"

"Very interesting!" I replied.

"I should think so, sir. It is your own book you are reading."

"My book?"

And indeed I was holding in my hand the work on the "Great Submarine Depths." I did not even dream of it. I closed the book, and returned to my walk. Ned and Conseil rose to go.

"Stay here, my friends," said I, detaining them. "Let us remain together until we are out of this block."

"As you please, sir," Conseil replied.

Some hours passed. I often looked at the instruments hanging from the partition. The manometer showed that the Nautilus kept at a constant depth of more than three hundred yards; the compass still pointed to the south; the log indicated a speed of twenty miles an hour, which, in such cramped space, was very great. But Captain Nemo knew that he could not hasten too much, and that minutes were worth ages to us. At twenty-five minutes past eight a second shock took place, this time from behind. I turned pale. My companions were close by my side. I seized Conseil's hand. Our looks expressed our feelings better than words. At this moment the Captain entered the saloon. I went up to him.

"Our course is barred southward?" I asked.

"Yes, sir. The iceberg has shifted, and closed every outlet."

"We are blocked up, then?"

"Yes."

★ ★ ★

Thus, around the *Nautilus*, above and below, was an impenetrable wall of ice. We were prisoners to the iceberg. I watched the Captain. His countenance had resumed its habitual imperturbability.

"Gentlemen," he said, calmly, "there are two ways of dying in the circumstances in which we are placed." (This inexplicable person had the air of a mathematical professor lecturing to his pupils.) "The first is to be crushed; the second is to die of suffocation. I do not speak of the possibility of dying of hunger, for the supply of provisions in the *Nautilus* will certainly last longer than we shall. Let us then calculate our chances."

"As to suffocation, Captain," I replied, "that is not to be feared, because our reservoirs are full."

"Just so; but they will only yield two days' supply of air. Now, for thirty-six hours we have been hidden under the water, and already the heavy atmosphere of the *Nautilus* requires renewal. In forty-eight hours our reserve will be exhausted."

"Well, Captain, can we be delivered before forty-eight hours?"

"We will attempt it, at least, by piercing the wall that surrounds us."

"On which side?"

"Sound will tell us. I am going to run the *Nautilus* aground on the lower bank, and my men will attack the iceberg on the side that is least thick."

Captain Nemo went out. Soon I discovered by a hissing noise that the water was entering the reservoirs. The *Nautilus* sank slowly, and rested on the ice at a depth of 350 yards, the depth at which the lower bank was immersed.

"My friends," I said, "our situation is serious, but I rely on your courage and energy."

"Sir," replied the Canadian, "I am ready to do anything for the general safety."

"Good! Ned," and I held out my hand to the Canadian.

"I will add," he continued, "that being as handy with the pickaxe as with the harpoon, if I can be useful to the Captain, he can command my services."

"He will not refuse your help. Come, Ned!"

I led him to the room where the crew of the *Nautilus* were putting on their cork-jackets. I told the Captain of Ned's proposal, which he accepted. The Canadian put on his sea-costume, and was ready as soon as his companions. When Ned was dressed, I re-entered the drawing-room, where the panes of glass were open, and, posted near Conseil, I examined the ambient beds that supported the *Nautilus*. Some instants after, we saw a dozen of the crew set foot on the bank of ice, and among them Ned Land, easily known by his stature. Captain Nemo was with them. Before proceeding to dig the walls, he took the soundings, to be sure of working in the right direction. Long sounding lines were sunk in the side walls, but after fifteen yards they were again stopped by the thick wall. It was useless to attack it on the ceiling-like surface, since the iceberg itself measured more than 400 yards in height. Captain Nemo then sounded the lower surface. There ten yards of wall separated us from the water, so great was the thickness of the ice-field. It was necessary, therefore, to cut from it a piece equal in extent to the waterline of the *Nautilus*.

There were about 6000 cubic yards to detach, so as to dig a hole by which we could descend to the ice-field. The work was begun immediately, and carried on with indefatigable energy. Instead of digging round the *Nautilus*, which would have involved greater difficulty, Captain Nemo had an immense trench made at eight yards from the port quarter. Then the men set to work simultaneously with their screws, on several points of its circumference. Presently the pickaxe attacked this compact matter vigorously, and large blocks were detached from the mass. By a curious effect of specific gravity, these blocks, lighter than water, fled, so to speak, to the vault of the tunnel, that increased in thickness at the top in proportion as it diminished at the base. But that mattered little, so long as the lower part grew thinner. After two hours' hard work, Ned Land came in exhausted. He and his comrades were replaced by new workers, whom Conseil and I joined. The second lieutenant of the *Nautilus* superintended us. The water seemed singularly cold, but I soon got warm handling the pickaxe. My movements were free enough, although they were made under a pressure of thirty atmospheres. When I re-entered, after working two hours, to take some food and rest, I found a perceptible difference between the pure fluid with which the Rouquayrol engine supplied me, and the atmosphere of the *Nautilus*, already charged with carbonic acid. The air had not been renewed for forty-eight hours, and its vivifying qualities were considerably enfeebled. However, after a lapse of twelve hours, we had only raised a block of ice one yard thick, on the marked surface, which was about 6000 cubic yards! Reckoning that it took twelve hours to accomplish this much, it would take five nights and four days to bring this enterprise to a satisfactory conclusion. Five nights and four days! And we have only air enough for two days in the reservoirs? "Without taking into account," said Ned, "that, even if we get out of this infernal prison, we shall also be imprisoned under the iceberg, shut out from all possible communication with the atmosphere." True enough! Who could then foresee the minimum of time necessary for our deliverance? We might be suffocated before the *Nautilus* could regain the surface of the waves! Was it destined to perish in this ice-tomb, with all those it enclosed? The situation was terrible. But every one had looked the danger in the face, and each was determined to do his duty to the last.

As I expected, during the night a new block a yard square was carried away, and still further sank the immense hollow. But in the morning when, dressed in my cork-jacket, I traversed the slushy mass at a temperature of six or seven degrees below zero, I remarked that the side walls were gradually closing in. The beds of water farthest from the trench, that were not warmed by the men's mere work, showed a tendency to solidification. In presence of this new and imminent danger, what would become of our chances of safety, and how hinder the solidification of this liquid medium, that would burst the partitions of the *Nautilus* like glass?

I did not tell my companions of this new danger. What was the good of dampening the energy they displayed in the painful work of escape? But when I went on board again, I told Captain Nemo of this grave complication.

"I know it," he said, in that calm tone which could counteract the most terrible apprehensions. "It is one danger more; but I see no way of escaping it; the only chance of safety is to go quicker than solidification. We must be beforehand with it, that is all."

On this day for several hours I used my pickaxe vigorously. The work kept me up. Besides, to work was to quit the *Nautilus*, and breathe directly the pure air drawn from the reservoirs, and supplied by our apparatus, and to quit the impoverished and vitiated atmosphere. Towards evening the trench was dug one yard deeper. When I returned on board, I was nearly suffocated by the carbonic acid with which the air was filled—ah! if we had only the chemical means to drive away this deleterious gas. We had plenty of oxygen; all this water contained a considerable quantity, and by dissolving it with our powerful piles, it would restore the vivifying fluid. I had thought well over it; but of what good was that, since the carbonic acid produced by our respiration had invaded every part of the vessel? To absorb it, it was necessary to fill some jars with caustic potash, and to shake them incessantly. Now this substance was wanting on board and nothing could replace it. On that evening, Captain Nemo ought to open the taps of his reservoirs, and let some pure air into the interior of the *Nautilus*; without this precaution, we could not get rid of the sense of suffocation. The next day, the 26th of March, I resumed my miner's work in beginning the fifth yard. The side walls and the lower surface of the iceberg thickened visibly. It was evident that they would meet before the *Nautilus* was able to disengage itself. Despair seized me for an instant, my pickaxe nearly fell from my hands. What was the good of digging if I must be suffocated, crushed by the water that was turning into stone?—a punishment that the ferocity of the savage even would not have invented! Just then Captain Nemo passed near me. I touched his hand and showed him the walls of our prison. The wall to port had advanced to at least four yards from the hull of the *Nautilus*. The Captain understood me, and signed to me to follow him. We went on board. I took off my cork-jacket, and accompanied him into the dining-room.

"M. Aronnax, we must attempt some desperate means, or we shall be sealed up in this solidified water as in cement."

"Yes; but what is to be done?"

"Ah! if my *Nautilus* were strong enough to bear this pressure without being crushed!"

"Well?" I asked, not catching the Captain's idea.

"Do you not understand," he replied, "that this congelation of water will help us? Do you not see that, by its solidification, it would burst through this field of ice that imprisons us, as, when it freezes, it bursts the hardest stones? Do you not perceive that it would be an agent of safety instead of destruction?"

"Yes, Captain, perhaps. But whatever resistance to crushing the *Nautilus* possesses, it could not support this terrible pressure, and would be flattened like an iron plate."

"I know it, sir. Therefore we must not reckon on the aid of nature, but on our own exertions. We must stop this solidification. Not only will the side walls be pressed together; but there is not ten feet of water before or behind the *Nautilus*. The congelation gains on us on all sides."

"How long will the air in the reservoirs last for us to breathe on board?"

The Captain looked in my face. "After tomorrow they will be empty."

A cold sweat came over me. However, ought I to have been astonished at the answer? On March 22d, the *Nautilus* was in the open polar seas. We were at 26°. For five days we had lived on the reserve on board. And what was left of the respirable air must be kept for the workers. Even now, as I write, my recollection is still so vivid, that an involuntary terror seizes me, and my lungs seem to be without air. Meanwhile Captain Nemo reflected silently, and evidently an idea had struck him; but he seemed to reject it. At last, these words escaped his lips—

"Boiling water!" he muttered.

"Boiling water?" I cried.

"Yes, sir. We are enclosed in a space that is relatively confined. Would not jets of boiling water, constantly injected by the pumps, raise the temperature in this part, and stay the congelation?"

"Let us try it," I said, resolutely.

"Let us try, Professor."

The thermometer then stood at seven degrees outside. Captain Nemo took me to the galleys, where the vast distillatory machines stood that furnished the drinkable water by evaporation. They filled these with water, and all the electric heat from the piles was thrown through the worms bathed in the liquid. In a few minutes this water reached a hundred degrees. It was directed towards the pumps, while fresh water replaced it in proportion. The heat developed by the troughs was such that cold water, drawn up from the sea, after only having gone through the machines, came boiling into the body of the pump. The injection was begun, and three hours after the thermometer marked six degrees below zero outside. One degree was gained. Two hours later, the thermometer only marked four degrees.

"We shall succeed," I said to the Captain, after having anxiously watched the result of the operation.

"I think," he answered, "that we shall not be crushed. We have no more than suffocation to fear."

During the night the temperature of the water rose to one degree below zero. The injections could not carry it to a higher point. But as the

congelation of the sea-water produces at least two degrees, I was at last re-
assured against the dangers of solidification.

The next day, March 27th, six yards of ice had been cleared, four
yards only remaining to be cleared away. There was yet forty-eight hours'
work. The air could not be renewed in the interior of the *Nautilus*. And this
day would make it worse. An intolerable weight oppressed me. Towards three
o'clock in the evening, this feeling rose to a violent degree. Yawns dislocated
my jaws. My lungs panted as they inhaled this burning fluid, which became
rarefied more and more. A mortal torpor took hold of me. I was powerless, almost unconscious. My brave Conseil, though exhibiting the same symptoms
and suffering in the same manner, never left me. He took my hand and en-
couraged me, and I heard him murmur, "Oh, if I could only not breathe, so as
to leave more air for my master!"

Tears came into my eyes on hearing him speak thus. If our situation
to all was intolerable in the interior, with what haste and gladness would we
put on our cork-jackets to work in our turn! Pickaxes sounded on the frozen
ice-beds. Our arms ached, the skin was torn off our hands. But what were
these fatigues, what did the wounds matter? Vital air came to our lungs! we
breathed! we breathed!

All this time, no one prolonged his voluntary task beyond the pre-
scribed time. His task accomplished, each one handed in turn to his panting
companions the apparatus that supplied him with life. Captain Nemo set the
example and submitted first to this severe discipline. When the time came, he
gave up his apparatus to another, and returned to the vitiated air on board,
calm, unflinching, unmurmuring.

On that day the ordinary work was accomplished with unusual
vigour. Only two yards remained to be raised from the surface. Two yards
only separated us from the open sea. But the reservoirs were nearly emptied
of air. The little that remained ought to be kept for the workers; not a particle
for the *Nautilus*. When I went back on board, I was half suffocated. What a
night! I know not how to describe it. The next day my breathing was oppressed. Dizziness accompanied the pain in my head, and made me like a
drunken man. My companions showed the same symptoms. Some of the
crew had rattling in the throat.

On that day, the sixth of our imprisonment, Captain Nemo, finding
the pickaxes work too slowly, resolved to crush the ice-bed that still separated
us from the liquid sheet. This man's coolness and energy never forsook him.
He subdued his physical pains by moral force.

By his orders the vessel was lightened, that is to say, raised from the ice-bed by a change of specific gravity. When it floated they towed it so as to bring it above the immense trench made on the level of the water-line. Then filling his reservoirs of water, he descended and shut himself up in the hole.

Just then all the crew came on board, and the double door of communication was shut. The *Nautilus* then rested on the bed of ice, which was not one yard thick, and which the sounding leads had perforated in a thousand places. The taps of the reservoir were then opened, and a hundred cubic yards of water was let in, increasing the weight of the *Nautilus* 1800 tons. We waited, we listened, forgetting our sufferings in hope. Our safety depended on this last chance. Nothwithstanding the buzzing in my head, I soon heard the humming sound under the hull of the *Nautilus*. The ice cracked with a singular noise, like tearing paper, and the *Nautilus* sank.

"We are off!" murmured Conseil in my ear.

I could not answer him. I seized his hand, and pressed it convulsively. All at once, carried away by its frightful overcharge, the *Nautilus* sank like a bullet under the waters, that is to say, it fell as if it were in a vacuum. Then all the electric force was put on the pumps, that soon began to let the water out of the reservoirs. After some minutes, our fall was stopped. Soon, too, the manometer indicated an ascending movement. The screw, going at full speed, made the iron hull tremble to its very bolts, and drew us towards the north. But if this floating under the iceberg is to last another day before we reach the open sea, I shall be dead first.

Half stretched upon a divan in the library, I was suffocating. My face was purple, my lips blue, my faculties suspended. I neither saw nor heard. All notion of time had gone from my mind. My muscles could not contract. I do not know how many hours passed thus, but I was conscious of the agony that was coming over me. I felt as if I was going to die. Suddenly I came to. Some breaths of air penetrated my lungs. Had we risen to the surface of the waves? Were we free of the iceberg? No; Ned and Conseil, my two brave friends, were sacrificing themselves to save me. Some particles of air still remained at the bottom of one apparatus. Instead of using it, they had kept it for me, and while they were being suffocated, they gave me life drop by drop. I wanted to push back the thing; they held my hands, and for some moments I breathed freely. I looked at the clock; it was eleven in the morning. It ought to be the 28th of March. The *Nautilus* went at a frightful pace, forty miles an hour. It literally tore through the water. Where was Captain Nemo? Had he succumbed? Were his companions dead with him? At the moment, the manometer indicated that we were not more than twenty feet from the surface. A mere plate of ice separated us from the atmosphere, could we not break it? Perhaps. In any case the *Nautilus* was going to attempt it. I felt that it was in an oblique position, lowering the stern, and raising the bows. The introduction of water had been the means of disturbing its equilibrium. Then, impelled by its powerful screw, it attacked the ice-field from beneath like a formidable battering-ram. It broke it by backing and then rushing forward against the field, which gradually gave way; and at last, dashing suddenly against it, shot forward on the icy field, that crushed beneath its weight. The panel was opened—one might say torn off—and the pure air came in in abundance to all parts of the *Nautilus*.

"The Last U-Boat"

❦

BY STEPHEN PULEO

Based largely on research by attorney and naval historian Paul M. Lawton
(Excerpted from the book *Due to Enemy Action*)

Stephen Puleo's *Due to Enemy Action: The True World War II Story of the USS Eagle 56* is a drama that spans generations and two centuries. It begins in the Battle on the Atlantic in the 1940s, reaches a crescendo of action in 1945 during the closing weeks of the war, then concludes with a Purple Heart ceremony aboard the USS *Salem* in 2002. At the center of the tale is the torpedoing of the *Eagle 56* off the American coast in May 1945, *after* Germany's surrender. *U-853* either had not received, or chose to ignore, the radioed messages of the German command to cease operations. After sinking the *Eagle 56*, *U-853* went on to torpedo yet another ship, instigating a massive effort by the Navy to track down and sink the "rogue" U-boat.

 The Navy buried the truth about the *Eagle*'s sinking for years, but, as often happens, the truth has a way of surfacing. In the ceremony in 2002 appropriate honors were paid to the memories of those who perished in the sinking and the few who survived. Stephen Puleo's account is a stunning tribute to men who had to be remembered in a story that had to be told. In this excerpt from the book, we focus on the U-boat and watch the drama unfold as it heads for American waters to do whatever damage it can in the final weeks of the war.

Helmut Froemsdorf, twenty-three-year-old commander of the *U-853*, maneuvered his boat out of Germany's alternative operational center, one of five U-boats with orders to proceed to America's New England coast and wreak as much havoc as possible with Allied shipping.

Froemsdorf's orders had been issued by *Grossadmiral* (Grand Admiral) Karl Dönitz, formerly head of *Unterseeboote*, the German U-boat service, and now commander in chief of the *Kriegsmarine*, the German Navy. Froemsdorf was well aware of Dönitz's swift rise in the German high command, and knew the *Grossadmiral* was a trusted adviser of the Führer, Adolf Hitler. Like most U-boatmen, Froemsdorf admired and respected Dönitz, and would do most anything to please him.

Remarkably tall for a U-boatman—nearly six feet, five inches— Froemsdorf was bright and strong, an athlete, a skier, and a dancer. He was neither a member of the Nazi Party nor a fanatic, but he had great pride in the Fatherland, a brashness to accompany his ascendance to U-boat commander at such a tender age, and a determination to carve out a reputation for himself in the U-boat service, whose ranks were replete with Germany's most celebrated heroes.

One of those was the *U-853*'s previous commander, Helmut Sommer, whose heroics helped him and the boat achieve near legendary status when, on May 25, 1944, the *U-853* happened upon one of the most prized targets in the Atlantic, according to authors Henry C. Keatts and George C. Farr. While the *U-853* was surfaced to transmit a weather report, Sommer sighted the enormous profile of the *Queen Mary* filling the horizon, transporting American troops and goods to England. Usually, large ocean liners required no escorts; they were so fast that no U-boat could get into attack position unless she happened to be in the right spot. Immediately, Sommer had ordered the *U-853* to submerge and pursue, but the fast ocean liner easily outran it.

The *U-853* surfaced again to complete her interrupted weather transmissions. German intelligence believed these reports could help anticipate Allied plans to invade Europe from across the English Channel—an invasion the Germans knew was imminent by May of 1944, and one which would be heavily influenced by weather conditions. The *U-853* was suddenly attacked by three rocket-firing British planes. Instead of diving immediately, Sommer ordered his anti-aircraft guns into action, a daring strategy that briefly confused the attacking pilots. While the three planes regrouped for a second attack, the captain took the *U-853* down to safety.

Three weeks later, June 15, 1944—nine days after the Allied invasion on the beaches of Normandy, France—a hunter-killer group, comprised of the carrier USS *Croatan* and six destroyers, pursued the *U-853*. The Allied ships had located the U-boat by intercepting radio transmissions using high-frequency direction-finding (h/f-d/f, or "Huff-Duff") detecting equipment. For seventy-two hours, according to Keatts and Farr, aircraft from the carrier combed the area while the carriers waited for the U-boat to surface, which it would have to do sooner or later. Men on the waiting surface ships named the elusive *U-853* "Moby-Dick" after the great white whale that the fictional Captain Ahab pursued in Herman Melville's classic novel. During this same period, the *U-853* crew, in admiration of Sommer's skill in eluding attackers, nicknamed their boat *Der Seiltaenger*, or "Tightrope Walker."

Finally, on June 18, *Croatan*'s Huff-Duff equipment intercepted a weather transmission from the *U-853* only thirty miles distant. Within minutes, fighter planes from the carrier were strafing the deck of the surfaced U-boat. This time, the *U-853*'s anti-aircraft gun crews were less fortunate. Two crewmen were killed, and several others were wounded, including Sommer, who was riddled by slugs and fragments that ripped into his head, stomach, and arms. In all, Sommer was hit twenty-eight times, but he managed to stay alert long enough to give the orders to submerge just seconds before bombers arrived to finish off the *U-853*. The act became folklore in the U-boat service, and Sommer became a hero to his men.

The *U-853* limped back to her base in Lorient, France, on July 4 of 1944, sixteen days after the attack, but was forced to leave the base as the Allies advanced on the port city. With a temporary commander at the helm, she was transported to Germany, where she underwent repairs and was fitted with a *schnorchel* (snorkel), a retractable air intake and exhaust pipe that would permit operation of her diesel engines while submerged. The new device reduced the dangerous periods the U-boats had to spend on the surface charging their batteries. Soon thereafter, on September 1, 1944, Froemsdorf, the *U-853*'s twenty-three-year-old former executive officer who had performed well on the previous mission, assumed command of the 252-foot-long Type IXC/40 U-boat.

Though young, Froemsdorf understood that the world had changed dramatically in three short years.

In the first few months of 1942, German U-boats had operated boldly and with little resistance off the East Coast of the United States, inflicting physical and psychological damage on the Americans by sinking hundreds of ships just miles from her shores. German U-boat commanders dubbed it the "Great American Turkey Shoot" and the "Second Happy Time," a sequel to the resounding success U-boatmen had against British shipping in the summer and fall of 1940.

By mid-1943, though, the tide had turned, and the situation deteriorated quickly for the U-boats. The American president, Franklin Roosevelt, had called the United States home front to action. Her people and her factories responded by building ships and airplanes at astounding rates. The U.S. Navy soon developed a sophisticated convoy system whereby merchant ships were protected by warships both across the Atlantic and along the eastern seaboard. American fighter planes and bombers became the nemesis of the U-boats, which had operated in the early days primarily on the surface, submerging to stay hidden for a short time or to slip away undetected if enemy ships were in the area. Now, remaining on the surface was near suicide. The *U-853*'s snorkel meant it could remain submerged at periscope depth for most of the trip across the Atlantic—with just the top of the snorkel tube protruding above the surface—but the trade-off was that travel was unbearably slow. A slight miscalculation by the operator who controlled the boat's depth, or even a moderate amount of extra surface turbulence, would cause water to cover the snorkel cap, closing its valve suddenly and shutting off the flow of air. At that point, the U-boat's diesels, which needed a large amount of air, would suck the air from the inside of the hull unless they were immediately switched off. This could result in a dangerous buildup of carbon dioxide that could prove toxic to the crew. Froemsdorf and his men were protected from Allied planes while submerged, but the trip across the Atlantic would take them the better part of two months. The *U-853* would only be about halfway through its Atlantic crossing when Froemsdorf celebrated his twenty-fourth birthday on March 26.

Though they were now more the hunted than the hunter, the crew of the *U-853* possessed a strong sense of pride. The men had adorned the U-boat's black conning tower with the insignia of a trotting red horse on a yellow shield, which was technically against German Navy regulations, but a remnant of the boat's glory days under Sommer. Froemsdorf would try to recapture some of that glory for the *U-853*, though he knew

STEPHEN PULEO . **187**

his efforts would ultimately be in vain. With the Russians bearing down on Berlin from the East, and the Americans and British advancing from the West, the outcome of the war was no longer in doubt. Germany would keep fighting, but she could not win, and with each passing day, her options narrowed. Dönitz hoped that these recently dispatched U-boats could disrupt Allied supply lines enough to convince American president Franklin D. Roosevelt and General Dwight D. Eisenhower to reconsider their position—that only the "unconditional surrender" of Germany would be acceptable to end the war.

For Germany, the fighting was all but over. The intent of Froemsdorf's mission was to improve the prospects of the Fatherland's postwar future.

As the *U-853* headed westward toward the American coast in late February of 1945, Helmut Froemsdorf knew the chances for survival were slim for him and his crew. The U-boat service suffered casualty rates approaching 85 percent, the highest of all the military branches, Axis or Allied. In the last three years, thousands of brave U-boatmen had met their deaths in watery graves, pummeled by bombs from Allied airplanes or depth charges from their ships. Not only was Froemsdorf's mission difficult, it was perilous; even if the *U-853* managed to record any kills, she would be hard-pressed to return to Norway safely.

Froemsdorf, a member of the U-boat class of 1939, hoped for some success, but in his last letter to his parents, even while expressing his pride at commanding the *U-853*, he portended a sense of doom: "I am lucky in these difficult days of my Fatherland to have the honor of commanding this submarine and it is my duty to accept . . . I'm not very good at last words, so good-bye for now, and give my sister my love."

★ ★ ★

Early March, 1945
Helmut Froemsdorf
Aboard the U-853, *halfway across the Atlantic*

Helmut Froemsdorf was reading the latest secret radio dispatch from Berlin. *Grossadmiral* Dönitz's message exhorted U-boat commanders to remain steadfast in their loyalty to the Third Reich's cause.

"Let us fly into the face of all those who want to give up, who adopt the silly motto 'It is no longer any use.' Those are the greatest weaklings. They are the ones who let themselves be led to the slaughter like patient cattle,"

Dönitz's message read. "Let us fly into the face of any German who now becomes the least bit shaky in his loyalty to the Nazi state and to the Führer. The motives for this are only fear, cowardice, and weakness. We are the strong and the faithful."

Froemsdorf, who would soon celebrate his twenty-fourth birthday in the cramped quarters of his U-boat, never publicly questioned his crew's loyalty, but was aware that he had two things working against him as a commander of men: his tender age, and former Commander Sommer's stellar reputation, which would be difficult for him to emulate. This alone would make it difficult for him to command the respect of his crew, a relationship "based squarely on the concept of a benign autocrat who is all-powerful but who nevertheless requires trust and confidence from below so he can rule effectively," in the words of author Jordan Vause. "There were no secrets" among men who "suddenly found themselves thrown together in a metal shell the size of a small apartment, in which they worked, ate common meals, literally slept in each other's bunks, grew rank and dirty together, and remained so for weeks at a time . . . each man knew everyone else intimately and soon found himself depending on everyone else for his life. If he made a mistake, others suffered for it . . . an enemy ship might escape, or the entire crew might die."

Indeed, it was this very intimacy that likely prompted Froemsdorf to suspect what he must not have known for certain: that several members of his crew questioned his leadership and feared his potential for recklessness. Before the *U-853* departed from Norway, twenty-year-old Machinist Mate 2nd Class Frederick Volk had written to his mother that he was worried about the mission because he had no faith in Froemsdorf. Theodore Woner, a *U-853* crewman who had missed the last cruise because of illness, later wrote that, "He [Froemsdorf] was a different personality [than Sommer] . . . at least some of the crew believed Froemsdorf was out to get a decoration." Even Sommer was concerned for the safety of his officers and crew under Froemsdorf's command. Sommer's wife would write later that her husband thought Froemsdorf was "very young and ambitious when he became commander. My husband asked him again and again not to act frivolously, for he knew the end of the war was near and . . . that all the fine fellows of his crew should survive."

Though he may have sensed his crew's misgivings, Froemsdorf knew nothing of these letters. For now, the correspondence he was most concerned with was the latest radio message sent by Karl Dönitz in Berlin:

"Let us show our enemies that the destruction of Germany will cost them more in blood, treasure, and time than they can withstand," the dispatch read. "Let us exert all our powers to the utmost, for example, by sinking as many ships as possible for the Anglo-Saxons in total disregard of risk. Then their doubts as to whether this unconditional defeat of Germany is practicable and not too costly will increase."

Froemsdorf did not know whether he would have the opportunity to fulfill Dönitz's desire to sink Allied ships. Nor could he have known how he or his crew would react under combat stress.

As he finished reading Dönitz's secret communiqué, as the *U-853* moved slowly and cautiously toward the Gulf of Maine, there was one other thing Froemsdorf could not have known: Within hours, in a highly secure room inside U.S. Naval Headquarters on Constitution Avenue in Washington, D.C., a small, select group of American naval intelligence officers—the enemy—would be reading the same message.

★ ★ ★

April 23, 1945, Noon
The "Secret Room"
Washington, D.C.

What John Scagnelli, Harold Petersen, Johnny Breeze, Ivar Westerlund, Oscar Davis, Fred Michelsen, Harold Glenn, Harold Rodman, John Laubach, and James Early didn't know—nor did anyone else aboard the *Eagle 56* or at Portland base command—was that hundreds of miles to the south, the Secret Room team had been tracking a German U-boat prowling the Gulf of Maine for most of April. Yet, in the last few days, the sub had made no radio contact with Berlin, so it was difficult for [Commander] Kenneth Knowles and his staff to pinpoint its movements. Knowles's last dispatch to Admiral Low, dated April 21, reported that two antisubmarine task forces were on the lookout for U-boats in the North Atlantic, and the Secret Room had also issued a general alert to operational base commanders to keep a sharp eye out for U-boats. This was particularly important since U-boats had sunk both a Canadian minesweeper and a freighter off the coast of Nova Scotia within the last ten days.

Knowles hoped that ships operating off the coast of Maine were paying close attention.

April 23, 1945, Noon
Aboard the USS Selfridge
Gulf of Maine

Lieutenant Commander J. A. Boyd, piloting the destroyer USS *Selfridge* in defense of Portland Harbor, was about seven miles away from the *Eagle 56*, when he noticed something highly irregular, and against all naval regulations: his navigational crew had tracked the PE-boat "at dead in the water" in Casco Bay, a dangerous condition to say the least. Even with Germany about to fall, the *Eagle 56* commander should have been more careful. With his ship at a complete stop, the PE captain left his vessel exposed to a possible U-boat attack, and all commanders had been warned of U-boats in the vicinity.

Actually, "exposed" was probably too mild a word—at a dead stop, the *Eagle 56* was a sitting duck.

April 23, 1945, 12:14 P.M
Helmut Froemsdorf
Aboard the U-853
Gulf of Maine

For two difficult months at sea, it is likely that Helmut Froemsdorf had dreamed of this moment. His boat had been forced to remain submerged like a frightened rabbit for virtually the entire trip across the Atlantic, crawling beneath the surface to avoid detection and likely destruction from Allied ships and planes, which had killed more than one hundred U-boats and their crews in the first four months of 1945. The fifty-five men aboard the *U-853* would be growing restless and irritable, eating bland food, breathing stale air, living and working in cramped quarters alongside shipmates who had not changed clothing or showered in weeks due to a lack of space for personal effects and restrictions on the use of freshwater.

Now, the time for cowering and restlessness was over; precision and daring were the orders of the day. Helmut Froemsdorf, who had turned twenty-four years old less than a month earlier, would truly come of age on this raw April day in the Gulf of Maine. He was operating the *U-853* under power of her electric motors as she crept, submerged, toward the *Eagle 56*, the U-boat's sound masked by the noisy wake of the American destroyer, *Selfridge*, seven miles away. Froemsdorf would have celebrated his good fortune.

The American subchaser was at a dead stop and made an easy target for the *U-853*'s torpedoes.

As he drew a bead on the *Eagle 56*, Froemsdorf may have recalled the glory days of his predecessors—of Sommer's bravery in the open Atlantic, of Hardegen's and Mohr's dramatic kills along the American East Coast during the Second Happy Time in 1942. He also may have thought about the last message he had received from Admiral Dönitz, on April 11, one that rose to the unwavering defense of Adolf Hitler, calling him the "single statesman of stature in Europe."

But perhaps it was the last portion of Dönitz's April 11 message that was uppermost in Froemsdorf's mind as he prepared to attack the *Eagle 56*, words that trumpeted the glory of the *Kriegsmarine* and its willingness to "fight to the end," words that heralded the bravery of its U-boat captains who would never "think of giving up [their] ship" and whose "bearing in the severest crisis of this war will be judged by posterity."

With the *U-853* less than six hundred yards from the *Eagle 56*, Froemsdorf ordered his torpedo crew to fire.

★ ★ ★

April 23, 1945
Gulf of Maine
Afternoon and evening

Within hours of the *Eagle*'s sinking, the waters off Casco Bay and Cape Elizabeth were being swept by a fleet of naval vessels, including the *Selfridge*, which had returned to the scene, and destroyers USS *Craven*, USS *Woolsey*, and USS *Earle*, the destroyer escort USS *Evarts*, and the Coast Guard-manned patrol frigate, the USS *Brunswick*. They were assisted by the USS *Eberle*, USS *Muskegon*, USS *Rinehart*, USS *Uniontown*, and the USS *Wingfield*. They conducted anti-submarine warfare operations well into the late evening, joined by aircraft from the Brunswick Naval Air Station. The *Craven*'s war diary for the day reported starkly: "Eagle boat exploded and sank in the area today. Cause undetermined, may have been enemy submarine."

By this time, however, the *U-853* had already crept off into the relative safety of deeper waters, submerged on her electric motors and concealed by the area's rough-bottom topography, far from shore.

★ ★ ★

April 24–28, 1945
Off the coast of Maine

The day after the *Eagle 56* exploded, the waters off the coast of Maine were teeming with ships conducting anti-submarine patrols, and they were assisted by patrol-bomber aircraft from the Brunswick Naval Air Station. USS *Muskegon*, USS *Earle*, USS *Eberle*, USS *Uniontown*, and the U.S. Coast Guard Cutter *92004* were hunting the U-boat off Monhegan Island, approximately fifty miles East-Northeast of Portland, when the Coast Guard cutter reported: "110 degrees magnetic, very likely submarine contact. Watch reports sub blew tanks."

The cutter's report seemed to confirm what the ship commanders and crews in the area had suspected when they watched the geyser of water spew from the exploding *Eagle*: a U-boat was patrolling the coast of Maine searching for American targets. Berlin was falling, the Third Reich was crumbling, but German U-boats continued their last desperate patrols in U.S. waters.

The search continued into the early afternoon, when, at just past 3:00 P.M., the USS *Muskegon*, part of the same patrol group, reported: "Sighted smoke on surface from no visible source . . . all hands to General Quarters . . . presumed to be enemy submarine using *schnorchel* (snorkel) . . . proceeding to investigate." Again, the patrol group could not locate the U-boat, but U.S. ships hunted into the evening and early hours of the morning of Wednesday, April 25, 1945, when at 3:50 A.M., the Coast Guard cutter reported: "Sub contact. Can hear electric motors and blow of tanks." The contact was lost, but nine hours later, according to historian Paul Lawton, at 12:50 P.M. on the 25th, the *Muskegon* reported that a sound contact at 72 fathoms (about 430 feet) at the mouth of Penobscot Bay was "classified as possible bottomed submarine" with "strong echoes." The *Muskegon* fired a full complement of Hedgehog depth charges with negative results. But, as she chased the contact further, she blew a gasket on a steam line to the galley and had to discontinue the search to make repairs. The *Earle* and *Eberle* maneuvered in the area and made several subsequent depth-charge attacks, and the *Muskegon* returned to the search after she completed repairs. The warships formed a scouting line at 2,500-yard intervals and swept the vicinity several times without regaining any good sonar contacts. In addition, a U.S. Navy blimp was dispatched to the area from the Naval Air Station in South Weymouth, Massachusetts, but her airborne magnetic anomaly detection (MAD) gear malfunctioned, and unable to acquire a contact, she returned to her base.

On Thursday, April 26, 1945, an air patrol squadron from Quonset Point, Rhode Island, Naval Air Station, flying anti-submarine patrol over the Gulf of Maine, picked up a blip on the radar screen at about 3:00 P.M. "The radar said there was a submarine sitting on top of the water about 40 miles away charging their batteries," said air crewman William Heckendorf. "We homed in on it and saw the oil slick on the water where it had been sitting. We dropped our sonar gear and picked up the sound of a submarine's engine. We pinpointed the sub and dropped two 500-pound depth charges. About five minutes later the ocean was full of debris and oil." Paul Lawton speculated: "It is possible that the U-boat attacked by the airboat was the one that torpedoed and sank the *Eagle 56*. It was a common ploy for U-boat commanders to discharge oil and fire debris out of their torpedo tubes to confuse attackers into believing they had destroyed the prey, thereby ending the attack."

If that was the case, Commander Froemsdorf's ploy was successful. The *U-853* was still at large and dangerous.

None of the patrol-group ships knew it, but Commander Kenneth Knowles and the F-21 U-boat Secret Room were also tracking the *U-853* through the Gulf of Maine. On April 24, it evaluated as "possible" the Coast Guard cutter's report of a U-boat contact near Monhegan Island. In an April 25, 1945, Secret Dispatch numbered 251515 to the Commander of the Eastern Sea Frontier, Knowles drafted a message that, in part, stated: "one [U-boat] possibly 3600 6930 moving West to SW from radar contact 250153Z alternatively Gulf of Maine from PE incident." Three days later, on April 28, another secret COMINCH dispatch added: "one [U-boat] possibly . . . in Gulf of Maine from attack 271438Z (PE incident)."

At some point, probably after April 27, the *U-853* departed the Gulf of Maine and slowly headed south past Cape Cod and into Rhode Island Sound, according to Paul Lawton. For security reasons, however, the highly classified information from the Secret Room—about the presence of the *U-853* in the area of the *Eagle 56* sinking—would not be shared by the Office of Naval Intelligence with the Court of Inquiry investigating the loss of the *Eagle* and the death of forty-nine of her officers and crew members.

★ ★ ★

May 1–2, 1945
Germany

On the evening of May 1, General Helmuth Weidling, the commandant of the city of Berlin, ordered his troops to stop fighting the Russians to end the senseless bloodshed. In a message to his troops, he wrote: "The Führer committed suicide on April 30, 1945, thereby abandoning all those who swore loyalty to him . . . I am ordering an immediate halt to all resistance. Every hour you continue to fight prolongs the terrible suffering of Berlin's civilian population and of our wounded. By mutual agreement with the High Command of the Soviet Army, I order you to stop fighting immediately."

Nevertheless, on May 2, Dönitz—far removed from the catastrophic conditions in Berlin—dispatched a message to all military forces, including his U-boat commanders, that demanded their loyalty and continued resistance. The communiqué, which was intercepted by Kenneth Knowles's team in the United States sub-tracking room in Washington, D.C., read in part:

> My comrades! The Führer has fallen. True to his great purpose of saving the culture of Europe from Bolshevism, he dedicated his life and met a hero's death. In him, we have lost one of the greatest heroes of German history. In awe and grief, we lower the flag for him. The Führer designated me as his successor and Chief of State and Supreme Commander of the Armed Forces . . . I must continue the battle against the English and the Americans as long as they obstruct me in the prosecution of the battle against Bolshevism . . . I demand discipline and obedience . . . Only through the unconditional execution of my orders will chaos and ruin be avoided. [Any German military man] is a coward and a traitor who now shirks his duty and thereby brings death and slavery to German women and children . . . German soldiers, do your duty. The life of our people is at stake.

Yet, despite the bravado in his May 2 message, in the final hours of the Third Reich, Dönitz feverishly sought to accomplish two goals from his northern outpost headquarters: end the war against the Western Allies as soon as possible, while simultaneously saving as many German people as possible from the Soviets. "He sent every available naval and merchant vessel to the Baltic ports still in German hands, with orders to bring out every refugee he could," wrote authors Samuel Mitcham Jr. and Gene Mueller. "The troop units still fighting were ordered to cover the evacuation of the refugees and then escape to the west themselves. It has been estimated that two million civilians escaped Soviet captivity in the eight days that Dönitz prolonged hostilities."

Thus, in the first two days of May 1945, a bizarre contrast was playing out on land and under the sea. In Berlin and across Germany, Hitler's fighting men were laying down their arms and German civilians were literally running for their lives to escape the dreaded Russians. Yet, thousands of miles away, German U-boats—including the *U-853*—were still prowling the East Coast of the United States, desperately looking for the final kills that could salvage a measure of pride and, perhaps, concessions for Germany in her final hours.

★ ★ ★

May 5, 1945
Germany

Across the Atlantic Ocean, from his headquarters near the Danish border, Admiral Karl Dönitz issued a message to his U-boat commanders vastly different in tone than Knowles's. [Commander Kenneth Knowles in a congratulatory message anticipating the war's end.] Whereas the American Secret Room commander celebrated victory, Dönitz acknowledged heartbreaking defeat to his beloved U-boat commanders.

On May 3, still trying to surrender as many forces as possible to the British and Americans rather than the feared Russians, Dönitz had sent a special emissary to British commander Bernard Montgomery proposing that the three German armies facing the Red Army in the north surrender to Anglo-American forces. "The German aim was to avoid, at all costs, surrendering to the Russians, and to stall for time in order for as many Germans as possible to escape to the west to avoid certain Red Army retribution, which had already been unleashed in an orgy of mass killings, rapes, and plunderings," military historian Carlo D'Este wrote. Montgomery asked Eisenhower, who formally rejected the proposal, stating that any German surrender must be "unconditional and simultaneous" in all theaters. However, as Eisenhower later recalled, as a "tactical" matter, he authorized Montgomery to accept the military surrender "of all forces in his allotted zone of operations . . . including those in Holland and Denmark." The agreement took effect at 8:00 A.M. on May 5, and as part of the terms, Dönitz agreed to direct all U-boat skippers to cease fire and prepare to surrender.

He radioed to them on the morning of May 5:

My U-boat men!

Six years of U-boat warfare lie behind us. You have fought like lions. A crushing material superiority has compressed us into a very narrow area. A continuation of the struggle is impossible from the bases that remain. U-boat men, unbroken and unashamed, you are laying down your arms after a heroic battle without an equal. In reverent memory, we think respectfully of our fallen comrades, who have sealed with death their loyalty to the Führer and the Fatherland. Comrades, maintain in the future your U-boat spirit with which you have fought at sea bravely and undeviatingly through the long years for the welfare of the Fatherland. Long live Germany! Your Grand Admiral.

It was Dönitz's final message to his undersea warriors, many of whom were still unswervingly loyal to him to the end. Not everyone believed it. Heinz Schaeffer, commander of the *U-977*, was incredulous when he picked up Dönitz's signal in the English Channel. "He did not believe that Dönitz was responsible for it; it was the work of an impostor, or the *Grossadmiral* had been forced to do it," wrote Jordan Vause, who quoted Schaeffer as saying, "I couldn't conceive it possible that our leaders had sunk so far as to send out official orders to surrender."

But Herbert Werner, commander of the *U-953*, received Dönitz's message with a sense of welcoming relief, which he described many years later:

"The Admiral who had led the U-boats to glory and to disaster mourned for the faithful who lay on the bottom and gave thanks to those few survivors of the monstrous battle. This was the message that put an end to the suffering. It admitted defeat for the first time. The murdering had finally come to an end. Henceforth, we would be able to live without fear that we had to die tomorrow. An unknown tranquility took possession of me as I realized that I had survived. My death in an iron coffin, a verdict of long standing, was finally suspended. The truth was so beautiful that it seemed to be a dream."

For Dönitz, who had begun the war with glorious dreams of U-boat dominance and remarkable early successes, but had since seen horrible deaths claim thousands of his beloved U-boatmen and two of his sons, this last message summed up both his irrepressible pride and the wrenching pain and bitterness that consumed him at war's end.

Because Ultra records remained classified until after Dönitz's death, the grand admiral was at least spared the humiliation of knowing—though he may have suspected—that U.S. Navy cryptographers in Washington, D.C., as they had been doing since 1942, intercepted even his final radio message to the

U-boats, decoded it, and sent it along to Kenneth Knowles in the sub-tracking Secret Room. Knowles quickly prepared and distributed a memo to F-20 watch officers explaining the procedure that U.S. and British warships should follow in anticipation of the widespread surrender of German U-boats.

★ ★ ★

May 5, 1945, late afternoon
Off Point Judith, Rhode Island

U-boat commanders Herbert Werner and Heinz Schaeffer may have responded in markedly different ways to Führer Dönitz's surrender message, but it is at least clear that they received the dispatch. Did *U-853* commander Helmut Froemsdorf, submerged off the coast of Rhode Island, ever hear Dönitz's signal instructing U-boat commanders to cease hostilities?

It is possible that Froemsdorf's radio equipment was damaged by one of the depth-charge or Hedgehog attacks conducted by the *Selfridge, Muskegon, Evarts,* or *Eberle,* in their pursuit of the *U-853* as she departed the Gulf of Maine. Yet, it is just as likely that Froemsdorf foolishly disregarded Dönitz's order, balked at surrendering, and decided to go down fighting.

The real answer will never be known.

What *is* known to history is that on Saturday, May 5, 1945, at just past 5:30 P.M., *after* Dönitz's order to surrender, the *U-853* spotted and locked in on another easy target: the aging 5,400-ton collier *Black Point,* moments after she had passed the Point Judith, Rhode Island, Coast Guard Station lighthouse on her way to Boston to deliver a load of soft coal. *Black Point* captain Charles Prior had just picked up 7,700 tons of coal in Newport News, Virginia, and was steaming northeast, unescorted, for the Edison power plant at the L Street wharf in South Boston, by way of the intracoastal waterways of Long Island Sound, Rhode Island Sound, and eventually, the Cape Cod Canal. "That day in 1945 was foggy along the eastern seaboard and merchant ships were not equipped with radar," noted *The Boston Globe.* "Twice during his steam up Long Island Sound, Prior lost sight of his own bow and had to anchor." In addition, Prior was not in convoy, nor had he been for several weeks now that the U-boat threat was considered minimal.

By late afternoon, however, the seas had calmed, the fog had lifted, the sun had emerged, and Prior was standing on the *Black Point's* bridge. The *Globe* reported: "The only other traffic in sight, far off to starboard, were two small freighters, a tugboat pulling lazily at three barges, and the Yugoslavian freighter *Karmen*." Captain Prior was about to light a cigarette when a huge explosion rocked the ship. As glass shattered and doors splintered around him, Prior's first thought was, "Jesus, we've hit a mine." The explosion blew away forty feet of the ship's stern and she began to sink fast. Naval historian Paul Lawton wrote: "Merchant crewman Joseph Raymond Tharl later recalled that he had been belowdecks, eating his regular Saturday dinner of franks and beans in the galley amidships [when the explosion occurred]. He raced to the radio room and started transmitting an SOS distress signal, as Captain Prior struggled to pry the stunned third mate Homer Small's hands from the ship's helm. Captain Prior then rushed to secure the ship's records and gave the order to abandon ship. In the excitement and confusion following the explosion, several sailors were crushed and injured or killed as lifeboats swung wildly from their davits . . ."

By 5:55 P.M., both the 40-foot stern section and the 230-foot bow section had sunk beneath the waves. Eleven crewmen and one armed guard went down with the ship.

The freighter *Karmen* rescued the thirty-four survivors, including Captain Prior, and quickly broadcast an alarm after her crew members witnessed an inexplicable sight that left no doubt that the explosion aboard the *Black Point* was not caused by any mine, but an enemy torpedo. For some reason, once again, the *U-853* had mysteriously surfaced, this time for a few minutes. Officers and crewmen aboard the *Karmen* saw several *U-853* crewmen off her aft deck, and some later said that the U-boatmen were trying to deploy a yellow inflatable raft or retrieve something from the water; however, within moments, the *U-853*'s crew "scrambled back down the hatches," according to Lawton, and the U-boat quickly dove from view as the *Karmen* broadcast her SOS radio distress signal.

★ ★ ★

Four Boston-bound American warships, heading to port for repairs and provisions, heard the alarm broadcast by the *Karmen*: the *Ericsson*, the *Moberly*, the *Amick*, and the *Atherton* all began to chase the *U-853*. Other U.S. warships, including USS *Action*, USS *Barney*, USS *Breckenridge*, USS *Blakely*, USS *Newport*, the USS *Restless*, and the USS *Semmes* soon arrived on the scene and established a barrier patrol around the search area to prevent the U-boat from escaping her hunters. Further south, destroyers USS *Baldwin*, USS *Frankford*, and USS *Nelson* received a dispatch from the Commander Eastern Sea Frontier to join the hunt for the *U-853*.

As the net of surface ships drew tighter around the German U-boat, the relatively shallow waters and flat-bottom topography of Rhode Island Sound also worked against her, failing to offer the protective cover she enjoyed off the craggy coast of Maine, where it was much more difficult for SONAR to detect submarines. There was one spot, about nine miles south of the sinking of the *Black Point*, that the American hunters believed the U-boat might choose to hide. In this area, known as East Ground, a steeply rising shoal could allow a submarine to lie alongside and escape a destroyer's detection. In addition, according to Navy Ensign D. M. Tollaksen, son of the *Moberly*'s commanding officer, "there was a possibility of a wreck in the area, which would further confuse the search . . . once the above course of action was deemed most likely for the German submarine skipper to follow, the search plan was set up to sweep across this area and back."

The search plan worked. At approximately 8:15 P.M. on May 5, the USS *Atherton*, skippered by Lieutenant Commander Lewis Iselin, picked up a sound contact on the *U-853* as the U-boat crept slowly south on her electric motors, close to the bottom, attempting to escape detection. At just before 8:30 P.M., the *Moberly* dropped thirteen magnetic depth charges on the sound contact, one of which detonated. The USS *Ericsson* arrived on the scene to join the *Atherton* and *Moberly* in their search and follow-up attacks on the SONAR contact. The *Atherton* made two subsequent Hedgehog attacks before marking the area with a lighted buoy, and breaking off the attack to conduct repairs and reload her Hedgehog spigot launchers. The three warships regained sound contact quickly, this time presuming it was the U-boat lying dead in the water at a depth of one hundred feet with her propellers silent. At a quarter to midnight on May 5, *Atherton* fired a pattern of Hedgehogs, and "evidence of a hit began to well up to the surface, indicating the *U-853* had been damaged, if not destroyed," Paul Lawton wrote.

Moberly sonarman second class Richard I. Duburg, recalled: "After the attack our searchlights in the dark revealed air bubbles and oil welling to the surface with bits of wood, cork, and dead fish, a rubber inflatable raft, life jackets tied in knots, wooden flagstaff, a pillow with an embroidered duck on the corner, the Captain's cap, and a whiskey wood crate . . ." The *Atherton* picked up the contact again after this attack and held it for about twenty minutes while circling the area. "There was no noticeable movement of the submarine," Tollaksen wrote.

The *Atherton* attacked again in an attempt to split the sub's pressure hull, dropping a pattern of depth charges set to explode at 75 feet in water that was between 100 and 128 feet deep. After the attack, at 1:00 A.M. on May 6, the *Moberly* and the *Atherton* turned on their searchlights and saw additional debris and dead fish. At 2:41 A.M., the *Atherton*, which had circled the area every twenty to thirty minutes to keep track of the position of the contact and hunt for more wreckage that might have come to the surface, reported that there were three pools of oil coming from the submarine which were spaced about thirty feet apart. The *Moberly* reported that an oil slick and much debris extended half a mile from the position of the last attacks. The *Ericsson* and the *Atherton* began searching for evidence of the submarine's destruction, and found "a large number of German escape lungs and life jackets, several life rafts, abandon-ship kits, and an officer's cap which was later judged to belong to the submarine's skipper," Tollaksen recounted.

Between 5:30 and 6:00 A.M. on May 6, two U.S. Navy blimps, *K-16* and *K-58* from Lakehurst, New Jersey, arrived on the scene to search the area of the debris field and diesel oil slick, photograph the area, and mark the position of the stricken submarine with smoke and dye markers. The *K-16* soon made a strong sound contact on the *U-853*, marked the position, and reported that the target was stationary. At that point, the destroyers made additional Hedgehog and depth-charge attacks to crack the hull of the submarine and bring up more debris to the surface. "From time to time, the attacks would be discontinued and boats lowered to pick up more wreckage," Tollaksen described. "*Ericsson* recovered a chart desk, a life raft, a rubber hood for foul-weather gear, and some bits of cork."

Blimp *K-16* dropped a sonobuoy on an oil slick, and SONAR operators in both blimps heard sound which they described as a "rhythmic hammering on a metal surface which was interrupted periodically." About ten minutes later, they heard "a long, shrill shriek and then the hammering noise was lost in the engine noise of the attacking surface ships."

Could the hammering have been the last desperate poundings of any surviving *U-853* crew members, begging the attacks to stop? Some U-boat commanders have described the concussive force and deafening blasts of depth-charge and Hedgehog attacks as the equivalent of being inside a 55-gallon metal drum while several people are bashing the sides of the drum with sledgehammers. According to Paul Lawton, the trapped *U-853*, lying dead on the bottom, underwent a sixteen-hour-long deluge of twenty successive Hedgehog and depth-charge attacks, during which more than fifteen tons of explosives were dropped on the crippled U-boat, including two hundred depth charges. Her crew members would have endured unimaginably horrific pain and trauma from the terrible pounding that she absorbed as she lay helpless. "I don't think there's a hull that took a bigger beating during the war," reported *Atherton* commander Lewis Iselin years later. Writers Henry Keatts and George Farr noted: "The monstrous detonations of Hedgehogs and depth charges would have pounded against the U-boat with sledge-hammer blows. The crew was probably thrown about inside like toys until concussions finally blew the pressure hull open and the sea rushed in."

At 10:45 A.M., Task Force Commander F. C. B. McCune, aboard the *Ericsson*, declared the U-boat "sunk and on the bottom," but still the bombardments did not cease. The vessel *Semmes* was given permission to enter the area to test her new experimental SONAR gear on the bottomed submarine. Marker buoys were dropped and the vessels made practice Hedgehog runs. Finally, at 12:24, the *Ericsson* marked the position of the dead submarine with a buoy line and the attacks were discontinued. Years later, the *Boston Globe* would quote a former U-boat crew member as speculating that "it is entirely possible . . . that several Germans [in the *U-853*] in the airtight forward compartments would have survived all the practice runs and were still alive when the bombing stopped at 12:24 P.M. By then, the men may have gone insane. Their deaths would have come from suffocation, as the world above prepared to celebrate peace."

McCune later expressed surprise that the U-boat made no attempt to surface or fire her torpedoes, an indication that she was probably critically damaged early in the attacks. Otherwise, Froemsdorf likely would have blown his ballast tanks and surfaced to give his crew at least a fighting chance to escape before the *U-853* was destroyed. Instead, he apparently had little choice but to play possum on the bottom, hoping the attacking ships would be convinced of a kill and leave, allowing the U-boat to inch away and perhaps live another day.

His last desperate strategy failed utterly.

On the afternoon of May 6, 1945, diver Edwin J. R. Bockelman from the Navy salvage and rescue vessel *Penguin* descended 130 feet to the bottomed U-boat to confirm the kill and examine the wreckage. He landed on the U-boat's conning tower, reported massive damage to her hull, and found her hatch crammed with the bodies of several German naval officers and crewmen wearing escape equipment. Despite the danger from many unexploded depth charges surrounding the wreck, Bockelman recovered the body of one dead crewman—twenty-two-year-old seaman Herbert Hoffmann—from the conning tower, which he brought to the surface as evidence of the kill.

Before he returned to the surface, Bockelman identified the boat by its number, *U-853*, painted on her conning tower. Although there is no historical document that confirms it, Bockelman likely spotted something else painted on the conning tower: the red trotting horse and yellow shield insignia of the *U-853*, the "red and yellow markings" that *Eagle 56* crew member Daniel Jaronik had seen as he abandoned ship and later testified about during the Court of Inquiry.

All fifty-five officers and crewmen aboard the *U-853* were lost; Froemsdorf's final, meaningless attack on the *Black Point* led to a horrible death for himself and his crew.

In all, the *U-853*'s attacks killed sixty-one men aboard the *Eagle 56* and the *Black Point*, bringing the total dead from these incidents to 116 Americans and Germans in the final two weeks of World War II. The *U-853*, the final German U-boat sunk in the Battle of the Atlantic, had been responsible for the final German kills of an American warship and merchant ship.

As to the question of whether Froemsdorf's radio equipment did or did not pick up Dönitz's final "cease-fire" message, the German U-boat archives would report years later that, while there was no radio message from the *U-853* after the *Eagle 56* was destroyed, there was a brief message from the U-boat to Berlin that did get through after she sunk the *Black Point*. This indicates, but does not *prove*, that Froemsdorf received the cease-fire message and foolishly chose to disregard it; it does confirm that his radio was working for at least a brief period afterward.

Whether the cocky U-boat commander was unaware of the cease-fire and the war's end, or risked the lives of his brave crew in a fool's mission—knowing that he would never be able to outrun American pursuit or be allowed to surrender after sinking the *Black Point*—is a mystery whose answer is forever lost with Froemsdorf at the bottom of the Atlantic Ocean.

An answer to another mystery was also lost when the *U-853* and her crew were destroyed: why she surfaced after torpedoing the *Eagle 56* and the *Black Point*. Paul Lawton and other historians have speculated that she was required to surface after failing to maintain proper "trim control" after launching her torpedoes. "In order for a U-boat to maintain proper 'trim' (the control of a submerged submarine's depth and equilibrium), the crew had to regularly track the boat's displacement (weight) throughout her patrol," Lawton explained, "including daily measurements of fuel, food, and freshwater consumption, garbage, human waste, and the discharge of ordnance (torpedoes, mines, artillery, and anti-aircraft munitions) . . . rapid and extreme changes in the boat's buoyancy and trim . . . such as that resulting from a submerged torpedo launch, required excellent training, experience, and discipline, in order to keep the boat from broaching the surface, potentially exposing herself in a vulnerable position, and compromising some of the tactical advantage obtained from a submerged attack . . . anything short of perfect execution could cause the boat to sink below periscope depth, or rise uncontrollably [above] the surface . . . this phenomenon was not uncommon with inexperienced U-boat officers and crewmen, particularly those lacking sufficient experience in the firing of live, or practice, torpedoes . . ."

Lawton and others have also cited alternate explanations for the *U-853* breaking the surface after her attacks, including the "intentional, though highly dangerous acts of defiant bravado by the young Commander Froemsdorf" to view the results of his kills, or "his desire to get a better view of the destruction he inflicted for the purpose of battle damage assessment."

One final perplexing question may never be answered: Why were *U-853* crew members attempting to launch an inflatable life raft after sinking the *Black Point*? Did Froemsdorf order the launch, and if so, for what reason? Or, did some *U-853* crew members, fearful that Froemsdorf's torpedoing of the collier would lead to their deaths, decide to defy their commander and attempt, albeit unsuccessfully, to abandon their U-boat and take their chances on being plucked from the ocean by an American ship?

"The Story of the Kursk"

BY ROBERT MOORE

(Excerpted from the book *A Time to Die*)

In August 2000, much of the stress and bitterness of the long Cold War between the Soviet Union and the free world had receded into the pages of the history books. The Berlin Wall was gone; the threat of a global conflict between Russia and the West seemed a chilling memory instead of a current possibility. Yet, for Russia as for the United States, missile submarines capable of mass destruction still roamed the oceans.

One such vessel was the nuclear submarine *Kursk*, the pride of Russia's elite Northern Fleet. She was three days into a training exercise in the Southern Barents Sea when disaster struck.

The full, gripping story of the remarkable drama inside the *Kursk* and of the desperate rescue efforts had never been told until Robert Moore's book was published in the United Kingdom and went on to become an international bestseller. In a journalistic coup, Moore obtained the story of what actually happened from interviews with top Russian military officials and scientists, and documents found on the sunken vessel.

For forty-eight hours, from early on Thursday, August 10, until Saturday, the Northern Fleet exercise went broadly according to plan, although there were a number of highly visible technical problems and weapons failures. Several surface warships fired missiles at target barges over the horizon to test the launch systems and the crew training. The *Peter the Great's* first firing went spectacularly wrong, an SS–N–19 missile crashing into the sea a short distance from the ship. Engine failure was suspected, since commanders deliberately chose to use their oldest missiles first. The second launch went much better, the dummy warhead landing extremely close to the target, near enough for observers in patrol boats to describe it as a "complete success."

The pressure to send positive news to the Defense Ministry was intense, and Admiral Popov obliged by giving a prerecorded television interview expressing deep satisfaction with the performance of the ships and submarines and describing the maneuvers as a resounding success. The crews, he added, were heading home.

As premature congratulatory statements go, this would take some beating, for the exercise was not quite over. All four submarines—the attack subs the *Kursk*, the *Boriso-Glebsk*, and the *Daniil Moskovsky* and the SSBN the *Karelia*—still had to go through their paces.

The attack submarines were tasked to fire torpedoes, and the *Karelia* was to launch a ballistic missile. On board the Northern Fleet submarines, the commanding officers were preparing for the tactical phase of the war games, when they would maneuver within their pre-assigned "patrol boxes" and try to avoid detection by the Russian surface ships. The Fleet gave prizes to the submarine crew that performed best, and there was a good-natured rivalry between the commanding officers for the awards.

As the sun rose higher in the clear Arctic sky that Saturday morning, the *Peter the Great* and her support ships surged through the sea on a westerly heading. The group's exact movements were kept secret, to introduce an element of surprise. Before long, the ships turned around, sweeping back on a southeasterly heading. All the submarines were now deployed in their firing areas, and each captain signaled to the Fleet command that he was waiting for the final phase of the exercise to begin.

The *Kursk* signal—"We are ready for torpedo firing" was received at 8:51 A.M.

This would be the final communication from the *Kursk* until she reported the completion of the test. Each submarine was under strict instructions to stay within her specified exercise area. This eliminated the possibility of a collision and would also help the surface ships detect the presence of a Western spy sub. Any acoustic contact moving quietly below the waves but outside the designated patrol boxes could be regarded as a hostile Western submarine.

The whole focus of the *Kursk's* operations now shifted to the forward two compartments, which housed the command center and the torpedo room. The rest of the submarine simply existed to transport the weapons to the firing point, and now the flair, tactical skill, and cool nerves of the commander took center stage.

Captain Lyachin liked to stand in the heart of the central command post in the run-up to a torpedo launch, watching over his team and absorbing information from those around him. The officers were excellent professionals, and their mood was upbeat. In each compartment, there were men he completely trusted, a bond forged during the long Mediterranean patrol nine months before. He had the comfort of knowing that extra technicians were working in the torpedo room, and he was not bothered by the presence in the control center of several senior, shore-based staff officers, who had joined the sub for the exercises.

In a properly worked-up submarine, the atmosphere is calm and professional at this time. Submarine commanding officers say that the perfect attack is conducted in a taut, efficient, and ruthlessly clinical manner. But for Russian submarine COs, with much less training than their Western counterparts, a weapons launch is an anxious affair. Despite his confidence in the crew, Lyachin was well aware of the heightened risks that resulted from the atrocious condition of the Fleet's infrastructure. Even as he concentrated on the flow of orders and preparations leading up to his imminent order to fire, he had to wrestle with a number of disturbing questions. These were doubts that preoccupied all Russian sub commanders. Were the test torpedoes being reused too often? Had a warhead been destabilized during poor handling? Were the safety rules about weapons storage being strictly enforced?

Once the *Peter the Great* penetrated the *Kursk's* designated area, and Lyachin was satisfied with his line of attack, he would order the launch of two special practice torpedoes in quick succession. The warheads had been removed from the weapons, and in their place devices had been installed to record the speed, direction, and depth of the torpedoes. In addition, a safety feature was fitted to each, which ensured that they would run too deep to risk hitting a surface ship. Flotation devices would bring the torpedoes to the surface at the end of their runs.

An alarm rang throughout the submarine, one short burst, then a long one lasting twenty seconds, the signal for the crew to man their battle stations. A voiced command from a senior officer then explained the reason for the alarm:

"*Uchebnaya trevoga. Torpednaya ataka.*"

"Practice alarm. Torpedo attack."

The *Kursk* moved into position for the launch. A torpedo slid into the larger 650mm tube, on the starboard side, with a sharp hiss of air and the sound of the tube's breech door closing behind it. In the torpedo room, all appeared well. In keeping with common practice during firings, the reinforced, watertight doors between the command center and the torpedo room were opened, which helps to minimize the change in pressure and to dissipate the noise of a weapon's launch.

Just before 11:30 A.M., Lyachin was making the final calculations of the firing geometry and choosing the precise timing of the attack.

The chain of events that would soon unfold was triggered not by Lyachin but by an unforeseen development in the first compartment's torpedo room, a crowded workspace filled with weapon racks. With their distinctive green-and-gray steel casings, the torpedoes lie on shelving, their propellers wrapped in protective covering. A narrow walkway down the center allows the technicians to inspect the weapons, but it's a tight squeeze.

Modern torpedoes are built with the same basic design as the primitive versions of eighty years ago: At the front lies a warhead, and behind that is a propulsion system to drive the torpedo through the water as well as a guidance system to steer the weapon to its target. In the earliest days, when the torpedo was proving itself as a weapon during the First World War, the warhead featured a fuse that was triggered to explode when it collided with a ship's hull. The torpedo's propulsion was driven by either compressed air or an electric motor. The new generation of underwater weapons are much more devastating, designed to travel much faster, to carry greater destructive power over increased range, and to pursue a target actively. They are ultra-high-performance machines that, once released, engage in a dramatic sprint toward an ever-shifting target in the ocean. Some naval engineers compare the race to a cheetah's pursuit of an antelope—the hunter following every desperate twist and turn of the prey, all the time closing in for the kill.

The search for extreme performance in an underwater weapon has heightened dangers. High-speed and long-range torpedoes require huge quantities of energy; the energy stored in the propulsion section of a modern high-performance torpedo exceeds even that of the warhead. The engineering challenge is how to tame this energy until the moment of launch.

In the 1920s, propulsion engineers came up with the idea of powering a torpedo by using a conventional fuel, such as kerosene, and giving it an immense energy boost by mixing it with an oxidant. That combination would result in a furious but contained chemical reaction. The best theoretical choice was liquid oxygen, but it was judged far too dangerous and volatile to store inside a submarine. Second best was hydrogen peroxide, known in its highly concentrated form as high-test peroxide (HTP).

The first Russian HTP torpedo was known by the strictly functional name of "53-57," the 53 referring to the diameter in centimeters of the torpedo tube, the 57 to the year it was introduced. Moscow's military leaders, adhering to a deep-seated belief that bigger was better, committed themselves to building ever more powerful weapons. Driven by Cold War competition, they ordered the development of a larger more potent HTP torpedo. The result was the 65-76 torpedo. As the name suggests, the weapon would be launched from 65cm tubes, and it was introduced in 1976. The torpedo found a place throughout the Russian fleet of nuclear-powered multipurpose submarines. The *Kursk* was carrying two of them on the morning of the test. One had just been loaded into the starboard's tube number four, and would be the first practice torpedo fired. The second weapon due to be launched that day was a USET-80, a smaller but powerful torpedo that uses an electric propulsion system.

Once the firing countdown is under way, the launch technicians run through a strict checklist of preparations:

- confirm the outer torpedo tube door is securely shut; double-check it by opening a valve and making sure the water is not under high pressure;
- secure the inner door in the open position; check if the empty torpedo tube is clear of debris;
- check the torpedo's latch claws are attached; remove the safety covers and pins in the torpedo's nose;
- observe closely as the hydraulic lifts align the torpedo with the 65cm tube on the starboard side.

At this point, the weapon glides forward into the torpedo tube, immense power contained within a deceptively simple casing. The intercom to the command center is kept open to allow for a constant dialogue with officers in the second compartment as the final series of checks continues in the torpedo room:

- remove the protective covers from the propellers and from the steering at the rear of the torpedo;
- allow the torpedo to slot home; connect the control cables;
- shut the inner door; flood the tube.

Seawater rushes into the torpedo tube until the pressure is equal to that of the outside ocean. The torpedo room then waits for the captain's instructions to open the outer door in the external hydrodynamic hull, breaking the clean shape of the submarine's bow.

Then they wait for the order to fire.

In the command post at this time, all eyes are on the captain. Perhaps only a fighter pilot has the same single-handed ability to shape the outcome of a mission as that of a submarine commander. Although there is an intense camaraderie on board—more than one hundred highly trained professionals working as a team, each with a very specific responsibility—as soon as a torpedo launch or missile firing is being prepared, or when a submarine is involved in combat or an emergency, the commanding officer makes all the big decisions. One man alone in the attack center determines the fate of the submarine and the success of the mission.

In no other walk of life can a man in his thirties or early forties be thrown into such a demanding and lonely job as commanding a nuclear submarine, where panicking under pressure can have catastrophic results. Once at sea on covert patrol, submarines are expected to communicate only in absolute emergencies. The commanding officer of a ballistic-missile submarine is on his own, with sufficient power to annihilate large parts of the planet.

Lyachin opted to launch his exercise attack on the *Peter the Great* cruiser from periscope depth. Firing a torpedo from deeper is an option, and in war, when preserving the submarine's covert status is a matter of survival, that may be the most desirable tactic. But it is much easier to engage a target when your periscope and masts are breaking the surface—like going into a fight with your eyes open. Lyachin tracked the *Peter the Great* with all the *Kursk*'s sensors: the periscope, the sonars, and the electronic intercepts of the surface ship's radar. He confirmed the identity of the target, matching the *Peter the Great*'s passive sonar signature to his library data. Everything was ready for the attack.

The latest target information flashed down the control cable attached to the torpedo's guidance system. On the appropriate command, the motor of the 65-76 would start up, and as it gathered momentum, compressed air would eject the torpedo from the tube and hurl it into open water. Then, once safely clear of the submarine, the propulsion system would kick in, the HTP and the kerosene igniting in their virulent chemical reaction, driving the torpedo toward its target at thirty knots.

Captain Lyachin had no reason to know the service history of the practice weapon that lay in tube number four, which at any moment he would send hurtling on its way toward its target. The torpedo was manufactured in 1990 in the Mashzavod factory in Alma-Ata, the biggest city in Kazakhstan and lying deep in Soviet Central Asia. In the possession of the Northern Fleet since January 1994, when it had last been serviced, the torpedo had never been used before, unlike so many of the other practice weapons. Technical documents refer to this particular 65-76 torpedo by the factory manufacturing number 298A 1336A PV. But no paperwork revealed its greatest and most terrifying secret: Deep within the casing, over a period of six years, corrosion had invisibly begun to weaken internal metal and plastic components, including gaskets perilously close to the tank that contained the HTP.

The torpedo had been loaded onto the submarine on August 3 by two of the *Kursk*'s technicians, Senior Midshipman Abdulkhadur Ildarov and Senior Lieutenant Alexei Ivanov-Pavlov. The base supervisor was absent, so they signed the required documents themselves, confirming that the weapon was now the responsibility of the *Kursk* crew.

From the moment they signed for the torpedo and winched it through the loading hatch and into the first compartment, Ildarov and Ivanov-Pavlov unwittingly transformed the *Kursk* into a potential disaster zone. The horrifying destructive power of a compromised HTP torpedo had become devastatingly clear forty-five years earlier.

On a sparkling midsummer's morning in 1955, the British Royal Navy's submarine *Sidon* was in Portland harbor, moored alongside a depot ship. With her crew at "harbor stations," HMS *Sidon* was about to proceed to sea, and all her hatches were shut except at the conning tower.

Suddenly, inside her number three tube, a twenty-one-inch torpedo known by its nickname, "Fancy," exploded without warning. Debris was hurled backward into the torpedo room, and toxic fumes swept through the submarine, killing twelve men. HMS *Sidon* began flooding. Nearby ships made desperate attempt to keep her afloat, but less than thirty minutes after the explosion she sank.

The accident triggered an exhaustive investigation by the Royal Navy, and for many years the results of the inquiry were kept secret. The Admiralty Board believed that high-test peroxide had leaked out of a pipe and reached the catalyst chamber of the torpedo. Its top-secret report concluded the HTP droplets may have ignited on "an oily or greasy surface . . . [and] violent combustion and consequent rise of pressure burst open the torpedo tube." Six men died from blast and burn injuries; the other six were killed by the thick, poisonous fumes of carbon monoxide that quickly filled the submarine.

At first glance, hydrogen peroxide, H_2O_2, seems an extraordinarily benign liquid, colorless and odorless. As the chemical formula indicates, it is just water (H_2O) with an extra oxygen atom. But when it comes into contact with certain metals, such as copper, the reaction is fast and furious as it tries to eject the additional oxygen atom, producing immense amounts of heat. Copper is found in brass and bronze, both of which were used in the construction of the torpedo tube, and investigators realized that if the hydrogen peroxide leaked while a torpedo was in position for launch, the chemical reaction would begin.

What shocked the investigators was the fact that twelve men had died and a submarine had been lost—without the torpedo warhead even detonating. All the destructive power had been in the propulsion system. The Royal Navy decided then and there that hydrogen peroxide was too volatile to be stored within the unforgiving confines of a torpedo room, and never again did a British submarine go to sea with weapons that used HTP.

Russia's Northern Fleet had issued no such edict. Aboard the *Kursk*, the 65-76 torpedo lay silently in its tube. Poised for launch, the potent HTP chemical cocktail was ready for ignition.

★ ★ ★

Seven men were crammed into the small passageways of the torpedo room that day, including Mamed Gadjiev, the only civilian on board. He was from Dagestan in the Russian Caucasus, and he worked in a rundown factory that produced many of the Navy's torpedoes. A talented and serious man in his mid-thirties, Gadjiev's engineering background was in aeronautics. He had studied in the Ukraine before switching to the plant on the shores of the

Caspian Sea, to be close to his wife and two teenage daughters. Gadjiev was aboard the *Kursk* to supervise a test of a new battery for the USET-80 torpedo, the second weapon that was to be launched that Saturday morning.

As he stood in the torpedo room, listening to the crew run through the launch checklist, his technical knowledge and engineering's instinct would have given him no advance warning that something was going terribly wrong. The reservoir of colorless HTP was seeping through gaskets deep inside the casing of the 65-76 torpedo. Although an inexorable chemical reaction had begun, it must have been invisible to those in the torpedo room.

The explosive power needed to drive a thirty-five-foot-long, five-ton torpedo at a speed of thirty knots for up to fifty miles was about to annihilate the forward compartment of the *Kursk*. As the reaction accelerated, Gadjiev may have experienced a few seconds of paralyzing horror, fleetingly aware of the enormous destructive forces that were building.

The torpedo exploded in a massive fireball at exactly 11:28.27, with a force equivalent to 220 pounds of TNT. The blast registered 1.5 on the Richter scale—the size of a small earth tremor.

With the torpedo doors still shut, the energy burst backward into the compartment, traveling at more than a thousand feet a second, engulfing all seven men in a rush of flames.

Mamed Gadjiev, Abdulkadur Ildarov, Alexei Zubov, Ivan Nefedkov, Maxim Borzhov, Alexei Shulgin, Arnold Borisov.

They were incinerated with merciful speed, by forces of overwhelming power.

★ ★ ★

Immediately behind the torpedo room, in the second compartment, lies the operational heart of the submarine, where thirty-six men were at their posts. Normally, the command center is manned by thirty-one officers and sailors, but on this voyage an additional five senior, shore-based officers were monitoring the performance of the submarine and her command team. In the control room, at the periscope or close by, stood Captain Lyachin. Next to him sat Sergei Tylik, the twenty-four-year-old with submarining in his blood, watching over his sonar and acoustic equipment.

The explosion ripped through the second compartment with fury, throwing men from their posts and hurling them against the machinery and pipework that surrounded the control room. Submariners who have experienced depth charges talk of their harrowing psychological impact: the fear, the uncertainty of what happens next, the sense of having nowhere to hide. This explosion was on a much greater scale, and *inside* the submarine.

Security forces use stun grenades to incapacitate people because the intense noise and flash of light overwhelms and numbs the human mind. Lyachin, Tylik, and all those around them had been subjected to the shock of a stun grenade multiplied a hundred times. Their shock and disorientation must have been complete. They were in no position to halt the sequence of explosions, ruptures, and avalanching electrical failures that doomed the submarine.

No one who has experienced explosions in a submarine on this scale has survived to relate the horror. The firsthand accounts that come closest are therefore those of the explosions of close-range depth charges. Few have recalled the unique psychology of being in peril in a submarine more vividly than Lothar-Günther Buchheim, who sailed in the German U-boat fleet during the Second World War. He has described the horror of successive concussions, the crew waiting for the hull to rupture, and the fatal rush of the icy ocean:

> The impact has knocked two men down. I see a mouth shrieking, flailing feet, two faces masked in terror. . . . My skull seems under the same extreme pressure as our steel skin. . . . I see and feel everything going on around me with astounding clarity. . . . I hear screams that seem to be coming from a long way off. . . . I want to lie down and hide my head in my arms. No light. The crazy fear of drowning in the dark, unable to see the green-white torrent of water as it comes bursting into the boat. . . .

Lyachin had no time to assess events. Even if he had shouted out orders, he would not have been heard. The explosion ruptured the eardrums of all those in the forward areas of the submarine. The noise of the detonation was itself intensified as hydraulic and compressed air running in pipes throughout the submarine burst into the compartments.

Behind the command center, in the third compartment, lay the *Kursk's* radio room, the most secretive part of the submarine, accessed only with special keys and codes. Experienced Oscar II officers say that the communications equipment is set up so that when the submarine is at periscope depth, with her antennae extended, an emergency signal can be sent by punching just four or five keys. Commanding the radio room was Andrei Rudakov, the officer who was taking legal action against his own admirals to ensure the sailors were paid on time. Trained in the Pacific Fleet, regarded as tenacious and capable, Rudakov is described by his friends as a man who would have excelled in a crisis.

The *Kursk*'s masts were all extended, just penetrating the ocean surface. At this depth and position, Rudakov appeared to be in an excellent position to dispatch an immediate SOS. But no emergency communication was sent—neither on Northern Fleet encrypted channels nor on international distress frequencies. The radio room must have been badly damaged and Rudakov incapacitated, probably thrown to the deck and severely disoriented.

In the few seconds after the explosion, in horror and confusion, Lyachin and some of the men in the command center must have struggled to regain their bearings. Despite injuries, they would have scrambled to assess the damage and open the air valves in order to bring the *Kursk* to the surface. Blowing air into the ballast tanks is a simple task that requires merely pressing a button on the control console. This would certainly have been the first action of any senior officer on board. But apparently it was already too late for that. If someone did reach and press the button, the submarine was too damaged to respond.

Even the emergency buoy, which is recessed into the casing of the outer hull, failed to function. The device is linked to sensors that detect a range of emergency conditions, such as increasing pressure inside the submarine, flooding, or fire, all of which should automatically trigger the buoy's release, sending it shooting upward on a cable. On reaching the surface, an antenna begins to transmit distress signals. Once the buoy is located, rescuers need only follow the cable down to the seabed to locate the missing submarine. Some Northern Fleet specialists claim that the *Kursk*'s buoy had malfunctioned so many times that it had been welded down; others suggest that the sensors were destroyed by the explosion before they could trigger the buoy's release. The startling truth is that during the *Kursk*'s 1999 Mediterranean voyage, there had been so much concern that the buoy would accidentally deploy and reveal the sub's position to Western naval forces that the release mechanism in the third compartment had been overridden. Even during this summer exercise in home waters, the mechanism lay deliberately disabled. The operating key in the machine that controlled the buoy had been removed.

If Lyachin and his senior officers had time to think that their predicament could not get any worse, they had only to glance at the depth gauges, which were still operating, to discover that the *Kursk* was now being driven downward by her own power and by the weight of the water that was pouring into the forward compartments through broken internal pipework.

The shallow water of the southern Barents Sea now presented its own grave danger. A lack of depth is a hazard in submarine operations, depriving a commanding officer of any margin for error. Even if Lyachin managed to make command decisions, he was desperately short of time. The average depth of the Barents Sea is 720 feet, and there are areas south of Bear Island where it reaches just under 2,000 feet. But the *Kursk* was in water only 375 feet deep. Instead of several minutes in which to save his submarine, Lyachin had only seconds.

In the wrecked torpedo room, the laws of physics were remorselessly at work. The inexorable reaction of fuel and HTP cannot be halted; it is self-sustaining, like an avalanche. Torpedoes give you no second chance. Extinguishers and other firefighting equipment, even if you have time to deploy them, are worthless. The reaction will only stop only when the chemicals—in this case, 2,200 pounds of HTP and 1,100 pounds of kerosene—are used up. The forward compartment became a giant combustion chamber: the fuel-fire of the torpedo, the mix of kerosene and high-test peroxide, raging to an incredible heat. The torpedo racks, the patchwork of wiring, the steel bulkheads, and the casings of the remaining twenty-three weapons began to melt. The torpedoes—not the practice weapons, but the actual warload—were either still lying jammed on their racks or were strewn among the debris from the explosion.

The warheads were, essentially, cooking.

Explosives suffer spontaneous combustion at around four hundred degrees Celsius (725°F.) The temperature in the torpedo room was soaring well into the danger zone.

The uncontrolled dive of the submarine lasted exactly 135 seconds, before the second explosion tore through the compartments. It is estimated that the *Kursk* traveled around a quarter of a mile between the detonations, descending 350 feet. The 23,000-ton ship crashed into the seabed at only a slight angle but with shuddering force.

The second detonation was a truly seismic event, nearly 250 times greater than the initial blast. All the warheads and the fuel in the remaining torpedoes ignited almost simultaneously, an explosion that registered 3.5 on the Richter scale. Scientists who have studied the seismic patterns generated by this second explosion say that it occurred at the same depth as the seabed—at 375 feet. That suggests, but does not prove, that the second detonation was triggered by the crash into the seabed rather than the warheads reaching spontaneous combustion. In fact, either could have been true. The fire inside the torpedo room was generating an inferno, temperatures now reaching several *thousand* degrees.

The pressure hull is far stronger than the internal bulkheads that separate the compartments. The high-strength, high-yield steel of the hull can withstand pressure up to a depth of 3,200 feet, whereas the bulkheads would yield at a tenth of that. But the scale of this second explosion made such distinctions barely relevant. The second blast ruptured the hull only a fraction of a second after the forward compartment's bulkhead was demolished. Directly above the torpedo storage area, on the starboard side, the shock wave tore out ten square feet of the pressure hull. The thick steel was punched out, as if by a giant fist. The outer hydrodynamic hull, just a third of an inch thick, stood no chance.

The shock waves then raced through the ocean, hammering into the seabed. Into a compartment that had been devastated by fire and explosion now roared icy Arctic waters, just a few degrees above freezing and under sufficient pressure to cut a man in two. Had the boat been close to the surface, the torpedo compartment, with its twenty-one-square-foot hole in the hull, would have filled up at a rate of 24,000 gallons a second; at a depth of nearly 375 feet, under the additional water pressure, the compartment filled up much faster. In just sixteen seconds, it was entirely flooded. The sailors and officers in the command center who had survived the first explosion stood no chance now. With the bulkhead destroyed between the torpedo room and the second compartment, they faced a crushing wall of water.

The second blast left all four forward compartments shattered. Rudakov and his team of twenty-four officers and sailors in the third compartment were protected only by the steel bulkhead that separated them from the control room, and that was ripped open as if it were made of paper. The fourth compartment, home to the kitchen, the canteen, and many of the living and sleeping quarters of the submariners, was wrecked. Those trapped here included Oleg Yevdokimov, the young chef who had regarded his transfer to the *Kursk* as a blessing because Captain Lyachin's watchful eye meant he would escape the bullying that was so prevalent elsewhere in the Russian armed forces.

As the shock wave punched its way through the large fourth compartment, the successive internal bulkheads began to slow the velocity of the blast. The explosion now became a titanic contest between the tremendous force of the blast and the engineering rigor of the submarine. The question was how far the destruction would extend back into the aft of the *Kursk*. The fifth compartment housed the twin nuclear reactors. They were encased by walls of extraordinary strength, surrounded by five inches of hardened high-grade steel, capable of resisting pressure to 3,200 feet, the same resilience as that of the inner hull.

The shock waves wreaked havoc in the first four compartments, smashing through the bulkheads up to the nuclear reactors. There, the bulkhead held. It was buckled and twisted, but, astonishingly, the steel held. An earlier generation of Russian *atomshiks* had scornfully described their submarines as "nuclear tractors," because of the rudimentary engineering that surrounded the reactors. But there was no mocking the construction of the *Kursk*. Against all the odds, a team of designers and engineers had built in a huge safety margin, and their work had passed the supreme test. The blast was halted at the most critical point, before the shock waves dislodged the control rods. If those rods had not been driven safely home in time, the reactor would have continued running, and without proper water circulation they would have become hotter and hotter. In a short time, the fuel could have melted its way through the reactor, a highly radioactive lump burning into the seabed and poisoning the ocean.

The world had come one bulkhead away from a nuclear disaster. Five inches of precious steel made sure this was a submarine accident, not a regional disaster.

In the event, the control rods were driven safely home, either by an automatic safety mechanism or by a sailor reacting with lightning speed to the impending disaster. Either way, the nuclear reactors "scrammed," automatically shutting down. The pressure in the steam plant plummeted as the turbogenerators stopped. The batteries in the forward compartments were destroyed. The *Kursk* now lay inert on the seabed, without electrical power.

Broken bodies floated in flooded passageways. Driven into the upper part of the bow compartment's ceiling were the remnants of the 65-76 torpedo that had been in the starboard tube. One of the sailors in the command center was blown backward and upward with such power that his corpse was later found embedded in the ceiling of the second compartment.

The submarine herself was over 500 feet long, so she was resting at a depth far less than her own length. Had she done the impossible and ended up resting vertically, some 130 feet of the submarine would have reared above the surface. The escape hatch over the ninth compartment would have been several yards above the waves.

With compartments one to five flooded, both hulls punctured, and her twin 190-megawatt reactors shut down, the *Kursk* was fatally wounded. The crowning achievement of the legendary Rubin design bureau in St. Petersburg and the Sevmash shipyard on the White Sea lay devastated on the bottom of the Barents Sea.

She had taken a decade to design, three years to build, and just 135 seconds to destroy.

For the survivors in the stern compartments of the crippled submarine, the ordeal was just beginning. One hundred meters separated the point of the explosion and the sixth compartment just aft of the nuclear reactors. The engineers at the shipyard on the White Sea had spoken of the boat's "survivability," and in one sense they had been proved right. It seems inconceivable that any other submarine in the world would have afforded the chance of life to so many of her crew after twin explosions of this size. What occurred to the *Kursk* was the worst nightmare imaginable for the Sevmash shipyard and the Rubin design bureau, but it was also their most remarkable achievement.

The sixth compartment was manned by five sailors led by Captain-Lieutenant Rashid Ariapov, the young married officer from Uzbekistan whose wife had told him just a few weeks earlier that she was pregnant with their first child. He was in charge of the submarine's propulsion systems. The seventh and eighth compartments housed the team in charge of the main engines and turbogenerators, a further sixteen men, led by Ariapov's friend Dmitri Kolesnikov and Sergei Sadilenko, both men with the rank of captain-lieutenant. In the final compartment, the ninth, three more sailors served as mechanics.

Just before the torpedo launch, we know, two of the sailors in the stern had moved forward, and one crew member had come aft, leaving twenty-three men behind the protective wall of the reactors. They had heard the standard warning bell and listened to the command post notifying them of the imminent firing.

The sailors in the aft must have been thrown to the deck by the shock waves, and waited in horror as the submarine buckled and convulsed, alarms ringing out. The sound of tearing steel screeched through the ship. In all four aft compartments, depth meters would have told them that the *Kursk* was rapidly plunging downward. Communication links with the control room were severed, leaving the sailors in the aft isolated and terrified. They can only have guessed at the horrors that were being inflicted on their colleagues and friends farther forward. There was no way for them to know what had happened, but they must have deduced that either there had been a massive collision with a ship or submarine, or else one of their own torpedoes or missiles had detonated.

For the first few moments after the second explosion, they were thrust into a world where survival was completely out of their own hands. Had the pressure hull ruptured over the stern, they would have faced instant death. The physics of the explosions and the work of designers in St. Petersburg and engineers in an Arctic shipyard several years earlier were determining whether they would be alive in a few seconds' time. They must have stared desperately at the bulkheads and hatches, waiting to see if these protective barriers would withstand the shock waves and the crushing pressure of the outside ocean.

By the time the submarine had slammed into the seabed, carving a shallow channel in the silt, the *Kursk* had lost communications, heating, ventilation, and all but emergency lighting. The hydraulic and electrical systems had collapsed. The twenty-three sailors were entombed.

As they lay on the deck, or clutched at machinery to maintain their balance, the deafening echoes of the detonations faded away. Amid the baffling horror of what they were facing, they still had no comprehension of the ordeal that now lay ahead.

Editor's postscript: As the world and the Russian people, especially family members and friends of the Kursk *crew, watched and listened in ever-growing despair, efforts to rescue the survivors in 375 feet of water proved to be beyond the Russian Navy's capabilities. The 23 surviving crewmen and officers had perished by the time the* Kursk *was eventually boarded. Their plight and names were recorded on the sunken vessel by Captain-Lieutenant Dmitri Kolesnikov and in individual notes by the crewmen. Their survivors on shore were outraged at rescue attempts they felt were too little, too late. The entire tragedy is fully told in Robert Moore's compelling book.*

"A Narrow Escape"

BY COMMANDER WILLIAM R. ANDERSON, USN
WITH CLAY BLAIR, JR

(Excerpted from the book *Nautilus 90 North*)

Launched at the famed Electric Boat facilities in January 1954, with an appropriate champagne bottle christening by First Lady Mamie Eisenhower, America's first nuclear submarine began a journey that would reach its pinnacle on August 3, 1958, when it surfaced at the North Pole after an undersea journey. The *Nautilus* would go on to complete the first transpolar voyage from the Pacific to the Atlantic.

The complete story of the *Nautilus*'s major journeys—to "boldly go where no man has gone before" as they say on "Star Trek"—is compellingly told by the boat's captain and Clay Blair, Jr., in *Nautilus 90 North*. This excerpt takes you aboard the *Nautilus* as she faces a frustrating setback, then goes on to complete the ultimate sea voyage.

With the western door locked, I intended to try the other, circling south around St. Lawrence Island, and then north off the coast of Alaska. We would pass over extremely shallow water in spots, which would force us to cruise part of the time with our sail, or perhaps the entire upper hull, exposed, thus increasing our chances of being detected. But we had no other choice.

By 0600 the following morning, we had completed our withdrawal from the Siberian ice. We ascended vertically to obtain a fix on St. Lawrence

Island. There was little or no wind, and no ice in sight. However, at that moment, unexpectedly, the sonar reported ice off the bow. Incredulous, I wheeled the scope around. The "ice" turned out to be two sea gulls bobbing in the water. It was reassuring to see how amazingly sensitive our ice detection gear could be. Later, with these instruments we picked up and tracked another bird, a diving cormorant.

By noon, when we again came to periscope depth to ventilate the boat, the weather was foggy, the visibility less than a thousand yards. We obtained one last fix on St. Lawrence Island and were on our way. As soon as possible I passed the word to the crew that I had decided to give up the western door and would try the Alaskan route. To a man, I'm sure, they shared my disappointment that we had not been able to drive straight through to deep Arctic seas on the first try. I also told them that we would be cruising through shoal water, and that we might run on the surface. Typical comment: "I hope it's not on my watch."

The crew was in good spirits, but the gnawing suspicion that all was not well returned to worry me. The leak had been stopped. There had been no further sign of fire. But new omens had come along to replace these. Our well-laid plan to enter the pack through the western door had backfired. The master gyrocompass, out most critical piece of navigating equipment, was behaving peculiarly.

We circled St. Lawrence Island to the east, and returned north following the Alaskan coast. The water was shoaling rapidly. We eased up to eight-five feet. Even at that depth, the fathometers showed only forty-five feet of water beneath the keel. Later that evening we rose to sixty-five feet, the top of our sail just barely underwater. The Conning Officer, Paul Early, kept a continuous watch through the periscope. The water was too shallow to duck under anything. We would have to maneuver around. We were moving at painfully slow speed.

A series of minor crises suddenly befell us. First, the master gyrocompass failed completely. However, our initial reaction of concern soon gave way to one of confidence. With the compass out of commission, the small malfunction which we had not previously been able to detect now made itself clearly evident. Raymond McCoole, who would soon be promoted to Ensign, and his assistant, Roland L. Cave, went to work.

Not long after that, Paul Early sighted a mast on the horizon, almost dead ahead. I was called immediately. I rushed to the periscope, all the while hoping that our sail, which was now partly out of water, had not been sighted. My first impression on viewing the distant object was that it was a snorkling submarine. "But what was it doing in these deserted waters?" I thought. "Could it be Russian?"

We closed in on the target rapidly, prepared for any eventuality. But very soon we breathed easier. The target turned out to be a drifting log with two projecting roots which made it appear very similar to a submarine with two periscopes extended. We were abreast of the mouth of the Yukon River and, as time passed, we spotted many such logs. Only a couple of hours later we came upon one so close that there was no time to retract the periscope, which struck the log a glancing blow. Fortunately, no damage was done.

By early afternoon we had once again reached the high latitude mark for the cruise. The weather was moderately clear, sea temperature well above freezing, and no sign of ice. The news that we might now proceed northward under far more favorable conditions spread like wildfire among the crew. Spirits rose.

Late in the afternoon the rugged features of King Island—just south of the Bering Strait—loomed in our periscope cross hairs. We turned west, reaching for deeper water, hoping to traverse the radar-scanned Strait at periscope depth or more. That evening, when Conning Officer Bill Lalor reported a few chunks of ice, we zigged north, leaving the ice on our port beam. Shortly afterward, we saw a massive mile-wide floe which protruded above the water several feet. We were now at the entrance of the Bering Strait, gateway to the Chukchi Sea and the Arctic beyond.

The newspaper continued, as usual, to pepper the officers, the crew, and our equipment.

> *Overland.* North American's N6A Inertial Navigator had us going overland, across the northwest Cape of St. Lawrence. Actually, it was a short cut. Only three miles across.
>
> *Matinee.* Dr. Lyon remarked at the Father's Day matinee: "Wonder what Dr. Kinsey's report of the crew will be now?" You had better watch it, Doc (Lyon, that is), or Doc (Kinsey, that is) will have the AMA after you.
>
> *Flash.* Rank seems to mean a lot nowadays even among the passengers. Even Rex Rowray had involuntarily given up his rack. Can we find something for Dr. Lyon to do so Rex can get some rest?

Shortly after midnight, June 17, we sighted the Diomede Islands fifteen miles ahead—Big Diomede, Russian-owned, and Little Diomede, American-owned—population, one Eskimo village. Soon after, the Siberian and Alaskan coasts loomed up through the haze. We remained at periscope depth in those shallow and restricted waters. There was no ice in sight except a few chunks near the Siberian coast. The seas were running about four feet high with numerous whitecaps. Conditions appeared most favorable for an undetected transit through the narrow, radar-scanned gap.

Actually, our trip through the Strait was accomplished with unexpected ease. We ran at periscope depth, and at 0530 our bow sliced into the waters of the Chukchi Sea. Like the Bering Sea south of the Strait, the Chukchi is flat and shallow, varying between 105 and 170 feet. Four hundred miles north across the Chukchi lay the deep Arctic Basin. If we could reach the Basin without bumping up against deep-draft rafted ice, I knew we had it made.

We threaded our way northward, trying to keep in at least 135 feet of water. A few hours after entering the Chukchi, we sighted our first piece of ice, dead ahead, range five miles. It was a lone floe measuring about thirty by fifty feet, projecting some ten feet above the water. Its irregular shape suggested a sailing vessel. The sun reflected a multitude of light greens and blues from its surface. It was a captivating sight. However, we had learned the year before that ice is equal in strength to a poor grade of concrete, so we changed course to give the floe a wide berth. We soon spotted other floes. We zigged and zagged, until at 0925, it appeared that ice covered the horizon as far as one could see. There was no choice then—we had to submerge. I ordered a depth of 110 feet.

We cruised at moderate speed, passing under occasional floes and chunks. At longitude 168 degrees 39 minutes west we crossed the Arctic Circle. Once again all our crew members were entitled to be called Bluenoses, although, to tell the truth, it was pretty hard to visualize cold weather in our 72-degree home.

Our feeling of elation at having reached this significant position was soon brought up short. The waters began to shoal dangerously. Since ice reports had been sporadic, I decided to ease up and see if we could safely cruise on the surface. After carefully checking the ice detection gear, I ordered the "ice pick"—one of the radio antennae—raised. As we inched up, I watched the antenna through the periscope. If it bent over, it would be a certain indication of ice overhead and I would still have time to "pull the cork."

Ascending slowly, to our great fortune, we found clear water all around. I gave orders to keep the boat on the surface. Since we were far from land, the risk of being detected was small. In shallow, unknown waters like the Chukchi, we could actually make better speed on the surface, and I was anxious to recover the time we had lost in our fruitless probe of the western door.

Dodging an occasional floe, we logged ninety miles in seven hours. Finally, at latitude 68 degrees 30 minutes north, the Conning Officer reported that the horizon was completely covered with ice. After a brief surveillance of this vast, seemingly endless ice barrier, we concluded that it was the long-sought, supposedly predictable polar pack itself. Relieved, and ringing with enthusiasm, Nautilus submerged to creep beneath it. At that time we did not expect to see daylight or open water again until we rose on the other side of the world near Greenland.

At first everything went smoothly. Ice covered only about 5 per cent of the surface and this was unerringly picked up by our supersensitive sonars. Some of the larger chunks had keels down to twenty feet—fifty feet above the top of our sail. Beneath the keel we had a good forty feet of water. To most submarine sailors this might be considered close quarters, but with our previous ice experience on the Nautilus we were not overly concerned. In fact, we felt safe in increasing speed to eight knots. But every man was alert at his station.

After an hour or so of watching the topside sonar recorder-pen trace the underside contour of the ice, I was convinced that we were indeed clear of the unpredictable shore ice and were well under the polar pack. We had traveled some 1,383 miles under this type of ice in our 1957 cruise and we knew it well. I authorized the Conning Tower to boost our speed to ten knots. Then I strolled down to the Crew's Mess to watch the movie, ironically titled *Hot Blood*.

In a very few minutes the long hours of tension began to tell. I returned to my cabin, lay down, and dozed.

At 2300, Tuesday, June 17—eight days out of Seattle—my doze was interrupted by the calm but emphatic words of Lieutenant Bill Lalor crackling from my cabin speaker. "Captain. Will you come in, please?" I hurried to the Control Room.

When I arrived, Bill reported matter-of-factly that Nautilus had just cruised under ice sixty-three feet thick! The ink tracing showed that the ice had passed only eight feet above the sail. I quickly ordered a swing to the left and a depth increase to 140 feet, a maneuver that would bring us to within twenty feet of the ocean floor. While we were turning, Alfred Charette, Sonarman First Class, quietly reported two massive ridges of ice lying directly ahead. Nautilus was almost under the first of the ridges.

I ordered speed slackened to dead slow. Our sonar revealed that the gigantic block under which we hovered was over a mile wide. Not in many years had I felt so uneasy in a submarine. Obviously, it was urgent that we move away from that ice. Fighting to keep an even tone in my voice, I again ordered the rudder put hard over.

As we crept into our turn, the recording pen wavered downward. All of us—Rex Rowray, who was operating the equipment; Bill Lalor, who was co-ordinating and checking on the ship's course, speed, and depth, together with sonar reports; and myself—stared transfixed. Then slowly the pen receded. We all breathed easier. We had cleared the monstrous hunk by twenty-five feet.

But we were still in trouble. Our instruments told us an even more formidable barrier lay just ahead. I stared in disbelief at its picture on sonar. The books said this couldn't happen!

Slowly—very slowly—we moved forward. My eyes were glued to the recording pen. Downward it swooped again—down, down, down. I reflexed, as if to pull my head into my shoulders. How I wished I could do the same with Nautilus! The small boy trying to squirm beneath the fence would soon be stuck. The inevitable consequences could be severe damage to our ship—perhaps even slow death for those on board.

I waited for, and honestly expected, the shudder and jar of steel against solid ice. The recording pen was so close to the reference line which indicated the top of our sail that they were, for what seemed like hours, almost one and the same. I—and others in the Attack Center, I am certain—turned for assistance to the only Person who could help us.

In pure agony we stood rigidly at our stations. No man moved or spoke. Then suddenly the pen, which had been virtually stationary, slowly moved upward. The gap between the ice and Nautilus was widening. We had made it! We had cleared—by an incredible five feet—a mass of ice big enough to supply a hundred-pound block to every man, woman, and child in the United States.

It took only a second's reflection for me to realize that Operation SUNSHINE had already totally and irrevocably failed. Not even Nautilus could fight that kind of ice and hope to win. To the north of us lay many miles of even shallower water and possibly even deeper ice. There was no question about it. The only sane course was south. Reluctantly I announced my decision to the crew. I told them we would exit the pack, send off a radio report to the Chief of Naval Operations, Admiral Burke, and ask for further instructions.

I spent a long time drafting that message. After so many months of anxiety it was heartbreaking to have to report that our first probes had showed that we could not get through. It was clear that we would have to stand off and take a long look. I tried to make the report to the point, adding my firm belief that the operation would be feasible later on—after the ice boundary had receded to deeper water. And we needed more information. The world about us—the darkness below the ice—was as unmeasured as the far side of the moon.

Toward midnight, Rex Rowray came into the Wardroom for a cup of coffee. He joked about how much he had aged watching the ice recorder for those few tense minutes. I told him I had aged a great deal, too, and I had, literally. It was my thirty-seventh birthday.

★ ★ ★

Peary describes the polar pack near the North Pole as a "trackless, colorless chaos of broken and heaved-up ice." Sir John Ross had this to say: "But let them remember that sea ice is stone, a floating rock in the stream, a promontory or an island when aground, not less solid that if it were a land of granite." They were right. But little did they dream of Nautilus, U. S. Navy, nuclear power, 1958.

Saturday morning, August 2, found 116 people running along at four hundred feet at cruising speed on course 000 true, just about forty-four hours short of culminating the most thrilling and adventurous cruise any sailor ever embarked upon. Overhead the ice was almost solid and incredibly rough, projecting downward as much as sixty-five feet from the surface, but averaging ten to fifteen feet thick. It would be less than honest to say that one can submarine under it with total abandon.

At first Frank Adams and I stood "watch and watch," which meant that one of us was up and about at all times. When my co-skipper took over, I could turn in for a few hours of sleep, knowing that the ship was in experienced and capable hands.

As we plunged deeper under the pack, I thought: *Where is the point of no return? Here? A hundred miles from here? A day's journey away? At the Pole itself, perhaps?* Frankly, I did not know. But I had computed it to be at the "Pole of Inaccessiblity," the geographic center of the ice pack, about four hundred miles below the true Pole. But who cared? We were safe, warm, and comfortable in our home beneath the sea.

Morale was high and excitement at fever pitch. Once we had reached deep water beneath the pack, all hands felt that from then on out it was a run for "home." Although our ship's log read eighteen knots, Chief Machinist's Mate Stuart Nelson, who by then was nicknamed "Stop Leak," scampered forward from the Engine Room to ask if the engineers couldn't make "just a couple more going-home turns." I ordered twenty knots. The whole ship seemed to purr along contentedly.

"Boy, this is the way to explore," remarked Robert N. Jarvis, Hospitalman First Class. Pipe in hand, a cup of coffee beside him, he took his ease between atmosphere analyses. "Pinging up and down and all around at twenty knots, fresh air all day long, a warm boat, and good hot food—we sure have the situation in hand. I'd hate to walk across these ice fields up there to the Pole the way Admiral Peary did it."

Though most of us considered the North Pole a desirable objective, our primary mission was to cross from the Pacific Ocean to the Atlantic Ocean, blazing a new northwest passage. Actually, from the standpoint of compass performance, it might have been preferable to avoid the Pole, to ease around it at lower latitude. However, the route across the Pole was the shortest and fastest. Besides, who could resist the temptation to cross the North Pole when it was so close at hand?

Dr. Lyon remained glued to his sonar equipment hour after hour, watching the recording pens trace the contour of the underside of the ice. His new instruments displayed the ice in far greater detail, and with much greater accuracy, than the machines we had used in 1957. In fact, it was at this point that we discovered that the ice pack was far thicker than we had estimated in 1957, and that pressure ridges (ice forced downward when two massive floes press against one another) projected down to 100 or 125 feet. As we sped along, Dr. Lyon's instruments collected in each hour more precise data on the ice and the Arctic Basin floor than have been assembled in all history. When he finally left the ship, he had accumulated two trunkfuls of data.

And what of peaks rising abruptly from the uncharted ocean floor? Our detection equipment kept a sharp "eye" on these obstacles. We found several. At latitude 76 degrees 22 minutes north, in a region where there are no charted soundings, our fathometer, which had been running along fairly steadily at about 2,100 fathoms, suddenly spiked up to 1,500 fathoms, and then, to my concern, to less than 500.

I camped alongside the fathometer for several hours, intently watching the rugged terrain as it unfolded beneath us. I saw incredibly steep cliffs—undersea ranges—rise thousands of feet above the ocean floor. Several times I ordered speed slackened, then resumed, as a promontory leveled off or descended as rapidly as it had risen. The shape of these undersea mountains appeared phenomenally rugged, and as grotesque as the craters of the moon.

As I paced from instrument to instrument, Chief Hospitalman Aberle arrived with the latest atmosphere analysis. He reported our air vitalization machines were working well enough to maintain an atmosphere averaging 20 to 30 parts per million carbon monoxide, 1.0 to 1.5 per cent carbon dioxide, and between 20 and 21.5 per cent oxygen. These figures were all within, or below, safe limits.

At latitude 83 degrees 20 minutes north we passed abeam of the geographical center of the ice pack, the "Ice Pole" or "Pole of Inaccessibility." Before the day of nuclear-powered submarines, the name was probably fitting. It may now have to be changed.

It has been reported that for the crew Nautilus "hung motionless in time and space." Nothing could be further from the truth. Every man aboard was acutely aware of our rapid and inexorable movement north. As the hours passed, each watch squad gasped at our astonishing progress. Men remained transfixed at the electronic machines clocking our track mile by mile, or before the television set on which they could watch the ice passing overhead like beautiful moving clouds. A mixture of suspense, anticipation, and hope was discernible throughout the ship. Few could sleep. Many of us had been praying for the successful attainment of our goal, and now, God willing, it appeared within our reach.

Our psychiatrist, Dr. Kinsey, went about his work methodically and mysteriously, probing for, I suppose, those men who were afraid. Each day, to a random group of volunteers, he distributed cards containing a series of questions, such as "Do you feel happy?" If a man did not feel happy, he was supposed to indicate by writing a single "V" on the card. If he felt slightly happy, he wrote "VV." Three V's meant that he was in fine spirits, and four V's signified total enchantment. Personally, it made no sense to me. I was not one of the select volunteers.

The main fear within me was that which we all shared: a materiel failure, such as that which occurred in 1957, which would force us to turn back. Every man on board examined and re-examined his instruments and equipment. Vigilance, they all knew, would prevent a small fault from becoming a casualty that would terminate the voyage or leave us stranded beneath the ice.

I did not—could not—sleep. I wandered restlessly about the ship, occasionally taking a peek through the periscope. I was surprised on these observations to see phosphorescent streaks in the water. This is a phenomenon common in tropic waters. It seemed unusual to me to find these streaks in water so cold that the outside of our Engine Room sea-water pipes was covered with thick layers of rime ice.

As I walked about the ship, taking the measure of the crew, I listened as the men spun tales and cracked jokes.

One crewman, recalling the time when Nautilus paid a memorable visit to New Orleans, captivated his shipmates with this story:

"I was headed back for the ship early in the morning. We'd spent most of the evening in the Monkey Bar in the French Quarter. Well, it's about dawn, and I'm walking down this deserted street. Suddenly, out of the corner of my eye, I saw a panhandler crossing the street headed full speed in my direction. He stopped me and asked for a quarter. I looked this bird in the eye and said, 'Look, bud, I'm working this side of the street. You stay on your own side.' Well, I wish you could have seen his face. He was really shook."

In another compartment, two crewmen on watch were talking.

"Joe, do you know who man's best friend is?" Bill asked.

"Well, I always heard it was a dog," Joe said.

"That's not so," Bill said.

"Well, if the dog isn't, then who is?" Joe asked.

"Lady alligators," Bill explained. "You see, every year these lady alligators come up on the beach and they lay about 1,000 eggs. Then, they tell me, the lady alligator turns around and devours about 999 of the eggs she laid."

"How does that make her man's best friend?" asked Joe.

"Well, Joe, it's like this. If that lady alligator didn't eat those 999 eggs, we'd be up to our neck in alligators."

In spite of this lighthearted talk, every man was alert for an emergency. The leads or polynyas were infrequent, but the position of each was carefully plotted, so that if it became necessary to surface, we would know where to find an opening. James H. Prater stood watch in the Torpedo Room, carefully bleeding just the right amount of oxygen into the hull. Nearby was Richard M. Jackman, prepared to make all torpedo tubes ready on an instant's notice, if it became necessary to blast a hole through the ice. We were ready, but the possibility of a casualty seemed remote. Indeed, I had never seen the ship's machinery function so perfectly. Our "out of commission" list reached a new low. It was as if Nautilus herself had found peace and contentment beneath the ice. If she could have filled out one of Dr. Kinsey's cards, it would have contained four V's, or five, or six, for every question.

Shortly after midnight, August 3, we passed latitude 84 degrees north. Since we had entered compass-baffling waters, we made preparations to guard against longitude roulette. At that time we placed our auxiliary gyrocompass in a directional gyro mode so that instead of seeking north, it would tend to seek the line we were following, a Great Circle course up the Western Hemisphere, across the Pole, and south again to the Eastern Hemisphere. This was the track I intended to cruise. When our master gyrocompass began to lose its north-seeking ability, as it would when we approached the northernmost point on earth, then we intended to shift to the auxiliary. Thus we would have something to steer by in the darkness below—something to lead us out on our track south.

In order to insure that all of the gyrocompasses remained properly oriented, we made all course, speed, and depth changes extremely slowly. For example, when we came near the surface to decrease water pressure on the hull (this is desirable in operating the garbage ejector), we rose with an angle of one or two degrees, instead of the usual twenty to thirty degrees. Once we changed course twenty-two degrees. So gradual was the shift that six minutes elapsed before we had settled on the new heading. Some wag had suggested that when we neared the Pole we might put the rudder hard over and make twenty-five tight circles, thus becoming the first ship in history to circle the earth nonstop twenty-five times. Any such maneuver was, of course, out of the question.

As we rapidly closed in on the North Pole, Tom Curtis, manning the inertial navigator, which constantly plotted our position by electronics, made minute adjustments to insure that his complex instrument was operating properly. At 1000 we crossed latitude 87 degrees north, breaking our record of last year, and with the passing of each new mile, we moved farther north than any other ship in history.

Two hours south of the Pole, a wave of unchecked excitement swept through Nautilus. Every man was up and about, and unabashedly proud to be aboard. Frank Adams, staring intently at the electronic gear, uttered a word often employed by Nautilus men who have exhausted all ordinary expressions to sum up their reaction to the never-ending Nautilus triumphs: "Fandamn-tastic."

★ ★ ★

When we crossed the Pole, of course, no bells would ring, nor would we feel a bump. Only our instruments could tell us how close we had come. Since we had made the decision to cross the Pole, we were determined to hit it precisely on the nose. Along with Navigator Shep Jenks and his assistant, Chief Petty Officer Lyle B. Rayl, I had stationed myself in the Attack Center, and although we were almost as far north as man can go on this planet, we were literally sweating over the charts and electronic position-indicators, making minute, half-degree adjustments at the helm.

The hour by Nautilus clocks, which were still set on Seattle time, was 1900, or seven o'clock in the evening. Our nuclear engine, which up to then had pushed Nautilus more than 124,000 miles, was purring smoothly. Our electronic log, or speedometer needle, was hovering above twenty knots, the depth-gauge needle about four hundred feet. Our sensitive sonar indicated that the endless polar ice pack was running between eight and eighty feet thick. Above the ice, we imagined, the polar wind was howling across its trackless, barren stamping ground, grinding massive floes one upon the other.

By then we had been under ice for sixty-two hours. Obviously, it was not possible to take the usual fix on heavenly bodies to determine our position, so we were navigating primarily by dead reckoning. This means that we were spacing our speed and course on the chart and plotting our position every half-hour or so, accordingly. Our bottom soundings, sometimes useful in submerged navigating, did not help, of course, in this uncharted, unsounded area. Our precision fathometer had indicated differences of as much as eight thousand feet at those rare points where soundings were made, so we could not rely on it. Our only check on our navigating was the inertial navigator. At the exact moment we crossed the Pole, we knew, the instrument would give a positive indication. Tom Curtis moved closer to his dials and scopes as we drew near.

A mile south of the Pole, I told Jenks to inform me when we were four tenths of a mile from the Pole as indicated by the electronic log. The mileage indicator was moving rapidly. It was only a matter of seconds. Nautilus crewmen had gathered in the Attack Center and the Crew's Mess.

On Jenks' mark, I stepped up to the mike of the ship's public-address system:

"All hands—this is the Captain speaking . . . In a few moments Nautilus will realize a goal long a dream of mankind—the attainment by ship of the North Geographic Pole. With continued Godspeed, in less than two days we will record an even more significant historic first: the completion of a rapid transpolar voyage from the Pacific to the Atlantic Ocean.

"The distance to the Pole is now precisely four tenths of a mile. As we approach, let us pause in silence dedicated with our thanks for the blessings that have been ours during this remarkable voyage—our prayers for lasting world peace, and in solemn tribute to those who have preceded us, whether in victory or defeat."

The juke box was shut off, and at that moment a hush literally fell over the ship. The only sound to be heard was the steady staccato of pinging from our sonars steadily watching the bottom, the ice, and the dark waters ahead.

I glanced again at the distance indicator, and gave a brief countdown to the crew. "Stand by. 10 . . . 8 . . . 6 . . . 4 . . . 3 . . . 2 . . . 1. MARK! August 3, 1958. Time, 2315 (11:15 p.m. Eastern Daylight Saving Time). For the United States and the United States Navy, the North Pole." I could hear cheers in the Crew's Mess.

I looked anxiously at Tom Curtis. He was smiling. The inertial navigator had switched precisely as expected, positively confirming that we had crossed the exact North Pole. Curtis sang out: "As a matter of fact, Captain, you might say we came so close we pierced the Pole."

I stood for a moment in silence, awe-struck at what Nautilus had achieved. She had blazed a new submerged northwest passage, vastly decreasing the sea-travel time for nuclear submarines from the Pacific to the Atlantic, one that could be used even if the Panama Canal were closed. When and if nuclear-powered cargo submarines are built, the new route would cut 4,900 miles and thirteen days off the route from Japan to Europe. Nautilus had opened a new era, completely conquered the vast, inhospitable Arctic. Our instruments were, for the first time, compiling an accurate and broad picture of the Arctic Basin and its approaches. Nautilus' achievement was dramatic proof of United States leadership in at least one important branch of science; and it would soon rank alongside or above the Russian sputnik in the minds of millions. Lastly, for the first time in history a ship had actually reached the North Pole. And never had so many men—116—been gathered at the Pole at one time.

I was proud of what Nautilus had done, yet I felt no sense of personal triumph or achievement. That we had reached the Pole was the work and support of many people. My reaction, frankly, was an overwhelming feeling of relief that after months and months of preparation and two unsuccessful probes we had finally made it.

Precisely at the Pole, for the record, I made note of some statistics which may or may not prove useful. The water temperature was 32.4 degrees Fahrenheit. The depth of the sea was 13,420 feet, exactly 1,927 feet deeper than reported by Ivan Papanin, a Russian who landed there, he claims, in an airplane in 1937. (In 1909 Admiral Peary had found the depth "greater than 9,000 feet.") At the exact Pole our ice detectors noted a pressure ridge extending twenty-five feet down.

After crossing the Pole, I made my way forward to join in the "North Pole Party" in the Crew's Mess. My first act was to pay modest tribute to the man who, more than any other, had made our historic voyage possible: the President of the United States. A few minutes before, I had written him a message. It concluded: "I hope, sir, that you will accept this letter as a memento of a voyage of importance to the United States." In the Mess, before seventy crew members of Nautilus, I signed this letter, and one to Mrs. Eisenhower, who had christened the ship.

★ ★ ★

Although one goal—the North Pole—had been achieved, we had yet another and even more significant one to realize: the first complete transpolar voyage from the Pacific to the Atlantic. The long leg of the journey was done. If all continued to go well, we would reach open water in the Greenland-Spitsbergen portal within a day and a half.

Without changing course we were now heading due south. The master compass was secured and slewed around. Slowly it began to settle on the new meridian. The auxiliary gyro still indicated course north because, as a directional gyro, it was simply pointing out in space, rotating at the same rate as the earth. How the Helmsmen complained to find themselves steering south by a compass that still pointed north!

I had been requested by the Chief of Naval Operations to send him a brief message after we crossed the Pole—if we could find a polynya or lead large enough to permit us to surface. I drafted the message. It was short and to the point: "Nautilus 90 North." We searched in vain for a polynya. The ice overhead was deep, thick, and closely packed. I stuffed the Top Secret message in my pocket.

With life on board Nautilus once again slipping into a familiar routine, we hurried on at better than twenty knots, making "liberty turns" as the sailors call it when headed toward port. By 0700, August 4, with the Pole 240 miles behind us, the master gyro at last settled on the true meridian. Our Helmsman, Daniel Brigman, breathed a sigh of relief. Now on course south he could actually steer south. The inertial navigator continued to check perfectly with our "dead reckoning position."

After the master gyro had settled and appeared to be operating perfectly, I felt safe in ordering a change in course. I asked the Navigator for a heading to the opening between Spitsbergen and Greenland. It was not a simple request. In order to steer an accurate course, we would have to change our heading one degree for each degree of longitude that we crossed. Because the longitudinal lines were so very close together (they converge completely, of course, at the true geographic Pole), we computed that there would be twenty-six changes—one every twenty minutes. So be it!

That evening, according to our "dead reckoning" navigator, Nautilus entered waters that we had probed on our 1957 cruise. Our charts were covered with soundings—those that we had compiled on our first trip under the ice. Oddly enough, the readings on our fathometer did not match those on the chart. A slight uneasiness permeated the navigation party. After studying the information available, I concluded that we were west and north of our dead reckoning position. Therefore, I ordered a slow course change that would aim us slightly east of south—toward Spitsbergen.

A few hours later, at 0400 on August 5, we cruised under a small patch of open water. Soon afterward our sonars picked up a giant ice floe measuring twelve miles from stem to stern.

"Are you certain?" I asked, making a beeline for the sonar instrument. This kind of ice was not at all typical of the ice we had encountered in this region the year before. Then it had been mostly block and brash—not twelve-mile floes!

At that moment our fathometers registered 2,400 fathoms—a depth far greater than the reports we had been receiving, or had observed on our trip the year before. I glanced at the chart. The only sounding approaching 2,400 fathoms was near the Pole. I wondered: Had our equipment failed? Had we been running in circles? It seemed impossible. Too many things were checking. I shrugged off my concern, thinking we had simply discovered another weird ice characteristic—and one more new hole in the ocean floor.

However, a few moments later, we received from the bathythermograph another startling—or, I should say, downright unnerving—report, indicating that the outside sea-water temperature was getting not warmer, as we had expected on our run south, but colder. In a flash our uneasiness built up to genuine apprehension. *We couldn't possibly be near northern Greenland,* I thought. *By now we would already have run aground!* A terrible—now ridiculous—thought crept into my mind: *Have we actually been trapped in a game of longitude roulette? Are we exiting into some strange sea? Possible the East Siberian Sea?*

While I was pondering those questions, the Conning Officer reported that we had just passed under a patch of clear blue water. I raced for the periscope. Through the glass I could see a steady intensity of blue-green. Completely absorbed, I studied the water. One minute passed—then five—then ten. Meanwhile, the detection equipment reported "all clear overhead."

I ordered speed slackened and we ascended to periscope depth slowly—just in case we had been fooled by a thin layer of ice. I stopped the ship and then backed down. Up went the starboard whip antenna—our "ice pick." We inched toward the surface. Through the scope I could see wave motion. Then the periscope broke the surface, and brilliant sunshine streamed into the glass.

As I backed away, temporarily blinded by the glare, Lieutenant Ken Carr said, "Captain. The sun always shines on Nautilus."

I scanned the surface of the water carefully, noting several small chunks of ice. But there were no large floes. Reluctant to expose the periscope to possible damage, and anxious to give the Radiomen as much antenna height as possible, I ordered the ship surfaced.

From the size of the waves and the swells, we were certain that we were in an open sea. The water seemed similar to that we had encountered in the Greenland Sea in 1957. As we carefully scrutinized the ice, bending around us to the west and south, we tentatively concluded that we had reached the edge of the pack. Although we were fairly sure of our position, I have learned that in polar navigation it is best to be from Missouri. I waited anxiously as the navigators computed our position by observations of the sun.

We worked our way south, meanwhile, dodging a very large floe, evidently one that had become detached from the pack. In contrast to the dirty floes we had seen on the other side, the ice was brilliantly white. We passed a small seal lazing in the sun atop a small, private chunk of ice that had torn loose from a floe. As we rushed by, the seal seemed not in the least surprised or disturbed. In fact, he acted as though he saw submarines emerging from the polar pack every day.

After about an hour on the surface, Navigator Jenks reported our exact position which, to the relief of all, placed us just where we thought we were: northeast of Greenland. After a transit of 1,830 miles—ninety-six hours under the ice—we were only a few miles—far less than ten—from his dead-reckoning position. In my opinion, it was the most remarkable piece of ship navigation ever accomplished. I shook my head in amazement and uttered a Nautilus word . . . "Fan-damn-tastic!" Then I passed the word to the crew on the ship's public-address system and made my way down to the Radio Room to see if our message had been sent off.

Communications in the Arctic are, as previously noted, erratic. I found Radiomen Harry Thomas and Terrence Provost flipping switches and adjusting knobs to pull the last ounce of energy out of the transmitter. Using brevity codes, Provost got on the telegraph key and clicked out: "Any U. S. Navy radio station this is an unidentified station with two operational immediate messages." Provost sent the message over and over, but he could get no response. It was a frustrating experience. Here we were, possessed of momentous news, but no one would listen to us.

"Captain," cracked one of the men, "we should have brought some carrier pigeons with us."

I was on the verge of submerging the ship for a fast run south to a more favorable atmosphere when, finally, a weak signal came through. "This is U. S. Navy radio, Japan. Send V's so I can tune you in." In a few painstaking minutes we fired off our historic three-word message, "Nautilus 90 North." Soon the message was en route to Washington, via Japan.

As Provost shifted to the second message, Japan faded out and another station answered. This time it was U. S. Navy radio, Honolulu. Then Radio Londonderry broke in. We relayed the message to Honolulu and, shortly afterward, submerged, and set cruising speed for the Denmark Strait. Operation SUNSHINE, perhaps the most remarkable voyage in the history of man, had been completed.

From then on Nautilus moved fast, events even faster.

Months before, when Operation SUNSHINE first evolved, Captain Aurand, the President's Naval Aide, had told me that if the trip proved successful, the White House desired to release the information as rapidly as possible. To expedite the release, an extraordinary plan was drawn up. After

Nautilus left the ice pack, she would proceed to a secret rendezvous off Reykjavik, Iceland. (When Navigator Jenks stumbled over the name Reykjavik, one Nautilus sailor said, "Never mind how you pronounce it, just find it.") At that point, unobserved by ships and aircraft, Nautilus would stop and wait for a helicopter. When the helicopter came in sight we were to surface. Then I would leave Nautilus and climb aboard the helicopter, which would fly me to Iceland. There a plane would wait to lift me to Washington, where I would report directly to the President.

My feelings were mixed about this phase of Operation SUNSHINE. This would be an honor excelling all I had ever before experienced, or probably ever would experience in the future. It would provide an opportunity for me to see Bonny, who was waiting at our home in Mystic, Connecticut. It would give the finest Executive Officer in submarines, Frank Adams, a chance to step up, temporarily, to command what we both believe is the finest submarine in the world. My main concern was that during my absence the officers and men of Nautilus would find out that I was completely dispensable!

At dawn on August 7, the helicopter, an Air Force H-19, thrashed into the periscope field. I ordered three blasts on the surfacing alarm, zipped up my coveralls (to conceal my uniform), and slipped on a life jacket. As the bridge hatch cleared the water, Frank Adams assumed command of the ship. The H-19 pilot hovered the craft a scant five feet above our afterdeck. In seconds my gear was aboard. With the help of a crewman on the helicopter and a tall step, so was I.

On board the H-19, wearing flight coveralls, I found a friendly and familiar officer—Captain Peter Aurand. He gave me a warm getting and a message from the President, which said:

TO THE OFFICERS AND CREW OF THE NAUTILUS
Congratulations on the magnificent achievement—WELL DONE.

It was signed by Dwight D. Eisenhower.

We handed the message down to a Nautilus crewman. About fifteen minutes later the H-19 landed in Keflavik, directly alongside a Navy transport plane whose engines were turning over. Not more than a minute after that, the transport taxied down the runway and took off. As we moved south at four miles a minute the early morning light faded. My thoughts drifted back to Nautilus, which at that moment was steaming rapidly eastward, deep in the Atlantic, en route to Portland, England. I could visualize her—sleek, gray, sharklike on the outside, shiny, warm, and comfortable on the inside. For a brief moment my mind was flooded with visions of jagged ice profile recordings. And then, for the first time since departing Point Barrow, Alaska, six days before, I found restful sleep.

Soon the wheels of our plane touched down on the runway at Washington National Airport. A car was waiting, which took us to the White House. In another few minutes, to my astonishment, I was face to face with Bonny, who had been flown down from Mystic in another Navy airplane. I was still recovering from that surprise when someone whispered in my ear, "The President is waiting."

"Radar Sparring"

BY D. A. RAYNER

(Excerpted from the novel *The Enemy Below*)

U-boat versus destroyer—winner take all.

Portraying the simultaneous maneuvers and commands above and below the surface gives D. A. Rayner's *The Enemy Below* the atmosphere of a deadly duel, fought between two determined enemies. One is the captain of the British destroyer H.M.S. *Hecate;* the other the Kapitän of the U-boat *U-121.* (In the popular film version starring Robert Mitchum, the British destroyer is transformed into an American ship.)

As the action begins, the lone destroyer has picked up a radar contact of the U-boat running on the surface, and its commander and crew unaware of the danger bearing down upon it.

U-Boat *121* hurried over the sea. The vibration of the powerful Diesels shook her strong hull, and their clatter pervaded the whole boat. Driven into the waves regardless of the devastating motion, conditions aboard were indescribably vile. As her bow rocketed skywards men's innards would be left behind; as the lean ship breasted the waves' crest she would corkscrew wildly before plunging downwards—and once again stomachs would be in suspension. It was a motion that was sufficient to nauseate the toughest, and Korvettenkapitän Peter von Stolberg had a stomach that was never proof against such violent motion. Consequently, after refusing his supper, he had turned into his bunk, where, with pills, he had tried to calm the queasiness within him. Only necessity, the urgent necessity of getting to a given position on the deserted ocean by a given time, had caused him to make this high-speed dash on the surface. It had to be done, regardless of the discomfort to the crew and the possibility of damage to his ship, because Doenitz had said that he must be there on time. The Grand Admiral had emphasised his words with considerable deliberation. When he closed his eyelids to shut out the misery of his own and his men's condition, the Kapitän could see the shrewd dynamic face of his superior.

"You will be in position by noon, local time, on the 9th of September, Herr Kapitän—and nothing must stop you. Nothing!" The little man had slammed his fist on the polished top of the great desk behind which he sat. His eyes, which were of an unnaturally pale blue, with the irises completely surrounded by the whites, appeared like those of a bull-frog—about to pop out of his head. "Raider M has succeeded in capturing a complete set of the allied cyphers, which the enemy will bring into force on the 1st of October. It is true she is herself coming home, with a pleasant load of prisoners, after sinking over a hundred thousand tons of enemy shipping—but that is not certain enough for me. You understand? We must insure against the risk of her non-arrival. She has been instructed to photograph the cyphers and to transfer the films to you, for delivery to me here. You are to proceed direct to this position and, unless you yourself are directly attacked, you are not to engage the enemy—however tempting the target may be."

A few days later *U-121* had sailed from Brest with apparently plenty of time to make the rendezvous. But the first few days had not been entirely happy. A patrolling Liberator had spotted them on the second night out, and they had suddenly found themselves under the bright artificial moon of a parachute flare. A moment later the sea around them had erupted as the stick of depth-charges burst. Worse was to follow. A British escort group of sloops had hunted his boat relentlessly for three days before he had finally been able to shake them off. Thus they had been forced to make almost the whole of the first eight hundred miles submerged—surfacing only at irregular intervals and for just enough time to recharge their batteries. The continual air reconnaissance of the British Coastal Command was becoming beyond a joke. It didn't give a fellow a chance.

When at length the Kapitän had been clear of the aircraft, he had run into persistent bad weather, and the margin of seven days which he had thought he had in hand when he left Brest, had gradually been whittled down to no more than a bare eighteen hours to spare. For that reason, and that alone, he was driving his ship and his men unmercifully—at the same time he was extremely angry with his own body because of its frailty. He disliked the motion. He hated the stench of sickness that pervaded the boat. He longed for the calm of summer evenings in the Black Forest, and for mountains that rolled like dark-green waves, but did not fling the watcher about. The pill he had taken was working now. He felt drowsy and slept, rolling slightly from side to side. The expression of disgust still curled his lips—for he was a fastidious man.

Leutnant-zur-See Erich Kunz had the first watch. The Kapitän considered him to be a silly young man. Kunz was frightened of his Kapitän, and this made him appear to be more silly than in fact he was. Von Stolberg was from the aristocracy—Kunz from the Hitler Youth. They were poles apart in background, upbringing and in every other way. But Kunz was not concerned now with his Kapitän. He was concerned only with keeping himself as dry as possible, and that was a difficult enough job. Crash would go the long bow into the steep head sea flinging up the spray to whip over the exposed conning tower; then the wave, roaring aft along the deck, would break in fury against the four-inch gun, sending even heavier water pouring over the men that crouched in their inadequate shelter. There were three men whose duty kept them outside, Kunz, the officer of the watch, Karl Schott the signalman, and a seaman for lookout. It was, thought Kunz, a useless duty for all three; for in no direction could their water-laden eyes see a thing. But to say so to his commanding officer was quite beyond his capabilities.

A head and shoulders appeared above the conning-tower hatch. "Radar operator says it's time to swing her, sir."

"Very well." Kunz acknowledged the information, and down the voice-pipe ordered the alteration of course that would enable one of the quarter radar mattresses to cover the arc where the stern had been. Unlike a surface ship, whose radar aerial turned continually, the U-boats had "send and receive" radar mattresses that were fixed round the conning tower, each covering a certain arc. But because of the position of the anti-aircraft gun there was no mattress that covered the arc that lay ten degrees on either side of the stern. Consequently, when on passage, the routine practice was to swing the boat twenty degrees to one side once every hour to make sure that nothing was astern—and when this was ascertained to turn back once more to their previous course.

A moment or two later the head and shoulders reappeared.

"Anything to report?" Kunz asked.

"The ground returns from the sea are so bad that the screen's cluttered up with false echoes, Herr Leutnant."

244 . The Greatest Submarine Stories Ever Told

"Who is the operator?"

"Bauer."

Kunz nodded. "Very well." Willi Bauer was the signalman responsible for looking after the radar set. His report should be reliable.

"Bauer said that there seems to be a ghost echo eleven thousand metres astern—very indefinite."

"Anything would be in this weather. There no surface ships here, and if there are—we can't attack them."

"Shall I report to the Kapitän?"

"No, no. He will be angry if he is disturbed."

"Zum Befehl, Herr Leutnant."

"Tell Bauer to see if it's still there in an hour's time."

The head and shoulders disappeared and Kunz turned to the voice-pipe. "Bring her back on course," and he settled down to another hour of misery.

An hour later the ghost was still there.

"That proves it's something in the set—that machine is haunted with ghosts. Tell the hydrophone operator to see if he can hear any asdic transmissions, and report to me."

"Zum Befehl, Herr Leutnant."

Five minutes later the messenger was back again. "No transmissions audible, sir."

"Thank you." Kunz, satisfied that the radar had chosen this occasion to trot out one of the innumerable ghost echoes of which it was capable, prepared to do his utmost to keep himself dry.

And so it had gone on. From hour to hour, and from watch to watch. The longer that the echo stayed just where it was, the more likely it was to be a "ghost." For who had ever heard of an escort that, obtaining a radar contact had not rushed at it full tilt?

Kunz had been relieved at midnight by Oberleutnant Otto von Holem. There was no love lost between these two either. Kunz considered von Holem a useless sprig of the nobility, and the latter thought that Kunz was beneath contempt. The exchange had been as short as the necessity of duty permitted. At the last moment Kunz had paused half-way down the hatch. "Oberleutnant—there is a ghost echo on the radar, eleven thousand metres astern. I forgot to tell you."

"You have reported it to the Kapitän?"

"No. It was reported as a ghost, and has been there for three hours. It can be nothing else."

Von Holem was about to suggest with some acerbity that the Kapitän should have been told, when Kunz added from one rung farther down the hatch: "I thought you'd like the pleasure of starting a mare's nest."

"Verfluchter Kerl," von Holem murmured and turned to duck his head as a solid sheet of water flung itself over the conning tower.

Four hours later von Holem was relieved by the Executive Officer, Oberleutnant Heini Schwachofer.

"The weather improves."

"It's not quite so wet now."

The two officers stood side by side looking over the long bow as it creamed into a wave. But the wind was gone, and only a spatter of spray fell into the conning tower.

"Anything to report?"

"Nothing. A ghost echo turned up in Kunz's watch. Dead astern eleven thousand. I nearly reported it to the Kapitän, but it's so regularly there that I'm sure it is a ghost. It's been there for eight hours."

"I agree. It can't be the enemy. He's not the patient sort. Anyway, there are no escorts in this part of the world. Sleep well, Otto."

Von Holem lowered himself down the hatch.

The watch dragged on. A pale sheen flitted on the advancing face of the waves. The hull appeared darker and the phosphorescence paler—the dawn. Schwachofer stirred, easing cramped limbs.

"Signalman—coffee."

The man disappeared.

The cold light grew in intensity. The horizon of exact sight expanded, fifty metres—two hundred metres.

The signalman thrust a cup of steaming coffee into his hand.

"Ah!" The executive officer put salt-caked lips to the hot rim. The scent of coffee filled his nostrils. "Ah!" he said again with satisfaction.

The dawn of a new day crept over the ocean. It was lighter to the east. He glanced at his watch—twenty minutes past six—and turned again to look over the bow. The wave motion fascinated him as the seas creamed along the U-boat's circular hull and sucked at the long casing that ran up to the high bow.

Putting the binoculars to his eyes, he commenced a routine sweep. Jagged wave tops ahead, long valleys on the beam, the smooth backs of retreating waves astern, and . . .

"Zum Teufel!" He lowered his glasses, wiped them hurriedly, and looked again. Then he stretched out his hand and pressed the alarm for emergency diving stations.

The strident roar of the klaxon, that had not been heard for the last fortnight, filled the boat. In a moment the narrow central alley-way was full of men hurrying to their stations. They hauled themselves from their bunks, struggled into jackets, fastened trouser belts, grumbling and cursing. U-boat 121 had been caught with her trousers down.

★ ★ ★

"Submarine diving, sir." The cry was taken up by many voices.

"Commence asdic sweep. Steer two-four-oh. Note the time, Pilot. Yeoman, get a position from the navigator and get that signal off right away, Johnson is expecting it. Number One, sound off action stations and let me know as soon as the seven minutes are up." The Captain's orders came crisply and with certainty.

The telephone from the radar cabinet buzzed. The Captain raised the hand set. "Forebridge."

"Echo's faded, sir." Lewis's voice sounded tired.

"Thank you, Lewis. We've seen the U-boat submerge—and thank you for your work. It's been a damn' fine effort."

"Thank you, sir."

"Go and get your head down, man. I'll send for you if I need you."

"Aye, aye, sir."

The Captain replaced the hand set. While he had been talking he had been conscious of the clattering up ladders of many feet; the clang of iron as hatches were closed and clipped, and others, up which the ammunition would be sent to the guns, were flung open. Now the apparent chaos had subsided to the quiet efficiency of a prepared ship. The *Hecate* had drawn her sword, and the naked blade was bright in her hand. From many places came the reports.

"Coxswain at the wheel, sir."

"B gun cleared away, sir."

"Depth-charge crews correct, sir."

"Asdic hut closed up, sir."

"Plot closed up, sir."

"X gun cleared away, sir."

"Third boiler connected, sir."

It was, the Captain thought, an evolution that never ceased to thrill. Action stations sounded in the presence of the enemy: the incredibly intricate

ship coming under the control of one brain. Not that the one brain func-
tioned alone: it planned the action, but left the carrying out to trusted officers. Mentally he reviewed them. There wasn't one who could not be relied
upon to do his job.

The First Lieutenant touched his arm.

"Seven minutes, sir."

"In one minute alter course to port to one-eight-oh. Use thirty degrees of wheel. If she does not turn fast enough I'll stop the port engine. I
want her on the new course in two minutes."

"Aye, aye, sir."

The Captain moved apart from the other officers clustered on the
bridge. He felt an immediate desire to be alone—for he looked fear in the
face, and wanted to meet this new adversary alone. It was not so much
the personal fear of death, but the fear that his professional judgment might
prove to be at fault. Somewhere on the port bow and hidden by the waves, he
was sure that there was a lethal enemy preparing to strike at him, and through
him at the ship he commanded, and at the men who trusted him. For the first
time in the whole war he had the chance seriously to plan a meeting with the
enemy. Previous engagements had been fought on snap decisions and in-
tuitive actions. Parry had followed riposte into lunge with such speed that
serious thought had been impossible. This carefully calculated action was foreign both to his nature and experience.

The sun was breaking the horizon's rim. Pale gold light dispersed the
last of the dawn's shadow.

"Port thirty, steer one-eight-oh." The First Lieutenant's voice cut
across his thoughts and he moved towards the standard compass. The *Hecate*
began to heel, to lean over to starboard as her rudder bit into the water.
Looking astern, he saw the slick, satin smooth, already growing from her port
quarter.

The telephone from the asdic cabinet broke the silence. The Captain's arm shot out, and then remembering that he of all people must remain
calm, he slowly raised the hand set to his face. "Forebridge."

The asdic officer's excited voice came to him:

"Strong hydrophone effect on port bow."

"Bearing?" the Captain snapped.

"Difficult to say, sir. It covers quite a large arc. I'd say red three-oh to
right ahead."

The Captain looked at his First Lieutenant. "How's her head?"

"Passing two-one-oh, sir."

Captain to asdic cabinet: "Bearing now?"

Asdic cabinet to Captain: "Seems to be crossing the bow, sir. Approximate centre bearing red oh-five to green one-oh. Getting much louder, sir."

Captain to First Lieutenant: "How's her head?"

"Passing one-nine-eight, sir."

Captain down voice-pipe to the wheelhouse: "Stop port."

The voice-pipe answered: "Port engine stopped, sir."

Captain to First Lieutenant: "Half ahead port engine as soon as you're round to one-eight-five."

"Aye, aye, sir."

Captain to asdic cabinet: "Bearing now?"

"Green oh-five to green six-oh."

By the record of their instruments, the torpedoes had crossed their bows and were speeding into the barren wastes of the sea, where they would sink to the bottom and lie on the ooze to the astonishment of the deep-sea fish. But one could never be quite certain, unless one's eyes could confirm the tale told by the clever electrical machines.

"Captain, sir. Captain, sir." The bridge look-out on the starboard searchlight platform was pointing desperately towards the starboard beam.

Hurrying across the bridge the Captain lent over the starboard side to follow the look-out's finger. There, lying across the now blue and sparkling water, were two long white shafts that undulated as the waves crossed their path.

He came back to the compass platform. "Two torpedoes passed down our starboard side—half a cable clear." He felt good. He felt grand. He went to the voice-pipe that let to the plot. "Pilot, give me a course to a position two-one-oh degrees three miles from where she dived."

A moment's wait and then from the pipe the Scots accent: "Two-oh-eight, sir."

"Thank you," the Captain said, and turned to the First Lieutenant, who had just ordered the port engine ahead again. "Bring her back to two-oh-eight. We've drawn his fangs."

"Starboard thirty, steer two-oh-eight." The order was passed, and then: "Worked a treat, sir." His First Lieutenant's smiling face was raised to his. The blue eyes laughing in the tanned face. "I bet the Herr Kapitän is hopping mad."

"I hope so too. It may get him rattled—but I doubt it. He's the fighting type, or he'd never have sent those 'kippers' after us. He'll give us a run for our money."

Willis, the yeoman, approached him.

"Yes, Yeoman?"

"Message passed, sir. Johnson told me to tell you 'four minutes ten seconds dead,' sir."

"Thank you, Yeoman. Pass the word to Johnson that I'm very pleased indeed with the time. It's damn' good."

The *Hecate* was heeling now to port as she turned back to starboard after her enemy. Astern her wake showed clear—a gigantic S, the turns almost half a mile in diameter. Leaning against the voice-pipe to the wheelhouse, the Captain could hear snatches of conversation not meant for his ears.

"What I wants to know is, how the Old Man knew the bastard was going to try to kipper us?"

" 'Cos he's got a head on 'im, hasn't he—same as you? The difference is that he uses his. That's what he draws his pay for."

Laughing, the Captain flicked over the cover of the voice-pipe, cutting off further chance of eavesdropping.

The bell from the asdic buzzed warningly.

"Forebridge," the Captain said.

"Submarine echo bearing two-oh-eight, sir. Going away, extreme range."

"Nice job, Hopkins. Keep the plot informed." And to the plot: "Asdic has a target bearing two-oh-eight degrees, probably submarine. Extreme range. Plot the target."

"Aye, aye, sir. Plot the target."

★ ★ ★

Oberleutnant Schwachofer, after he had clipped down the heavy lower-conning-tower hatch, jumped the last four rungs to the deck and steadied himself by holding on to the ladder.

Already the boat's bow was sinking and the deck inclined downward. The clatter of the Diesels had gone, and in its place was the soft purr of the big electric motors. The Kapitän came from the doorway that led to the wardroom and through that to the engine and motor rooms. He was unshaven, and did not look well. His queasy stomach of the last twenty-four hours had given him pouches under his eyes. His hurriedly donned coat was unfastened and the trousers, in which he had slept, were crumpled.

"What is it?" He spoke in a voice that was louder than necessary, causing his Executive Officer to fear needlessly for the Kapitän's nerve.

"A British destroyer, Herr Kapitän."

"Nonsense! Did you sight her?"

"Indeed I did. Between four and five miles astern."

"To the eastward of us—up-sun. It is possible that she has not sighted us."

"I fear, Herr Kapitän," Schwachofer was going cautiously in spite of the obvious need to tell his senior everything that he knew, "that she has been tailing us since just after eight o'clock last night. We—that is first Kunz, and then the rest of us, thought that it was a ghost echo."

"Impossible." The veins were standing out in the Kapitän's neck. "Impossible." The blood was coursing into his face. The eyes were red with it. The Executive Officer had never seen such fury. "Impossible." Schwachofer drew back as if he feared his Kapitän would strike him.

The Kapitän shivered as, with a great effort, he fought for control and succeeded in achieving the mastery of his temper. But when he spoke the tone of his voice was unrecognisable for the usual friendly manner.

"Blöde Kerle. All of you. Almost ten hours. One hundred and forty miles you have brought the enemy. You know how important is our mission, and you lead him to our rendezvous. Is this how *U-121* obeys the orders of the Grand Admiral?"

"I'm sorry, Herr Kapitän."

"Mistakes cannot be rectified in war. Please God the Britisher makes a mistake. Four and a half miles. Bring the boat to ten metres at once. At once, you understand. I would use the periscope."

Both officers glanced at the depth gauge which already showed sixty metres. The Kapitän's standing order was that, on the sounding of the crash dive signal, the boat should be taken down to eighty metres.

The Executive Officer issued sharp orders. The bow whose dip had been growing less, now became level. The hiss of high-pressure air stowed in the big bottles under the deck could be heard expelling the water from the ballast tanks. The needle of the depth gauge stopped, hovered, and began to retrace its steps. Slowly at first, and then more quickly.

The Kapitän buttoned up his coat as he watched the gauge. One hand stroked his chin. He wished he could have been given time to shave. He did not like the men to see their Kapitän looking dishevelled.

Twenty metres. The needle crept more slowly now.

"Course two-one-oh. Four knots. Periscope depth, Herr Oberleut-nant—and be prepared to dive deep."

The hiss of the hydraulic rods, that brought the big attack periscope from its well, sounded through the control room. The eye-piece with its handles appeared above the deck. Bending, the Kapitän seized them. His back unbent as the periscope continued to rise. His eyes were fixed in the rubber eye-shield.

"Ten metres." Schwachofer spoke crisply. Now that his Kapitän was taking the offensive his own morale was returning. They'd sink the destroyer and then, in the rejoicing, they'd all be forgiven. He could even imagine that an unscrupulous Kapitän might claim to have lured the intruder along until daylight, so that he could torpedo it. He wondered just how scrupulous von Stolberg was. A strong disciplinarian, a good fellow, but a real Junker. Schwachofer was a sailor, born and bred in the Baltic timber trade; he would not altogether trust a "Von."

At the Kapitän's touch the periscope rose still higher until he was standing upright. Schwachofer watched von Stolberg's feet move flatly, gripping the deck which, now that they were at periscope depth, was feeling again the effect of the surface waves.

The Kapitän spoke. "She is not astern." A pause—then "Ach—I have her now, bearing green one-six-oh. A Western Approaches' destroyer. She has the white and light-green camouflage. Converted for escort work. One of the forward, one of the after guns, and the torpedo tubes have been taken out of her, so that she may carry more depth-charges."

"She was astern." Schwachofer volunteered the information.

"Then she makes her big mistake." The Kapitän's voice was gleeful. "Her captain is a clever man. He thinks to work out on my beam before he comes in to attack. An attack up my stern is so difficult for him. He will lose contact so long before he must fire his depth-charges, that I will avoid them. So he plans to attack from my beam. But, Schwachofer, I shall sink him. Kunz, start the attack table."

"Jawohl, Herr Kapitän." Kunz, its attendant officer, started the complicated electrical device which, when fed with the enemy's course, speed and range, would provide the angle of deflection. When this had been set on the sight in the periscope, it would enable the torpedoes to be aimed just the right amount ahead of the target, so that both should arrive at the same place at the same time. The Kapitän himself, knowing the length of the enemy, would decide on the amount of spread between one torpedo and the next.

"Müller," the Kapitän called the torpedo petty officer.

"Prepare numbers five and six tubes, set torpedoes to run at three metres at forty knots."

"Jawohl, Herr Kapitän." The man disappeared aft towards the two stern tubes.

"Kunz. Enemy's bearing green one-five-five. Course two-four-oh. Speed one-five knots. Range eight thousand five hundred."

The hush of excitement settled on every man in the boat. Their heart beats were caught up in the steady purr of the engines.

The periscope hissed as von Stolberg lowered it.

"Well?" he said, turning to Kunz.

"Deflection two-five degrees left, Herr Kapitän."

The Kapitän bent to the periscope handles and raised them slowly. "Stand by number five and six tubes."

"Müller reports number five and six ready, Herr Kapitän."

"Gut."

The periscope was nearly up now. The Kapitän was sweeping the horizon on either side of his target.

"The poor fool. He forgets that he is alone. For once—just once—I have a British escort in my sights, and I do not have to worry whether another is about to attack me. I have prayed for this so many times. Port ten, Coxswain, let her come round slowly. Ah—das ist gut—I enjoy myself. Stand by to fire. Fire six!" The boat lurched as the torpedo sped on its way.

"Torpedo running," Braun, the hydrophone operator, reported.

"Fire five!" the Kapitän ordered, and again the boat lurched.

"Torpedo running," Braun repeated.

"Kunz, what is the length of run?"

"One minute forty-eight seconds, Herr Kapitän." Kunz held a stopwatch in his hand.

Von Stolberg, his eyes glued to the periscope, answered: "Tell me when the first fish has been running for a minute."

"Jawohl, Herr Kapitän."

The tense-faced men gathered round the Kapitän in the control room saw his braced legs and back stiffen to rigidity, and heard an explosive "Du lieber Gott! He turns! He cannot see my torpedoes—but he turns under full helm."

"One minute, Herr Kapitän."

"You fool—this is all your fault," the Kapitän exploded, burning up his rising chagrin with a return to the original complaint.

The Executive Officer made a mental note that now there would be no bombastic reports written on this episode—and he smiled rather ruefully.

Watching the destroyer in the circular view of the periscope, von Stolberg saw that her bow was pointing directly towards him; and before he had seen the whole of her port side. She was still turning; as much of her starboard side was visible, as before there had been of the port. The target was already moving slowly to the *right* across the little black lines etched on the glass of the periscope—and the torpedoes had been fired with twenty-five degrees of *left* deflection. He had missed.

Kunz opened his mouth to tell his Kapitän that the first torpedo should be arriving. He caught Schwachofer's eye and hesitated. Slowly the latter shook his head and dropped the corners of his mouth. Kunz, who tried hard, only succeeded in irritating the two "Vons." Schachofer held that the freemasonry of the sea-service should override all other considerations. He was sorry for Kunz.

Von Stolberg whipped the periscope down. The hiss it made, as it slid into its well, sounded as if its pride was hurt. "Dive to eighty metres, Herr Oberleutnant. Silent routine. Warn engineer Kritz that we shall be shortly attacked with depth-charges."

In the last second before he lowered his periscope he had seen the destroyer's bows begin to turn back to starboard—towards him. The turn had not then been a lucky chance, but a deliberately timed and carefully thought-out maneuver. Such a possibility had not, until this last moment, appeared to be credible—and the Kapitän realised for the first time that he was up against another brain. In all his previous experience a target had been simply a target. The lumbering shapes of merchantmen had proceeded sedately along a straight line. His machines had calculated the angles. He had given the orders to fire when certain pre-requisites had been observed. Then, so long as his trained guesses at the target's course, speed and range were reasonably accurate, and provided the temperamental torpedoes ran correctly—hits were obtained: hits which in the fullness of time brought congratulatory letters and Iron Crosses. That this well-known procedure was not functioning any longer was an uneasy thought, that was quickly followed by one that was worse. Supposing the opposing brain were better than his own? For the first time in his life von Stolberg faced death, and knew it for what it could be.

"Asdic transmissions green one-six-five," Braun reported, spinning the polished wheel that directed the hydrophones, and before the Kapitän could acknowledge the information, added: "Closing. Propeller noises. Probably turbines, one-five-oh revolutions."

In the silent control room the waiting men, who hardly dared to breathe, would hear the sharp zip of the asdic transmissions that struck the U-boat's hull ten seconds apart. It was heard by them as the whisper of a whip about to be laid across their steel back.

"The Squalus Goes Down"

BY PETER MAAS

(Excerpted from the book *The Terrible Hours*)

The successful rescue of thirty-three crew members of the submarine *Squalus* after it plunged to the North Atlantic bottom in 243 feet of water was been called the most dramatic and successful in submarine history. The Navy officer who pulled together the rescue effort to save the entombed crew, against tremendous odds, an often sneering naval bureaucracy, and disbelieving naysayers, was Lieutenant Commander Charles ("Swede") Momsen. Peter Maas's *The Terrible Hours* is a dramatic, moment-by-moment account of the miraculous rescue engineered by Momsen to free the men from the crippled and partially flooded submarine. The time was May 1939, when escape devices on submarines and surface rescue techniques and equipment were still in their infancy.

This excerpt from the incredible story of the *Squalus* takes us aboard the boat in the Atlantic off the mouth of the Piscataqua River and the New Hampshire–Maine coast. For the crew of the *Squalus*, and their friends and loved ones ashore, "the terrible hours" are about to begin.

U p on the bridge with Naquin, the navigation and engineering officer, Lieutenant (j.g.) Robert Robertson, from a speck of a town in the Texas panhandle, took a fix with his sextant and told the skipper that they had less than a mile and a half to go before the *Squalus* reached her dive point.

In Navy time, it was 0830.

In the control room, executive officer Doyle said, "Inform the captain that the boat is rigged for diving." Yeoman Second Class Charles Kuney, over his battle phone, relayed the message to Naquin.

Still on the bridge, Naquin ordered, "All ahead, emergency!" He wanted every bit of momentum that the *Squalus* could muster and she strained forward, past sixteen knots. Next he ordered transmission of his final dive notification. In his cubicle, radio man Powell tapped out his second communication to Portsmouth that the sub was going down and that she would be submerged for one hour. Portsmouth immediately acknowledged. Powell signed off and started retracting his antenna.

Then Naquin ordered, "Stand by to dive." He took a final confident look around. Except for the two lobstermen he had passed earlier, now far astern, the *Squalus* was all by herself. He stepped down through the conning tower hatch, the last to do so, and with the help of his quartermaster, Frankie Murphy, he pulled it shut. You didn't have to know Murphy's last name to see all Irish in his freckled face. From the Charlestown section of Boston, he'd been home over the weekend, and his mother had remonstrated him for sleeping though Sunday Mass. "You should be on your knees thanking God you're still safe in that terrible thing you're sailing in," she'd said.

Just as they secured the hatch, Naquin heard the big klaxon honk the first diving alarm. His started his stopwatch and lowered himself down the narrow steel ladder leading to the control room.

Ten men were in the control room to begin the multiple operations that would send the *Squalus* beneath the waves.

Walter Doyle stood dead center toward the forward end of the compartment. From there, by swiveling his head slightly, he could see every essential diving control and indicator on the sub. Harold Preble was also present to observe the dive performance. By perching himself behind Doyle, one foot on a toolbox and the other braced against the bottom of the ladder coming down from the conning tower, Preble had nearly the same view. In each hand, he held a double-action stopwatch.

By the time the first klaxon sounded, Doyle had tested the number 1 periscope, had seen to it that the ballast-tank and air-pressure men were in place, and had the operators of the bow and stern diving planes check out the big fins extending out from the hull that worked in the sea like an airplane's wing flaps.

He had scrutinized the control board. It was called the "Christmas tree" and it confirmed the reports from Nichols and Patterson that the sub was properly rigged for diving. The board consisted of red and green lights. Each represented a specific aperture in the hull or superstructure. Green meant closed and watertight. Red showed that it was still open.

On the board only eight lights glowed red at Doyle among all the green. Four of them marked the exhaust valves for the diesel engines. One was for the flapper valve through which the radio antennae rose. Another was for the hatch above the conning tower that accessed the bridge.

The last two red lights were for the pair of yawning outlets—the main inductions—high up on the side of the conning tower right below the bridge deck that funneled air directly to the diesels and circulated more of it to the crew when the sub rode the surface. Both were covered by a perforated steel plate and they would remain open until the *Squalus* began her final glide down.

And that was about to happen. Everything would move very rapidly now. In the control room it grew hushed. Just an edge of tension had crept in.

Doyle directed the operators of the bow and stern planes to angle them at hard 'dive. Simultaneously, at his command, the main ballast tanks girdling the sub were opened to the sea. They would drag the *Squalus* beneath the surface. Still another tank, called bow buoyancy, was all the way up forward between the torpedo tubes there. It pulled her nose down during a dive. In addition, there were several smaller trim and auxiliary tanks for weight adjustment to maintain a steady, even keel under water.

The sea entered each of these tanks through a valve set in its lower side. On the upper sides there were also vents that allowed air pockets to escape so that the tanks would completely fill. When the sub was surfacing, the process was reversed. After the dive, the vents were closed and blasts of pressurized air from cylinders manned in the control room blew the seawater out through the same valves it had entered.

In quick succession, Doyle ordered the valves and vents opened on the bow buoyancy tank and on main ballast tanks 1 and 2. Next he had the valves on tanks 3 and 4 also opened, which would partially fill them. He held back on opening their vents until he was absolutely certain that the *Squalus* was sealed against the sea.

The control board would tell him that.

His eyes never left it. He saw the light for the hatch in the conning tower wink from red to green after Naquin and Murphy had dogged it down. So did the one for the antenna.

Then those for the diesel exhaust vents went green. In the control room, there was a startling silence when the diesels cut off. It made everybody's breathing sound very loud.

On the control room Christmas tree, only two lights still glowed red—those for the main inductions. They closed in tandem from the same hydraulic lever. Machinist's Mate Second Class Al Prien operated it this morning, as he did with the levers for the other valves and vents he was either opening and closing. He'd had the same duty on another sub before reporting to the *Squalus*. Prien now pulled the lever for the main inductions. Immediately, the last two red lights on the board turned green.

Lieutenant Doyle shut his eyes for one count and then looked at the board again. It was all green. The *Squalus* was secure. To make doubly sure, Carol Pierce, also an experienced machinist's mate, bled some air from one of the pressurized cylinder banks. If pressure built up inside the hull, it meant that the sub was airtight and therefore watertight.

From his station behind Doyle, Pierce announced, "Pressure in the boat, sir."

Doyle raised his right hand and extended two fingers.

At the signal, Chief Torpedoman Roy Campbell, the ranking enlisted man on board, pressed a button. The second *ah-ooo-gah, ah-ooo-gah* went off, the sound of the final klaxon dive alarm reverberating throughout the sub.

Driven by battery power, the *Squalus* slid down into the ocean. Outside, had anyone been watching, he would have seen the cold North Atlantic boil over her elongated hull, reach for her three-inch deck gun, and surge up around the base of her superstructure.

Then, suddenly, she was gone.

★ ★ ★

In the control room, after sounding the second dive warning, Chief Campbell instinctively glanced at the board and saw that it was green.

Yeoman Kuney, the control room talker, saw it was green. Kuney liked to bet with himself whether he would ever get word of a closing before it showed on the board. The board always won.

Al Prien, releasing his grip on the main inductions lever, saw that the board was green. So did Harold Preble, stopwatches in hand.

Just as the klaxon was honking, Oliver Naquin reached the bottom rung of the ladder from the conning tower. He, too, saw that no red lights registered on the board. Naquin stepped past Preble and joined his executive officer at the diving control station. He shifted his attention to the depth gauge indicator in front of him.

When it hit twenty-eight feet, the *Squalus* hesitated. This habitually happened during a dive. It signified the end of the sub's initial thrust from the surface. Now, against the mounting pressure of the sea, it took a few moments for her battery power to assert itself. Then she started to plunge down again.

At thirty feet, Preble said to Naquin, "Good, good. You're going to make it."

"This," Naquin replied, "is going to be a beauty."

The depth indicator moved faster . . . thirty-five feet . . . forty . . . forty-five. Up inside the conning tower, Frankie Murphy saw the sea flash over his eyeports.

Doyle ordered his bow and stern plane operators to gradually reduce the dive angle. He wanted the *Squalus* to level off at around sixty-three feet.

At fifty feet, their time target depth, both Naquin and Preble called out, "Mark!" They stopped their watches and compared the results. The time was a fraction over a second more than the sixty seconds Naquin had been aiming at.

"Good, good," Preble repeated.

Naquin smiled. It was better than he'd expected. He still had three weeks for crash-dive run-throughs, not only to get to a minute, but to get under it.

Automatically, he stepped to his number 1 periscope, gripped its handles and bent forward slightly to peer through its rubber-cupped eyepiece.

As he did, a strange fluttering sensation assailed his ears.

An instant later, talker Kuney's eyes went wide with disbelief. Not at what he saw, but at what he was hearing. For the first time word of something had come over his battle phone that wasn't reflected on the control board.

He cried out the stunning news. "Sir! The engine rooms! They're flooding!"

★ ★ ★

At the sudden cry from Kuney that the engine rooms were flooding, everyone in the control room froze, hypnotized by the Christmas tree board.

It was still unaccountably green.

This could not be happening! There was a moment of complete stupefaction on every face, the kind experienced by men who are absolutely certain that what is coming to pass could not possibly be. Yet it was.

Somehow, the dreadful thing was upon them. Despite what the control board was registering, the big main air-induction valve leading back to the now-dormant diesels had failed to close or, if it did, had opened again. With ferocious force, tons of sea were shooting into the engine rooms. It was as if a huge fire hydrant, wide open, had suddenly gone berserk. The fluttering sensation that Naquin had felt seconds ago was the rush of air being shoved violently forward by the ocean as it burst into the after compartments of the *Squalus*.

Naquin was the first to recover. "Blow all main ballast!" he shouted.

The words were barely out of his mouth before Walter Doyle called out, "Blow bow buoyancy!"

The still-mesmerized control room crew came to and scrambled into action. Al Prien, the machinist's mate manning the levers for the valves and vents during the dive, had already closed the ballast tank air-escape vents. Close by, Carol Pierce, who had bled air into the boat to make doubly sure it was watertight as the dive commenced, now slammed home the lever that would blow 3,000 pounds per square inch of air into the bow buoyancy tank. The air from his number 1 bank blasted off. Inside the control room, it made a soft whooshing sound. An instant later, he sent more pressurized air rushing into the main ballast tanks to drive the sea from them.

Two gunner's mates, Gene Cravens and Gavin Coyne, operating the bow and stern dive planes, immediately put them at hard rise.

Prien, having closed the ballast-tank air vents, stared down at the level that should have shut the main inductions. He clenched it, knuckles white, and tried to yank it farther toward him. But it wouldn't budge. It had gone as far as it could go.

Charles Kuney stood transfixed, his hands clapped over his phone receivers, pressing them tighter to his ears. The last thing he had heard from the after compartments was a desperate scream, "Take her up! Take her up!" Kuney couldn't tell which compartment the scream had come from.

The *Squalus* shuddered.

At eighty feet, for a tantalizing tick in time, she hung suspended between ocean floor and surface. Then she seemed to respond to the blowing of her ballast tanks. Her bow tilted upward. She even rose a little, her nose perhaps just breaking through the waves above. But the growing weight in her tail was too much. Inexorably, she began to slide stern first into the black depths of the North Atlantic.

The steep pitch of the *Squalus* came so suddenly that only by clinging to his number 1 periscope and bracing himself against the steel well of the second periscope directly behind him did Naquin remain on his feet. This was crazy, he kept thinking. How was it possible?

As Pierce was sending emergency blasts of air into the ballast tanks, Harold Preble rushed to his aid. Hanging on to the base of the gyroscope with one hand, the Portsmouth yard's test superintendent knelt beside Pierce and tried to activate a reserve cylinder of air to clear the tanks faster. He had to use a wrench to get the valve open. He was still struggling with it when a column of water hit him in the back of his neck, flattening him. Both Pierce and Chief Roy Campbell were struck by the same stream. Pierce, stumbling over Preble, grabbed the wrench and finished the job. But it didn't make any difference.

Campbell picked up Preble. Then he reached overhead to shut off a pipe in the ventilation system from which the water had shot out. By now the sea had found its way into the maze of pipes that ran the length of the *Squalus*. In the control room, jets of salt water sprayed from a dozen different places. The men worked frantically to close them off, seizing hold of whatever they could to stay upright.

Behind him, Chief Campbell heard an ominous hissing. He traced it to two toilet closets in the rear of the control room on the starboard side. Campbell groped through a billowing mist. It was coming out of a drainage line in the second closet. He had trouble turning the handwheel that would stop the leak because of the new packing around it. But finally he succeeded. Then he turned off every other valve he could find.

Across from Campbell, alone in his cubicle, radioman Powell was in the process of stowing his transmitter after sending the second dive message to Portsmouth when water gushed out of an air-supply blower in front of him. Powell reached for a valve in the pipe that he thought might stop the flow. Before he got to it, the water suddenly dwindled to a dribble. Powell figured that someone in the after battery must have closed another valve down the line. He sealed his anyway, and trying to maintain his balance, he staggered into the control room proper to find out what was happening. Overhead, the lights flickered, flared briefly and went out. The emergency lights came on, then they also began to flicker.

In the forward torpedo room, Lieutenant Nichols ordered Lenny de Medeiros to close the watertight door to the forward battery moments after learning that the engine rooms were flooding. As he did, he spotted Gerry McLees, head and shoulders sticking out of the passageway hatch leading down to the forward group of batteries. There didn't seem to be any problems in the compartment as far as he could tell.

When the bow rose so abruptly, de Medeiros thought that whatever the trouble was, it wasn't going to be so bad after all. The sub appeared to be on her way back to the surface.

Just then the dummy torpedo set up for a reload started to roll free. Loose in there with the *Squalus* now tilting so sharply, it would crush anyone in its path. Nichols, Torpedoman First Class Bill Fitzpatrick and a young seaman, Donny Persico, jumped for it and wrestled it back in place. Nichols finally threaded its nose ring with manila line and together the three men managed to lash down the wayward torpedo.

Some seawater mixed with air was sputtering out of the ventilation pipes, but it didn't amount to much. De Medeiros quickly shut the valves and the sprays of water stopped completely. By now, he could distinctly sense the backward slide down of the boat and realized that surfacing was out of the question.

He'd seen McLees in the forward battery. He couldn't remember where his other close pal, Lloyd Maness, was stationed for this dive. All he, like the others in the compartment, could do in the eerie silence was wait. And hope.

In the forward battery, as the *Squalus* struggled to rise, a coffeepot bounced across the pantry past one of the mess attendants, Feliciano Elvina. Elvina picked up the pot and tried to put it back on its stand, but it toppled over again. He finally placed it in a corner of the pantry deck. To his intense annoyance, water suddenly belched out of the faucet into the sink all over the dishrags he had squeezed dry a minute ago.

Muttering under his breath, Elvina stuck his head into the passageway to see what was going on. Everyone appeared to be yelling, but Elvina was no great shakes at English and he could not make out what they were saying. Then he spied the second mess attendant, his friend Basilio Galvan, back from finding out about the menu for the noon meal. Elvina looked at him in puzzlement. Galvan had been on submarines before and this was Elvina's first one. Galvan simply shrugged, however, and Elvina couldn't tell whether he was concerned. Galvan was both concerned and confused by the sudden turn of events, but as a veteran submariner in Elvina's eyes, he was determined not to show it. Finally Elvina just gave up, returned to the pantry and hunched down next to the coffeepot.

Allen Bryson, a machinist's mate, was on the forward battery phone when he heard the scream. Gerry McLees was about to close the passageway hatch over him when Bryson shouted out the news. McLees scrambled back up to see what was what.

Chief Electrician's Mate Lawrence Gainor had positioned himself at the aft end of the compartment to take voltmeter readings. He had yet to relay one of them to his recorder, a signalman named Ted Jacobs. But Gainor would have his hands full soon enough.

Sometimes a person's moment of truth comes so quickly that there is no chance to think about it. For Gainor, his twenty years of sub service came into instinctive play, triggered by whatever makes one man charge and another run, one man grapple with opportunity and another impotent.

At the first word of trouble, Gainor moved immediately to the watertight door between the forward battery and the control room, and with the help of Jacobs, he secured it. He could see the geysers of water spraying from the overhead network of pipes into the control room. Once the door was closed, he saw the water splattering against its eyeport. For all Gainor knew, the control room was flooded.

There was no time to dwell on it. As the forward battery lights began to flicker, he took another look at his voltmeters. They were discharging at a furious rate. Somewhere there was a bad short circuit.

He grabbed a flashlight and worked his way forward against the upward slant of the *Squalus* to the battery hatch. When he peered down into the well, he was greeted by a fearful sight. Solid bands of blue-white fire were leaping from battery to battery in eight-inch arcs. Stabbing through the darkness, they threw grotesque shadows against the sides of the inner hull. The heat was so intense that steam was pouring out of the battery cells and the rubber-compound insulation had begun to melt. As the boat continued her sickening drop, she was only seconds away from a gigantic explosion that would rip her apart even before she reached the bottom.

Without hesitation, Gainor lowered himself down there. The big batteries, six feet high, completely filled the space beneath the deck except for a narrow center walk. Alone, squinting against the fiery bands dancing around him, he crouched on the walk and groped for the master disconnect switches. Finally he located the starboard switch and yanked it clear. Next he bent to his left for the port switch. A terrifying arc over it spluttered and flashed in his face. One brush against it would send him to a horrible death. Gainor was sure that he would be electrocuted before he could reach the switch. He tried anyway, and with a last desperate effort he jerked it free. The fierce arcs vanished.

Gainor stayed put for a minute, gathering himself. Then he quietly made his way up the ladder.

In the after battery, Lloyd Maness would face an equally daunting task. Like Gainor, Maness was preparing to call off voltmeter readings. He also never got to the first one. For both Maness and his recorder, Art Booth, the early stages of the dive were perfectly routine. Booth had penciled in the dive time on his notepad. Together, they waited for the meter indicator to stabilize after the transfer to battery power. They could hear executive officer Doyle issuing his familiar commands in the control room.

All at once, the same movement of air that Naquin had felt swept by them. Then they heard Kuney's stunned cry that the engine rooms were flooding. All hell broke loose in the after battery. The lights went out. In the dim glow of the emergency lights, water was shooting every which way. Maness went right to his disaster station, the watertight door between the after battery and the control room. He stepped into the control room and got ready to swing the door shut.

As he did, Booth skipped past him.

Farther back in the after battery, Electrician's Mate First Class Jud Bland was manning the compartment battle phone. When he heard the incredible report come over it, he couldn't believe his ears. Then the water slammed into him. His initial thought was to close the valves in the overhead ventilation pipes. He wasn't quite sure where they were. After a dozen years with the surface fleet, not only was the *Squalus* his first sub, but he had not been on dive duty in the after battery before. As he felt for them in the gloom of the emergency lights, the *Squalus* lurched violently upward and sent him sprawling to his knees. By now he realized that she was long past the point where closing some valves would do any good. As the full impact of what was happening swept over him, Bland started toward the control room. Maness yelled at him to hurry.

Seaman Bill Boulton came on frantically behind Bland. One minute Boulton had been sitting at a mess table, idly staring into space, drying off after stowing gear topside. In the next, he was dumbfounded to see water streaming along the battery deck. For a moment, he could think only that the main-deck hatch above him had not been secured and he stood up reflexively to check it. Then he saw that the water around his feet was pouring in from the engine rooms. As he tried to puzzle this out, the sea rocketed in from pipes all over the compartment. And almost before he knew it, the upward pitch of the boat sent the water rolling back at him. It had already surged over the tops of his work shoes. Boulton splashed his way forward, more water springing suddenly at him in a terrifying crossfire. Dazed, Boulton stumbled blindly toward the control room. Then, all at once, he had passed Maness and fell into it.

At the far end of the after battery, Rob Washburn was still waiting for the pharmacist's mate, O'Hara, to give him aspirin for his cold when the water hit him. It shot out of the air blower over the medicine cabinet with explosive force, knocking Washburn to the deck on the port side of the compartment. He got back up just as the *Squalus* unexpectedly rose by her bow and was thrown headlong to the deck again. Once more, he managed to struggle up.

O'Hara was searching through his cabinet as the water gushed over his head, barely missing him. Then the bottles on the shelves started tumbling out. Instinctively, O'Hara tried to catch them. A moment later, he found himself sitting on the deck, water swirling at his waist. He flopped around and pushed himself up with both hands. He saw Washburn to his right and started to follow his erstwhile patient.

By this time, the slant of the *Squalus* was so steep that Washburn had to cling to the bunks lining the compartment as he worked himself forward hand over hand, O'Hara a few feet behind. Finally, he reached the control room. Lloyd Maness, holding the door, urged O'Hara on. At last, O'Hara also made it past him.

In the galley, Will Isaacs, the cook, waited impatiently for the *Squalus* to level off so he could switch his oven back on and get the meatballs going. A seaman, Alex Keegan, and a fireman second class, Roland Blanchard, were on mess duty helping Isaacs. When the dive began, Keegan had left to go to the crew's toilet across the passageway.

Isaacs and Blanchard never saw him again.

At the first klaxon alarm, Blanchard had started closing a valve in the hull ventilation line running through the galley. This was one of his regular dive assignments, and as had happened on previous plunges, he ran into difficulty trying to turn the stiff, new handwheel. There was a quick rush of escaping air and then the water followed, but there was so much pressure now that Blanchard couldn't budge the wheel at all.

After the sudden movement of air, Isaacs looked inquiringly into the passageway outside the galley. A solid stream of water smacked him in the face. He ducked away and glanced aft toward the forward engine room. The door to it was partially open and water was coursing through from the other side. Isaacs went immediately to the door and secured it. Then he straightened up to look through the eyeport. The sight was awesome. A great cataract was thundering out of the air-induction outlet above the diesels. It had already buried them. Isaacs stood there, transfixed.

In the galley, Blanchard had given up trying to turn the handwheel and stepped into the passageway. When the *Squalus* tipped upward, all the water in the after battery came racing down the deck toward him. Blanchard waded forward fighting the current, arms flailing wildly to keep his balance. He had gotten about a third of the way through the compartment when he slipped. His head went under and he felt himself being carried back again. At the last second, his hand clutched a steel stanchion. He hung on to it and with savage frenzy, he pulled himself up. Kicking off from the stanchion, he lunged desperately for the nearest tier of bunks. He got to it and dragged himself from one tier to the next. The water wasn't as deep here, but it kept pouring down from the overhead pipes and the footing was miserable. Up ahead of him, he saw the door to the control room begin to close. He yelled out. Maness heard him and eased the door open again.

For Isaacs, time was fast running out. But, his face pressed against the eyeport, he seemed unable to tear himself away from the frightful sight in the forward engine room. He could not see any crewmen in there, just the thundering ocean. Then he became aware of the icy water lapping around his waist. Before he could move, it had almost reached his armpits. He frantically propelled himself away from the door, actually swimming, and barged right into one of the mess tables hidden by the rising surge. Isaacs went under, but he had a hand around a leg of the table bolted to the deck and he came up spewing salt water from his mouth. He kept going and Maness, holding the door open an instant longer, saw him. Isaacs floundered into the control room and dropped to his knees, gasping for breath.

Now Maness could delay no more. Indeed, for agonizing seconds, it would appear that he had waited too long.

Twice he had paused before sealing off the control room, once for Blanchard, then for Isaacs. He peered into the blackness of the compartment. He thanked God that he couldn't see anybody else. To have closed the door in someone's pleading face would have been more than he could bear.

His task defied all odds. The door swung in from the after battery. It was oval and fitted into a steel frame that curved around the rest of the passageway. Normally, when the *Squalus* was on an even keel, it moved easily on its hinges. But now the ravaged sub was sagging by her stern at an angle of nearly fifty degrees. And Maness had to lift it toward him, almost as if it were a trap door. A trap door of solid steel, except for its eyeport, that weighed several hundred pounds.

He had to do it alone. There wasn't enough room for anybody to help him. Maness bent forward and pulled, the sea already spilling over the lip of the doorway. He strained harder, his feet braced against the sides of the door frame, beads of sweat full-blown on his forehead. The door began to swing up steadily, inch by inch. Then it stopped, neither moving up nor falling back.

Maness gritted his teeth. Summoning a last ferocious burst of strength, his arm and leg muscles quivering wildly, his shoulders threatening to pop their sockets, he heaved once more. And this time, the door shut.

On the other side was Sherman Shirley. He could only hope that there would still be a wedding, that Shirley was safely barricaded in the after torpedo room.

John Batick had made the wrong choice. Down in the well of the after battery instead of Gerry McLees, the hatch above him closed, he never had a chance.

A few moments later, in a swirl of trailing bubbles, the *Squalus* touched delicately on the North Atlantic floor, first her stern, then her bow. Inside, they hardly felt it. She had settled evenly on her keel, still slanting upward at an angle of about eleven degrees. Her emergency lights were out and she had no heat. She lay helpless in 243 feet of water. The temperature outside her hull was just above freezing.

In the control room, Chief Roy Campbell held a flashlight up to the eyeport of the door Maness had closed. An evil film of oily water rode against it on the other side. It was not quite eight-forty-five that morning. Less than five minutes had elapsed since the *Squalus* started her dive.

Up on the surface, it was as if she had never existed at all.

"Under a Carolina Moon"

BY BRIAN HICKS AND SCHUYLER KROPF

(Excerpted from the book *Raising the Hunley*)

As unlikely as the event may seem, the first sinking of an enemy ship by a submarine using an underwater weapon was carried out by the Confederates during the Civil War. On February 17, 1864, the USS *Hunley*, a submersible vessel with a captain and crew of seven operating a ram-type torpedo, successfully attacked and sank the USS *Housatonic* anchored four miles off Charleston. The *Hunley* never returned to base, and her fate was unknown. Nothing of the vessel was found at or near the site where the *Housatonic* had settled to the bottom. Interest in finding the *Hunley* and learning her fate was of course high among shipwreck divers for decades, but without success. Finally in 1995 an expedition of divers led by novelist Clive Cussler found the missing submarine lying under three feet of silt about a thousand feet from the spot where she had struck the *Housatonic*. Divers who eventually entered the sub found remains and artifacts of the crew. After careful planning, the sub was raised to the surface in 2000.

The Confederate plan to use an underwater attack boat was as dangerous as it was audacious. The first model killed a crew of five in one dive, and the second cost the life of the boat's inventor, Horace Hunley, and his crew of seven. On the *Housatonic*, the death toll was five. *Raising the Hunley* is the complete and remarkable story of this moment in Civil War history. This excerpt from the book focuses on the night of the attack.

T he moon hung over the Atlantic like a flare.

It was piercing cold on the beach at Sullivan's Island as the last flecks of daylight faded out of February 17, 1864. Lt. George E. Dixon cursed, but not necessarily about the weather. After three months of refurbishing the submarine, of training a new crew, of waiting for calm waters, it was time. Tonight the *Hunley* would attack the blockade. But Dixon was uneasy. There were complications. The bright moon shone like a spotlight on the water, possibly eliminating the tiny fish-boat's single advantage: surprise.

Still, there was no choice. Dixon knew he had tried the patience of the Confederate brass long enough. Since it had arrived in Charleston in August, the *Hunley* had spent more time at the bottom of the harbor than it had on patrol. When his latest leave from the Twenty-first Alabama Regiment was up in a few weeks, Dixon would be going back to Mobile. And that would be it for the *Hunley*—unless he could sink one of those blockade ships on the horizon.

As Dixon stood on the beach, tall and handsome, the sea breeze tousling his light-colored hair, he knew his time had come. The South Atlantic Blockading Squadron was strangling Charleston. The blockade could eventually threaten the entire Confederacy—unless, that is, he could do something about it. It was an enormous pressure on him. He was only twenty-four years old; he should have been nervous about the task before him. But as Beauregard had described him, Dixon was resolute. And he was confident. Above all else, Dixon had faith in the little submarine. He'd helped build it, tested it in Mobile Bay, and put it through more than two months of successful training in Charleston Harbor and the backwaters around Sullivan's Island. The submarine would work in the right hands. The previous accidents were the fault of the men piloting it. He and William Alexander had proved to Beauregard that the boat was not a death trap.

It was a temperamental piece of machinery, to be sure. Before the Lee spar had been fitted, when the submarine was still stationed in the harbor, there had been problems, even with Dixon commanding. One night the *Hunley*'s floating mine had got entangled in the David towing the submarine out to sea, nearly blowing both boats out of the water. That had been the fish-boat's last night in the harbor. After that the *Hunley* was moved to Sullivan's Island, a spit of sand on the north side of the harbor's entrance.

At the southern end of Sullivan's stood Fort Moultrie—which had battered Sumter into submission—and what few other buildings the island had. The *Hunley* was kept at the north end of the island, across Breach Inlet from Long Island (the modern-day Isle of Palms). It was a remote spot, away from the prying eyes of spies. Most important, it was close to the open ocean and was the only real departure point for the submarine to use and have any chance of reaching the Union fleet. It was when the *Hunley* was moved to Sullivan's Island that crew and submarine and environment jelled. The men fell into a simple pattern: they stayed together in an abandoned house in Mount Pleasant, 7 miles from the boat. Every other day they would make their way toward the ocean, take a rowboat or ferry over to Sullivan's, and walk along the beach to Battery Marshall, where the boat was moored. It was a long, dangerous walk, within sight—and firing distance—of the blockade, but it was much better than fighting the scrub of the barrier island. Besides, the view gave them more time to study the enemy.

The weather had been rough that winter, nor'easters chewing up the coast and turning the Atlantic into a mountain range of angry waves—no place for a submarine that could barely maintain buoyancy. On many nights they had contented themselves with practice and sailed the submarine through the safe water behind the island. Sometimes they would go out a few miles but only got close to the blockade ships occasionally.

One afternoon in January they had become comfortable enough with the boat to test its limits. Just off Battery Marshall on the inland side of the island, the crew took the submarine down and let it sink to the bottom. They wanted to know how long they could stay down without fresh air. After an attack they might have to submerge and lie still until favorable tides came around. Propelling the *Hunley* was hard enough work; fighting against the sea currents was nearly impossible.

Dixon believed they could hold out for about thirty minutes without refreshing their air; that was how long the candles lasted before expiring. But they would not know unless they tried, and on that day it was too rough on the open sea to venture out. After he filled the ballast tank, Dixon maneuvered the *Hunley* down softly in the mud. When the submarine settled into the muck, the men stopped talking and waited. It was daylight when the submarine went down, but very little of it filtered in through the submarine's ten deadlights—two rows of tiny portholes along the top of the hull. Within a half hour the candle flickered out, and the interior went blindingly dark.

The deal was that they would sit still until one crewman could not take it anymore. They had agreed that when the first man yelled "up," they would make for the surface. In the dark it seemed that time lost all meaning.

Occasionally Dixon would ask Alexander "How is it?" but other than that, silence. No one wanted to be the one to end the test. No one wanted to seem the weakest among a crew of daring—some said suicidal—volunteers. So they waited, all of them trying not to be the first to give the word.

Perhaps there was a single second when the last bit of oxygen had been used, when their lungs screamed out and the men's bodies told them they were out of time. At the same time every man in the crew yelled "up" in unison and furiously began pumping and cranking.

Soon the bow of the submarine was rising, reaching toward the surface, but the stern sat stoically in the mud. Alexander pumped the after ballast tank madly but quickly realized nothing was happening. It had happened before, and the Scot needed little time for adjustment. Working blind, he took off the pump's cap and felt seaweed clumped beneath the valve. He threw it out, put the contraption back together from memory, and began pumping. Soon the *Hunley* broke the surface, where Dixon and Alexander threw open the conning tower hatches, greedily sucking down the fresh Carolina air, letting it fill the boat. It was now dark. The submarine had been on the bottom for two and a half hours.

On the island the crew had been given up for dead. Word had already been sent to Beauregard that the third crew of the *Hunley* had perished, again on test runs. Dixon would have to correct that. Later. After the men had extricated themselves from their tiny ship, they stood on the dock and came to an agreement. They decided that if the *Hunley* ever became stuck, they would open the submarine's seacocks and end it. They would rather drown quickly at their own hand than suffocate slowly. It became the crew's pact, forged from shared experience. That day they'd been lucky. Alexander had saved their lives.

Alexander. He had become one of Dixon's closest friends; together they had shared the *Hunley's* entire history. But now Dixon was alone. Two weeks earlier Beauregard had ordered Alexander back to Alabama to build a new rapid-fire repeating gun for the Confederacy. Talent such as Alexander's was in high demand in the South as the fourth year of the war began. It was a tough separation for both men. The two had spent much of the Charleston winter together, Dixon the submarine's pilot, Alexander its first officer. Before going out in the evening, the two men would lie on the beach, a map and compass between them, and pick out targets. Their choices were limited; most of the Union fleet anchored farther than the crew could crank the boat's propeller. Or if they did get there, they wouldn't have enough energy to get back. In fact, fatigue had left them within hearing distance of the fleet on some mornings, the men turning the screw furiously while listening to some stupid Yankee singing to the rising sun.

Now, with Alexander gone, Dixon felt alone. He wrote letters to his old friend, keeping him informed as if he were still a member of the crew. In a couple of short messages sent to Mobile, Dixon told Alexander about weather conditions keeping the submarine docked, how the crew missed him. He let Alexander know about his replacement. Dixon wrote the notes in a void, during the time that normally he would have spent with his friend, scouting prey. Now that was one task he unhappily had to perform by himself. On this day he would write his last note to Alexander, telling him that the weather had finally co-operated. It was time.

As he silently watched the Union fleet, Dixon rubbed a bent coin he kept in his pants pockets. It was a $20 gold piece, and two years earlier it had saved his life. Now he fondled it constantly, rubbing it smooth with his thumb. He kept it with him always, took it with him everywhere. His girlfriend in Mobile had given it to him on the day he shipped out to the front lines. He had carried it into war. For a man in his early twenties, the gift meant much more than its monetary value. It represented his future. After the war he would be married and have a family of his own. He would settle in Mobile, where he'd been working on riverboats far from his native Kentucky before the fighting began. That's what he thought about when the coin was new and shiny and flat. And then came Shiloh.

Dixon's regiment stormed through the misty Tennessee predawn of April 6, 1862, eager to get the jump on the Yankees. It was a rare moment when the Rebels felt as if they had a good chance. But the Union fought back hard, its troops laying down a terrifyingly efficient spray of gunfire. The Twenty-first Alabama was hit harder than most regiments: five flag-bearers fell, one after another, that morning. Dixon was one of the first ones downed. The bullet smacked him high on his thigh. When he dropped, he thought he was dead—a fire sizzled in his leg. Soon the world went black.

When he awoke later, he found out just how lucky he'd been. The bullet had hit the coin, denting it, leaving it with a permanent warp. Twenty dollars had stopped the bullet and the gangrene that almost certainly would have followed. Queenie Bennett, his Alabama sweetheart, had saved his life from 400 miles away.

From that moment on, the coin was never out of Dixon's reach. He rubbed it absently sometimes, not realizing what he was doing. On other occasions he knew exactly what he was doing. The coin was his good-luck piece, if there was such a thing. Perhaps it represented something more to him, but he could not put it into words. Above all else, it was a comfort to him—a reminder of what was waiting for him, a sign that his work was not yet finished.

Dixon's unfinished business swung at anchor nearly 4 miles offshore. She was the USS *Housatonic*, a huge Union warship, steam-powered, triple-masted, and more than 200 feet long. She stood proudly on the horizon. But the *Housatonic* suffered from the luck of geography. Her place in the blockade was near Rattlesnake Shoal, at the north entrance of the channel, and her captain had a habit of coming in a little too close to shore to anchor. It was a mistake that would cost them. Perhaps Dixon smiled at that.

Nevertheless, he felt torn. His duty and honor were most important to him, and he'd told Beauregard he could do it. There was no backing out. But he longed for Mobile, for Queenie, and for his friends. Alexander's return to Alabama stirred those feelings. In addition, his comrades wanted him back. Capt. John Cothran of the Twenty-first Alabama—Dixon's regiment—had written to the young lieutenant, asking him to rejoin the company. Dixon politely declined. He was committed to the *Hunley*. Dixon wrote to Cothran on February 5, 1864:

> I am fastened to Charleston and its approaches until I am able to blow up some of their Yankee ships. I have been here over three months, have worked very hard, in fact I am working all the time. My headquarters are on Sullivan's Island, and a more uncomfortable place could not be found in the Confederacy. For the last six weeks I have not been out of the range of shells and often I am forced to go within close proximity of the Yankee battery. . . . If you wish to see war every day and night, this is the place to see it. Charleston and its defenders will occupy the most conspicuous place in the history of the war, and it shall be as much glory as I shall wish if I can inscribe myself as one of its defenders.

Dixon closed his letter to his friend with his most honest thought, an amazing display of candor: "I am heartily tired of this place." He knew what he had to do to erase that irritation. It was Wednesday, February 17, 1864. Time to go to work. Dixon walked around the end of the island to Battery Marshall for his appointment with history.

The submarine was moored at a wooden dock on the back of the island, very close to Breach Inlet, a rough stream rushing between Sullivan's and Long Islands. It took only minutes to reach the open water through the channel that the ocean—with the help of a hurricane—had cut between the two barrier islands. After months of trials, accidents, and bad weather, the submarine was ready. Earlier in the day Dixon had made final adjustments with the help of some of the troops stationed behind the earthen mounds of Battery Marshall. The spar system was working perfectly; the powder load had been increased to 90 pounds. When the David had had its first battle months earlier, 70 pounds had proved too small a charge to sink a Union ship. This, everyone was sure, would blow a hole in a warship big enough to drive a train through.

That evening it was cold, barely above freezing—to that point the coldest day of the year. The water was calm that night, almost glassine. The tide had turned sometime around six p.m., and the water followed its normal currents, rushing out through Breach Inlet toward the open sea. Within an hour the water was running swiftly, and what darkness the *Hunley* would enjoy that night had fallen. They would let the rushing tide carry the fish-boat out to sea.

Dixon gave the order to load up. It was not quite seven p.m. The men carried candles and a lamp into the submarine's dark, damp crew compartment. Even though it was cold, they would soon be working up a sweat that would leave them chilly, clammy, and uncomfortable. Among the crew, which had been together for three months, was Cpl. C. F. Carlson. A soldier from an artillery unit stationed in Charleston, Carlson had taken Alexander's spot on the crew. He'd had little training. In fact, he had scarcely been aboard the boat more than a half dozen times.

As Dixon climbed through the front hatch of the *Hunley*, he reminded Lt. Col. O. M. Dantzler, the commander at Battery Marshall, of the plan. Dixon would flash a blue phosphorus lamp when the *Hunley* had accomplished its mission. That would be the sign for the troops to start a signal fire on the beach, which the *Hunley* would use to steer home by.

And then Dixon closed the sub's hatch. It was the last time he was seen alive.

Lt. George E. Dixon had no idea the Yankees were expecting him. The only real surprise the *Hunley* had on its side was the exact date of the attack. The Union Navy knew about the fish-boat, had been on the lookout for it since January when two Confederate deserters reported its existence and described its inner workings to Rear Adm. John A. Dahlgren.

The two men had been present, oddly enough, at nearly every turn in the *Hunley*'s path from Alabama to the blockade that night. They were George Shipp and a man named Belton, both of whom had been drafted into the Confederate Army against their wishes. Belton was a mechanic from

Michigan who had worked his way south in the years before the war. When the South fired on Fort Sumter, Belton was running a train between Montgomery and Mobile, where the Rebels eventually put him to work. In the spring of 1863, he was laboring at Park and Lyons watching as the *Hunley* was built. Belton had seen nearly everything. In his report to Dahlgren, he mistakenly referred to the submarine as the *American Diver*, but he had everything else exactly right.

Belton had transferred to the navy and Charleston, believing that it afforded him a better chance to make his escape. He wanted to join the Union as a safe way of getting back to the wife he'd left in Ohio. In Charleston he served with Shipp on the *Indian Chief*. Shipp had been on the receiving ship for some time. In fact, he had seen the submarine's ill-fated dive with Hunley at the controls. Together the two men talked of escaping their miserable lives in the Confederate military. Soon a few others would join them. All they needed was the right break.

It happened on a foggy night in early January. Four of them took the captain's small launch and sailed away from the *Indian Chief*. But in their haste to get away, the men sailed up the Cooper River, not out to sea. They ended up in Shem Creek, a channel that ran through the middle of Mount Pleasant. In the rain, without food, the men hid in the marsh grass all the next day until nightfall, when they sailed the little boat out of the creek. The men sailed into the harbor and between the two forts, Moultrie and Sumter. They waved as they passed a Confederate picket boat.

As soon as the men met a blockader, they filed reports for Admiral Dahlgren. They told him about the Davids, about how strong Charleston's defenses were—everything the Union Navy needed to know. Dahlgren listened most closely, however, to the talk of this little boat that could submerge and plant an explosive charge on the belly of a Union ship. It, well, interested him.

On the deck of his flagship, the *Philadelphia*, moored off Morris Island, Dahlgren savored the information. Peering out over Charleston Harbor, where the church steeples spiked out of the landscape, Dahlgren marveled at how his life had turned around in a few short months. Just when it seemed that his career was over, salvation had come from the least likely source.

A year earlier Dahlgren had filled his days sitting in a Washington office peering out at the Anacostia River. He was one of the most important men in the Union Navy, but with each passing day, his chance of seeing combat was evaporating. Dahlgren was chief of the Bureau of Ordnance, and had been for nearly twenty years. During that time he had designed the most effective weapons in the Northern arsenal, including the lethal 15-inch smoothbores currently being fitted in the Union's monitors. The new wonder guns, shaped like a soda pop bottle, would smash anything the South could float. But at a moment when he should have been enjoying his greatest achievement, he was stuck at the Washington Navy Yard awaiting a command. He was suffocating under the weight of navy bureaucracy. He wanted to be on the open sea.

Not even his friendship with President Abraham Lincoln could help. On February 14, 1863, just a year before the *Hunley* would attack his fleet, Dahlgren found himself making a second trip to the White House in one day. Lincoln was brooding. The president had recently issued the Emancipation Proclamation but could not get the secessionist city of Charleston and its damnable defenders out of his thoughts. For nearly two years a city built almost on the Atlantic coast protected only by sand forts, a few thousand men, and an armada of small, sometimes homemade boats had fended off practically the entire United States Navy.

Dahlgren walked in as Lincoln was getting a shave. "He let off a joke," Dahlgren scribbled in his diary later, "the first I have heard for a long while." But he added, "Abe is restless about Charleston."

President Lincoln needed the political victory that would come from capturing the city that had started all this. He confided to Dahlgren that the Union's commander of the South Atlantic Blockading Squadron, Samuel du Pont, had let him down. Du Pont had done little to destroy Charleston. He had focused too much of his attention—and his guns—on Fort Sumter, which by now was little more than a pile of rubble. Within a few months Lincoln stopped complaining and did something: he gave his friend du Pont's job and a mandate. Break Charleston's will.

From the deck of the *Philadelphia*, that's just what Dahlgren planned to do. In January 1864, after hearing the tall tales of deserters, Dahlgren had mixed feelings. The inventor in him was impressed by the ingenuity of his adversaries; the commander, fearful that it might actually succeed. But now the advantage had turned again: he knew everything Beauregard planned to unleash against him and quickly issued new orders to the fleet.

"I have reliable information that the rebels have two torpedo boats ready for service," Dahlgren wrote, "which may be expected on the first night when the water is suitable for their movement. One of these is the 'David,' which attacked the *Ironsides* in October; the other is similar to it. There is also one of another kind, which is nearly submerged and can be entirely so. It is intended to go under the bottoms of vessels and there operate."

Dahlgren, a crafty sailor, wasted little time in coming up with his defensive plans. He ordered his ships to put chain netting along their hulls in hopes of foiling any chance the torpedo boat might have to get close and plant a bomb. He told ships' captains to change their anchorages occasionally, to keep the enemy off guard and to keep the Rebels from picking off weak vessels. He ordered guns trained on the water at all times and increased lookouts, especially when the water was calm. And he told them to take one last precaution.

"It is also advisable not to anchor in the deepest part of the channel, for by not leaving much space between the bottom of the vessel and the bottom of the channel it will be impossible for the diving torpedo to operate except on the sides, and there will be less difficulty in raising a vessel if sunk."

That order would save more than a hundred lives.

★ ★ ★

The crew of the sloop of war USS *Housatonic* followed Dahlgren's instructions to the letter; they thought they were ready. Besides, what little torpedo boat would dare take on such a massive ship? She lay at anchor just off Sullivan's Island, her bowsprit pointed defiantly skyward. She was one of the newer additions to the fleet, named after a New England river that emptied into the Long Island Sound just east of Bridgeport, Connecticut. The *Housatonic* had arrived at its station in the blockade in late September 1862 and by the winter of 1864 had proved itself a formidable warship. The *Housatonic* was one of the Union ships that regularly bombarded the city. Its crew had captured, or assisted in the capture of, at least two blockade-runners. Once, the guns of the mighty ship had run the *Chicora* and *Palmetto State* back into Charleston Harbor.

From land she cut an impressive profile. Her masts towered more than 100 feet above the decks, and she carried acres of sailcloth. The sloop ran fast on steam, and since the torpedo boat scare, her bunkers were kept filled with coal. She had a crew of 155 men—most of whom had bedded down by eight p.m. on February 17, 1864. If they didn't have the watch then, they would have to stand it early in the morning.

That night the *Housatonic*'s watch included six lookouts in addition to a handful of officers on deck. Even with that many men, on a ship with a beam of 38 feet, they were barely within hearing distance of one another. On the starboard corner of the bow, Robert F. Flemming, a black sailor, had just settled in for his watch. It was scarcely 8:40 p.m.; he'd been there little more than thirty minutes. It was a pleasant evening, and Flemming scanned the horizon quietly. Even though the temperature was only a few degrees above freezing, many members of the crew remarked that it felt oddly nice that night. Flemming was looking in the direction of Fort Sumter 5 miles away, catching the reflection of the moonlight shimmering on the water, when he saw it.

It was nearly 400 feet away—two ship's lengths—and looked like a log. A very big log. Remembering his briefing from a month ago, Flemming ran to report to the petty officer on the forecastle. Flemming had heard the warnings about the torpedo boat and was almost sure the queer log was really a Rebel fish-boat. But Lewis A. Cornthwait, an acting master's mate, was unimpressed by his excited lookout's report.

"It's just a log," he said, and ordered Flemming back to his post.

But Flemming, who had a sharper eye, argued with his superior officer. "It's not floating with the tide like a log would, it's moving across the tide."

Flemming called over the port lookout, C. P. Slade, for a second opinion. Seeing his men support each other, Cornthwait saw the possibility that they might prove him wrong. This spurred him to look again, this time using his spyglass. Not wanting to lose face, the officer repeated his earlier claim, "just a log."

And then he turned and ran aft, in a panic, toward the bridge. But by then the ship was already moving.

John Crosby, the ship's acting master, was on the *Housatonic*'s quarterdeck at 8:45 p.m. In the distance he could see the South Atlantic Blockading Squadron stretching along the coast, little lights from the decks flickering on and off. Just a mile away was the mightiest ship in the fleet, the *Canandaigua*, a ship that Crosby admired. It was calm, too much so. Peering toward the South Carolina coast, scanning for blockade-runners, Crosby saw something in the moonlight that registered oddly in his mind. He would later testify that at first he thought it looked "like a porpoise coming up to the surface to blow." It was less than 100 yards off the starboard beam. He called the quartermaster over. Do you see that? Is it a tide ripple? But when Crosby looked again, he realized that what he was seeing was no dolphin.

"Beat to quarters, slip the chain and back the engine," Crosby ordered, and went to alert the captain.

★ ★ ★

In the engine room the heat was sweltering. James. W. Holihan, as assistant engineer, had been on watch less than an hour but was already drenched in his own sweat. The engine room was under strict orders: keep heavy banked fires and 25 pounds of steam from six in the evening until six in the morning. That would allow the *Housatonic* to move from a dead stop to 7 knots— screaming speed for the ship—in just a few minutes. That was how it had to be: everything ready to go at a moment's notice. But the *Housatonic* didn't have that much time left. When the bells rang to signal the engineer to start moving, Holihan repeated the order: open the stop valves, back the engine.

And that's when the explosion knocked the 200-foot warship violently on its port beam.

Capt. Charles W. Pickering had been in his cabin working on the ship's charts when he heard the shouting. He thought a blockade-runner was coming. In his haste to reach the bridge, he had grabbed the hat of the ship's doctor, who was working with him. Realizing his mistake, he returned to the cabin for the proper hat. When he finally reached the deck, he repeated the order to slip the anchor chain and throw the engine in reverse: moving forward risked fouling the anchor chain in the ship's propeller. But going astern only gave the *Hunley* a better target.

The submarine was aimed straight for the mizzenmast of the *Housatonic* and moving at a steady rate of speed. On deck the crew could see an eerie yellow glow coming from little portholes in the fish-boat, although they did not know what they were seeing. Pickering told his crew to open fire and then took his own double-barreled shotgun loaded with buckshot and aimed at the *Hunley*'s front conning tower—where the biggest yellow target was glowing. By the time the submarine had been identified, it was too close, too low on the waterline, to train any of the Union ship's big guns on it. Dahlgren's new gun would be of absolutely no use to the *Housatonic*.

At first no one put the two incidents together. First, there was the noise. *Thud*. Many of the crew would later say they believed the ship had run aground in its attempted getaway. But with the dull sound, the ship moved only a little. It was almost imperceptible.

At the same time the odd thing in the water had stopped moving. Briefly it became an easier target and was showered with bullets and buckshot. Small-arms fire clanked off the hull of the mysterious boat. Then it started backing away, slowly at first, then faster. Between the shouting and the sound of the tide lapping at their ship's hull, the crew of the *Housatonic* could not hear the rope spinning from a partially submerged spool on the side of the submarine, easing out as slickly as fishing line.

The last thing any sailor on board the *Housatonic* remembered about the submarine was that it was about 50 to 80 feet off the starboard quarter when their world exploded. Pickering was still shooting when he felt his feet leave the wooden deck; he was airborne and the world went oddly silent. Perhaps he was deafened temporarily by the explosion.

If the *Housatonic* had moved only a little faster, she could have avoided being rammed by the *Hunley*, but the engines had made less than five revolutions when the torpedo that was rammed into the ship's hull detonated. Water immediately rushed into the engine room, followed by the sound of crashing timbers and metal. The ship lurched heavily to port, and many of the crew were tossed across the deck and into the sea. Most of the men had been in their bunks when the side of the ship disappeared; the whole incident took place in just a few minutes.

When 90 pounds of powder detonated in the *Housatonic*'s starboard quarter, she heaved mightily, like big game recoiling from a rifle shot. Instead of righting herself, the ship's hull just kept rolling to port. There was never any question, never any hope. She was going down.

Black smoke filled the air, but there was no fire. The explosion played itself out more like a depth charge. Splintered wood rained down on the Atlantic, and dozens of the crew soon found themselves in the cold, dark ocean. The sailors who remained on deck could feel the water creeping up their legs. Soon the ship would be underwater. Some went for the lifeboats, gathering up as many shipmates as they could. Others, including Captain Pickering, found themselves clinging to the ship's massive rigging. John Crosby, who had reached a gig, heard Pickering calling his name. The captain told Crosby to get all the men he could out of the water and then come get him. Together they would row to the *Canandaigua* for help. But the mightiest ship in the fleet was now nearly 2 long miles away.

The *Housatonic* had been anchored in water that, at low tide, was barely 25 feet deep—shallow water, just as Dahlgren had ordered. That would save most of the crew's lives. When the ship hit the bottom, its decks were less than 15 feet underwater; there was plenty of room in the rigging for the crew. Which is where they all ended up, waiting in a light Atlantic breeze for rescue. Some of them were naked, others in nightclothes. In five minutes the ship had sunk. Out of a crew of 155, only 5 died. The rest would live to tell the story a few days later at a Navy inquiry.

When the ship settled onto the silty floor of the Atlantic the night of February 17, 1864, those men hanging in the intricate webbing of the ship's rigging were briefly unsure of their fate. They could do little more than call out for help. Among the survivors was Robert F. Flemming, the man who had first seen the *Hunley* coming. The blast had left him unharmed, and he quickly scurried up the foremast. About an hour after the attack, as the *Housatonic* filled with seawater and settled onto the bottom, Flemming could see the *Canandaigua* coming for them towing the *Housatonic*'s launch. It was a comforting sight: they would be rescued, he knew.

Then he saw it. Just ahead of the *Canandaigua*, off the starboard bow of the *Housatonic*'s wreck, Robert F. Flemming saw a blue light shining on the water. He was sure of it.

On Sullivan's Island the Rebels saw the light, too, although they had no idea what events had precipitated it. Even a light ocean breeze masked noises 4 miles out on the water, and there was little or no fire from the *Housatonic*'s explosion. All those cold soldiers knew was, that was the signal. Immediately they began stoking a bonfire on the beach that could be seen a dozen miles out to sea. Had the Union Navy not been occupied at the moment, the sight of the huge fire burning on the beach might have puzzled the sailors on watch that night. They might have thought it was a victory celebration.

On land, however, the Confederates were oblivious to the chaos playing out on the water just a few short miles away. Cpl. D. W. McLaurin, a member of the Twenty-third South Carolina Volunteers, was one of the men on the beach that chilly evening. Earlier in the day he had been among the troops whom Dixon had ordered aboard the boat for last-minute adjustments to its equipment. It was a day McLaurin would never forget, but that night he didn't realize it.

From the edge of Sullivan's Island, the young soldier watched frantic signaling between the blockading ships as he threw driftwood on the fire. But McLaurin didn't put the two things together. None of the men did. They weren't expecting the *Hunley* to actually succeed. They were simply following orders and trying to keep warm, continually stoking the fire.

Over their shoulders the blue light called to them, twinkling brilliantly in the blackness. It would be the last confirmed sighting of the *H. L. Hunley* for 131 years.

Permissions Acknowledgments